Test Bank

Reflect & Relate

An Introduction to Interpersonal Communication

Second Edition

Steven McCornack

Prepared by
Charles J. Korn
Northern Virginia Community College

Bedford/St. Martin's
Boston ♦ New York

Manufactured in the United States of America.

4 3 2 1 0 9
f   e   d   c   b   a

For information, write: Bedford/St. Martin's, 75 Arlington Street, Boston, MA 02116   (617-399-4000)

ISBN-10: 0-312-57695-1
ISBN-13: 978-0-312-57695-0

Contents

Chapter 1: Introducing Interpersonal Communication

Matching

Match the concept, term, or theory with its correct response or definition.

A. channel
B. communication
C. communication studies
D. contexts
E. dyadic
F. feedback
G. fields of experience
H. impersonal communication
I. instrumental goals
J. interaction
K. interactive communication model
L. interpersonal communication
M. intrapersonal communication

N. linear communication model
O. mass communication and media studies
P. message
Q. noise
R. process
S. receiver
T. relationship goals
U. self-presentational goals
V. sender
W. speech and rhetorical studies
X. telecommunication studies
Y. transactional communication model

1. The process through which people use messages to generate meanings within and across contexts, cultures, channels, and media.
   H: Defining Communication, p. 6; C: factual/definitional; D: easy; L.O.: communication
   Answer: B. communication

2. People for whom a message is intended.
   H: Linear Communication Model, p. 9; C: factual/definitional; D: easy; L.O.: communication models
   Answer: S. receiver

3. Communication occurs through a series of interconnected actions.
   H: Defining Communication, p. 6; C: factual/definitional; D: easy; L.O.: communication
   Answer: R. process

4. A communicator's set of attitudes, values, and beliefs that are brought to a communication event.

H: Interactive Communication Model, p. 10; C: factual/definitional; D: easy;
L.O.: communication models

Answer: G. fields of experience

5. Practical goals you want to achieve through communication.

H: Interpersonal Communication and Specific Goals, p. 20; C: factual/definitional; D: easy;
L.O.: interpersonal communication needs

Answer: I. instrumental goals

6. The endless variety of communication situations.

H: Defining Communication, p. 6; C: factual/definitional; D: easy; L.O.: communication

Answer: D. contexts

7. How words are used to compel audiences to change or solidify their beliefs.

H: Table 1.1: Forms of Communication, p. 8; C: factual/definitional; D: easy; L.O.: forms of communication

Answer: W. speech and rhetorical studies

8. Research of communication within different contexts.

H: Table 1.1: Forms of Communication, p. 8; C: factual/definitional; D: easy; L.O.: forms of communication

Answer: C. communication studies

9. Communication between two (or more) people in which messages exchanged significantly influence their relationship.

H: Defining Interpersonal Communication, p. 13; C: factual/definitional; D: easy;
L.O.: interpersonal communication needs

Answer: L. interpersonal communication

10. History, current state, and critical analysis of mass media and culture.

H: Table 1.1: Forms of Communication, p. 8; C: factual/definitional; D: easy; L.O.: forms of communication

Answer: O. mass communication and media studies

11. Development, use, regulation, and impact of radio, television, the Internet, and other technologies.

H: Table 1.1: Forms of Communication, p. 8; C: factual/definitional; D: easy; L.O.: forms of communication

Answer: X. telecommunication studies

12. Demonstrates communication as a one-way activity.

H: Linear Communication Model, p. 9; C: factual/definitional; D: easy;
L.O.: communication models

Answer: N. linear communication model

13. An individual who generates information to be communicated.

    H: Linear Communication Model, p. 9; C: factual/definitional; D: easy;
    L.O.: communication models

    Answer: V. sender

14. The "package" of information.

    H: Defining Communication, p. 6; C: factual/definitional; D: easy; L.O.: communication

    Answer: P. message

15. Factors that impede messages from reaching their destination.

    H: Linear Communication Model, p. 9; C: factual/definitional; D: easy;
    L.O.: communication models

    Answer: Q. noise

16. Communication goals that are designed to ensure that a communicator is perceived in a particular way.

    H: Interpersonal Communication and Specific Goals, p. 20; C: factual/definitional; D: easy;
    L.O.: interpersonal communication needs

    Answer: U. self-presentational goals

17. A view of communication that considers feedback and fields of experience.

    H: Interactive Communication Model, p. 10; C: factual/definitional; D: easy;
    L.O.: communication models

    Answer: K. interactive communication model

18. The sensory dimension along which communicators transmit information.

    H: Defining Communication, p. 6; C: factual/definitional; D: easy; L.O.: communication

    Answer: A. channel

19. A view of communication that suggests communication is multidirectional.

    H: Transactional Communication Model, p. 10; C: factual/definitional; D: easy;
    L.O.: communication models

    Answer: Y. transactional communication model

20. Involving pairs of people.

    H: Defining Interpersonal Communication, p. 13; C: factual/definitional; D: easy;
    L.O.: interpersonal communication needs

    Answer: E. dyadic

21. Communication that has negligible impact upon people.

    H: Defining Interpersonal Communication, p. 13; C: factual/definitional; D: easy;
    L.O.: interpersonal communication needs

    Answer: H. impersonal communication

22. Goals which involve building, maintaining, or terminating bonds with others.
    H: Interpersonal Communication and Specific Goals, p. 20; C: factual/definitional; D: easy;
    L.O.: interpersonal communication needs
    Answer: T. relationship goals

23. An exchange or a series of messages.
    H: Defining Communication, p. 6; C: factual/definitional; D: easy; L.O.: communication
    Answer: J. interaction

24. Verbal and nonverbal messages used by receivers to indicate reactions to communication.
    H: Interactive Communication Model, p. 10; C: factual/definitional; D: easy;
    L.O.: communication models
    Answer: F. feedback

25. Communication involving only one person.
    H: Defining Interpersonal Communication, p. 13; C: factual/definitional; D: easy;
    L.O.: interpersonal communication needs
    Answer: M. intrapersonal communication

True/False

Please select whether the following statements are true or false.

26. The authors suggest that intrapersonal and interpersonal communication refer to basically the same phenomenon.
    H: Defining Interpersonal Communication, p. 13; C: conceptual; D: medium;
    L.O.: communication
    Answer: F

27. The "process" nature of communication suggests that everything that is said now will impact what is said and done in the future.
    H: Defining Communication, p. 6; C: conceptual; D: medium; L.O.: communication
    Answer: T

28. Even in our close personal relationships, we can communicate both impersonally and personally within the same interaction.
    H: Defining Interpersonal Communication, p. 13; C: conceptual; D: medium;
    L.O.: interpersonal communication needs
    Answer: T

29. Feedback and noise are the two additional components that make up the interactive communication model.
    H: Interactive Communication Model, p. 10; C: conceptual; D: medium;
    L.O.: communication models
    Answer: F

30. Content information is considered to be a form of meta-communication.

    H: Interpersonal communication conveys both content and relationship information, p. 15; C: conceptual; D: medium; L.O.: interpersonal communication needs

    Answer: F

31. A ballgame, work, or a classroom is an example of context.

    H: Defining Communication, p. 6; C: conceptual; D: medium; L.O.: communication

    Answer: T

32. Auditory, visual, tactile, olfactory, and oral are all examples of channels.

    H: Defining Communication, p. 6; C: factual/definitional; D: easy; L.O.: communication

    Answer: T

33. Quantitative approaches to research are most conducive to understanding the rich nuances of communication patterns.

    H: Research in Interpersonal Communication, p. 21; C: conceptual; D: medium; L.O.: communication

    Answer: F

34. In an I-It relationship we are less likely to treat others as objects.

    H: Defining Interpersonal Communication, p. 13; C: factual/definitional; D: easy; L.O.: defining communication

    Answer: F

35. The linear communication model conceptualizes communication as a simplistic one-way form of communication.

    H: Linear Communication Model, p. 9; C: factual/definitional; D: easy; L.O.: communication models

    Answer: T

36. The transactional model of communication is the most sophisticated, suggesting that communication is fundamentally a multidirectional process in which senders and receivers collaboratively create communication meaning.

    H: Transactional Communication Model, p. 10; C: conceptual; D: medium; L.O.: communication models

    Answer: T

37. Interpersonal communication competence consists of communicating in appropriate, effective, and ethical ways.

    H: Interpersonal Skills, p. 29; C: conceptual; D: medium; L.O.: issues of interpersonal communication

    Answer: T

38. According to your text, interpersonal communication is dynamic, meaning it is constantly in motion and changing over time.

    H: Defining Interpersonal Communication, p. 13; C: conceptual; D: medium; L.O.: interpersonal communication needs

    Answer: T

39. Impersonal communication tends to have a significant impact upon our thoughts, behaviors, and relationships.

    H: Defining Interpersonal Communication, p. 13; C: conceptual; D: medium; L.O.: defining communication

    Answer: F

40. Buber suggests that in an I-Thou relationship we embrace similarities, see things from others' perspectives, and communicate with honesty, resulting in feelings of closeness to others.

    H: Defining Interpersonal Communication, p. 13; C: conceptual; D: medium; L.O.: interpersonal communication needs

    Answer: T

41. According to Maslow's hierarchy of needs, one must resolve or meet social needs before self-actualization needs.

    H: Interpersonal Communication and Human Needs, p. 20; C: conceptual; D: medium; L.O.: interpersonal communication needs

    Answer: T

42. One cannot not communicate.

    H: Interpersonal communication can be intentional or unintentional, p. 17; C: conceptual; D: medium; L.O.: interpersonal communication needs

    Answer: T

43. Culture can include one's sexual orientation.

    H: Culture, p. 24; C: conceptual; D: medium; L.O.: issues of interpersonal communication

    Answer: T

44. Gender, unlike biological sex, is something that is learned.

    H: Gender and Sexual Orientation, p. 25; C: conceptual; D: medium; L.O.: issues of interpersonal communication

    Answer: T

45. Intrapersonal communication is different from dyadic because it only involves one person.

    H: Defining Interpersonal Communication, p. 13; C: conceptual; D: medium; L.O.: interpersonal communication needs

    Answer: T

46. Whether or not we intend to communicate, our words and actions can communicate meanings to others.

H: Interpersonal communication can be intentional or unintentional, p. 17; C: application; D: medium; L.O.: issues of interpersonal communication

Answer: T

47. Self-actualization needs include our desire to have others' respect and admiration.

H: Interpersonal Communication and Human Needs, p. 20; C: conceptual; D: medium; L.O.: interpersonal communication needs

Answer: F

48. According to research in interpersonal communication, differences in communication styles of women and men are more complicated than popular stereotypes portray.

H: Gender and Sexual Orientation, pp. 25–26; C: conceptual; D: medium; L.O.: issues of interpersonal communication

Answer: T

49. Relationship information is not a form of meta-communication.

H: Interpersonal communication conveys both content and relationship information, p. 15; C: application; D: medium; L.O.: principles of communication

Answer: F

Multiple Choice

Please choose the correct response to the following statements.

50. Auditory, visual, tactile, olfactory, and oral are all examples of kinds of
    A. media
    B. communication
    C. channels
    D. noise
    E. context

H: Defining Communication, p. 6; C: conceptual; D: medium; L.O.: communication

Answer: C

51. According to Maslow, which need is at the top, or apex, of his hierarchy?
    A. self-actualization
    B. ego
    C. security
    D. physiological
    E. social

H: Interpersonal Communication and Human Needs, p. 20; C: conceptual; D: medium; L.O.: interpersonal communication needs

Answer: A

52. An I-Thou relationship is characterized by all of the following EXCEPT
    A. embracing similarities
    B. sharing agreement on issues
    C. striving to see things from the other's point of view
    D. communicating honesty
    E. acting with kindness
    H: Defining Interpersonal Communication, p. 13; C: conceptual; D: medium;
    L.O.: interpersonal communication needs
    Answer: B

53. Interpersonal communication can be considered
    A. intentional
    B. unintentional
    C. irreversible
    D. dynamic
    E. all of the above
    H: Defining Interpersonal Communication, p. 13; C: conceptual; D: medium;
    L.O.: principles of communication
    Answer: E

54. Interpersonal communication involves all of the following characteristics EXCEPT
    A. dynamic
    B. transactional
    C. dyadic
    D. changes participants thoughts, emotions, behavior, and relationships
    E. impersonal
    H: Defining Interpersonal Communication, p. 13; C: conceptual; D: medium;
    L.O.: interpersonal communication needs
    Answer: E

55. According to the National Communication Association, all of the following are considered
    to be examples of ethical behavior EXCEPT
    A. withholding feelings and information in a significant interpersonal relationship
    B. communicating in an honest, accurate, and thoughtful way
    C. trying to both understand and respect others before evaluating or responding to their
       messages
    D. condemning communication that degrades people through intolerance, distortion, or
       intimidation
    E. sharing information, opinions, and feelings when dealing with significant relationship
       choices
    H: Interpersonal communication is intertwined with ethics, p. 19; C: conceptual;
    D: medium; L.O.: ethics of communication
    Answer: A

56. According to the text, what is the relationship between sexual orientation and communication?
    A. homosexuals and heterosexuals communicate similarly
    B. homosexuals and heterosexuals communicate differently
    C. gay men communicate like heterosexual women
    D. gay men communicate like heterosexual men
    E. none of the above

    H: Gender and Sexual Orientation, p. 25; C: conceptual; D: medium; L.O.: issues of interpersonal communication

    Answer: A

57. Qualitative research normally includes
    A. first formulating hypotheses
    B. making careful observations
    C. determining principles underlying observations
    D. both B and C
    E. none of the above

    H: Research in Interpersonal Communication, p. 21; C: conceptual; D: medium; L.O.: research in interpersonal communication

    Answer: D

58. Which of the following models of human communication is considered by your text to be the most elaborate, yet accurate, depiction of interpersonal communication?
    A. transactional communication model
    B. action communication model
    C. linear communication model
    D. interactive communication model
    E. field of experience model

    H: Transactional Communication Model, p. 10; C: factual/definitional; D: easy; L.O.: communication models

    Answer: A

59. Text messaging and e-mail exemplify which type of communication model?
    A. transactional
    B. interactive
    C. multidimensional
    D. linear
    E. none of the above

    H: Table 1.2, Communication Models, p. 11; C: application; D: hard; L.O.: communication models

    Answer: D

60. Which of the following was NOT an issue defined by your text as important to understanding interpersonal communication?
    A. culture
    B. sexual orientation
    C. online communication

D. biological sex

E. gender

H: Issues in Interpersonal Communication, p. 24; C: factual/definitional; D: easy;
L.O.: issues of interpersonal communication

Answer: D

61. Which need in Maslow's hierarchy has to do with the desire for self-esteem, power, and recognition?

    A. self-actualization

    B. ego

    C. security

    D. physiological

    E. social

    H: Interpersonal Communication and Human Needs, p. 20; C: conceptual; D: medium;
    L.O.: interpersonal communication needs

    Answer: B

62. Which of the following is NOT an element found in the linear communication model?

    A. sender

    B. noise

    C. feedback

    D. receiver

    E. channel

    H: Linear Communication Model, p. 9; C: factual/definitional; D: easy;
    L.O.: communication model

    Answer: C

63. Mark goes to the same coffee house almost every morning on his way to the office. He's never bothered to learn the barista's name and sometimes he fails to notice when someone else is working her shift. Mark's relationship with the barista can best be described as

    A. I-Thou

    B. I-It

    C. interactional

    D. intrapersonal

    E. linear

    H: Defining Interpersonal Communication, p. 13; C: application; D: difficult;
    L.O.: interpersonal communication needs

    Answer: B

64. Dyadic communication involves

    A. one person

    B. two people

    C. small group

    D. large group

    E. none of the above

Answer: B

65. Communication using e-mail, text messaging, chatrooms, and listservs is referred to as
   A. geographic communication
   B. online communication
   C. mediated communication
   D. intrapersonal communication
   E. impersonal communication

Answer: B

66. You are trying to persuade your communication professor to let you take a makeup exam
   because you missed the midterm examination. What interpersonal goal are you trying to
   meet?
   A. self-presentation goal
   B. relationship goal
   C. instrumental goal
   D. personal goal
   E. none of the above

Answer: C

67. Intrapersonal communication involves
   A. one person
   B. two people
   C. small group
   D. large group
   E. none of the above

Answer: A

68. Meta-communication involves
   A. communication with self
   B. communication with others
   C. impersonal communication
   D. communication about communication
   E. none of the above

Answer: D

69. If your romantic partner stops mid-sentence in the middle of a deep talk about your relationship and exclaims, "We need more toilet paper," this comment is an example of
    A. interpersonal communication
    B. intrapersonal communication
    C. impersonal communication
    D. interactive communication
    E. none of the above

    H: Defining Interpersonal Communication, p. 13; C: conceptual; D: medium;
    L.O.: interpersonal communication needs

    Answer: C

70. Culture is learned from
    A. media
    B. teachers
    C. parents
    D. peers
    E. all of the above

    H: Culture, p. 24; C: factual/definitional; D: easy; L.O.: issues in communication

    Answer: E

71. According to Maslow's hierarchy of needs, which need must be met before any others can be satisfied?
    A. self-actualization
    B. ego
    C. security
    D. physiological or physical
    E. social

    H: Interpersonal Communication and Human Needs, p. 20; C: conceptual; D: medium;
    L.O.: interpersonal communication needs

    Answer: D

72. You and your roommate are discussing who will get the larger bedroom in your new apartment, and you are willing to defer to his preference because your friendship means more than the slight difference in room size. What type of communication are you most likely using with your roommate?
    A. impersonal communication
    B. online communication
    C. I-It
    D. intrapersonal communication
    E. interpersonal communication

    H: Defining Interpersonal Communication, p. 13; C: application; D: difficult;
    L.O.: interpersonal communication needs

    Answer: E

73. Which need in Maslow's hierarchy has to do with feeling safe and having shelter?
    A. self-actualization
    B. ego
    C. security

D. physiological

E. social

H: Interpersonal Communication and Human Needs, p. 20; C: conceptual; D: medium;
L.O.: interpersonal communication needs

Answer: C

74. If you desire to be seen as trustworthy, caring, and credible by your new partner's parents,
which interpersonal goal are you trying to achieve?

A. self-presentation

B. relationship

C. instrumental

D. personal

E. none of the above

H: Interpersonal Communication and Specific Goals, p. 20; C: application; D: difficult;
L.O.: interpersonal communication needs

Answer: A

75. If Chris is trying to arrange a meeting with his partner of five years so that he can discuss
how he can terminate their relationship, what goal is he seeking?

A. self-presentation

B. relationship

C. instrumental

D. personal

E. none of the above

H: Interpersonal Communication and Specific Goals, p. 20; C: conceptual; D: medium;
L.O.: interpersonal communication needs

Answer: B

76. Which of the following is NOT a principle of interpersonal communication?

A. communication is reversible

B. communication can be intentional

C. communication has content information

D. communication has relationship information

E. communication can be unintentional

H: Interpersonal communication is irreversible, p. 17; C: factual/definitional; D: easy;
L.O.: interpersonal communication needs

Answer: A

77. Relationship information is primarily communicated

A. through verbal messages

B. through emotions

C. through nonverbal communication

D. both A & B

E. A, B, & C

H: Interpersonal communication conveys both content and relationship information, p. 15;
C: conceptual; D: medium; L.O.: interpersonal communication needs

Answer: C

78. Content information is primarily communicated
    A. through verbal messages
    B. through body language
    C. through facial expressions
    D. through emotions
    E. through nonverbal communication

    H: Interpersonal communication conveys both content and relationship information, p. 15; C: conceptual; D: medium; L.O.: interpersonal communication needs

    Answer: A

79. Which need in Maslow's hierarchy has to do with being accepted by others and feeling a sense of belonging?
    A. self-actualization
    B. ego
    C. security
    D. physiological
    E. social

    H: Interpersonal Communication and Human Needs, p. 20; C: conceptual; D: medium; L.O.: interpersonal communication needs

    Answer: E

80. "One cannot not communicate" means
    A. communication can be unintentional
    B. people can read into or give meaning to anything you say
    C. people can attach meaning to anything you do or don't do
    D. all of the above
    E. none of the above

    H: Interpersonal communication can be intentional or unintentional, p. 17; C: conceptual; D: medium; L.O.: interpersonal communication needs

    Answer: D

81. Quantitative approaches to research
    A. involve careful observation and description of events
    B. start with observation, followed by a hypothesis
    C. are better suited for learning the details and nuances of communication patterns
    D. often use controlled settings such as an experimental laboratory
    E. all of the above

    H: Research in Interpersonal Communication, p. 21; C: conceptual; D: medium; L.O.: communication

    Answer: D

82. The fact that interpersonal communication is dynamic suggests
    A. communication is in flux
    B. communication is always changing
    C. no two interactions with the same person will ever be the same
    D. no two moments within the same interaction will ever be identical
    E. all of the above

H: Interpersonal communication is dynamic, p. 18; C: conceptual; D: medium;
L.O.: interpersonal communication needs

Answer: E

83. Which of the following is NOT a factor in one's culture?
    A. nationality
    B. age
    C. sexual orientation
    D. gender
    E. none of the above

    H: Culture, p. 24; C: factual/definitional; D: easy; L.O.: issues of interpersonal
    communication

    Answer: E

84. The textbook suggests that which of the following is true about the relationship between
    gender and its impact upon communication?
    A. women and men communicate quite differently
    B. women and men communicate in similar ways
    C. women are more open and men are unable to disclose feelings
    D. men are more open and women are unable to disclose feelings
    E. none of the above

    H: Gender and Sexual Orientation, p. 25; C: conceptual; D: medium; L.O.: issues of
    interpersonal communication

    Answer: B

85. Your text presents a three-part model toward achieving healthy and satisfying interpersonal
    relationships. Which of the following is not part of that model?
    A. research
    B. outcomes
    C. skills
    D. knowledge
    E. none of the above

    H: Learning Interpersonal Communication, p. 28; C: conceptual; D: medium; L.O.: learning
    interpersonal communication

    Answer: A

86. Online communication can include all of the following EXCEPT
    A. multiuser discussion groups
    B. chatrooms
    C. instant messaging
    D. phone call
    E. e-mail

    H: Online Communication, p. 26; C: application; D: difficult; L.O.: issues of interpersonal
    communication

    Answer: D

87. Which of the following is NOT a factor that influences one's communication decisions?
    A. emotions
    B. one's perceptions of others
    C. sexual orientation
    D. self
    E. none of the above

    H: Gender and Sexual Orientation, p. 25; C: factual/definitional; D: easy; L.O.: elements of interpersonal communication

    Answer: C

88. Interpersonal communication competence is composed of
    A. ethics, effectiveness, and honesty
    B. ethics, effectiveness, and appropriateness
    C. effectiveness, appropriateness, and respect
    D. ethics, appropriateness, and clarity
    E. respect, honesty, and directness

    H: Interpersonal Skills, p. 29; C: conceptual; D: difficult; L.O.: elements of interpersonal communication

    Answer: B

Short Answer

Briefly respond to the following questions in full sentences.

89. Define communication.

    H: Defining Communication, p. 6; C: conceptual; D: medium; L.O.: communication

    Possible Answer: Process through which people use messages to generate meanings within and across contexts, cultures, channels, and media.

90. Identify the four domains of communication studies.

    H: Table 1.1: Forms of Communication, p. 8; C: factual/definitional; D: easy; L.O.: communication

    Possible Answer: Speech and rhetorical studies, communication studies, mass communication and media studies, and telecommunication studies.

91. Define communication studies.

    H: Table 1.1: Forms of Communication, p. 8; C: conceptual; D: medium; L.O.: forms of communication

    Answer: Research examining communication within various contexts, such as interpersonal, organizational, and intercultural communication.

92. What is gender?

    H: Gender and Sexual Orientation, p. 25; C: conceptual; D: medium; L.O.: issues in interpersonal communication

    Answer: Social, psychological, and cultural traits associated with one sex or the other.

93. When is it best to use quantitative research methods, and when is it most appropriate to use qualitative research methods?

    H: Research in Interpersonal Communication, p. 21; C: conceptual; D: medium; L.O.: communication

    Possible Answer: Qualitative approaches are best for uncovering rich, fine detail of communication patterns; quantitative methods are best used for determining frequencies and for examining factors that influence behavior.

94. Define interpersonal communication.

    H: Defining Interpersonal Communication, p. 13; C: conceptual; D: medium; L.O.: interpersonal communication needs

    Possible Answer: Dynamic form of communication between two (or more) people in which the messages exchanged significantly influence their thoughts, emotions, behaviors, and relationships.

95. What is intrapersonal communication?

    H: Defining Interpersonal Communication, p. 13; C: conceptual; D: medium; L.O.: interpersonal communication needs

    Possible Answer: Communication involving only one person, such as talking out loud.

96. Explain the difference between Buber's I-Thou and I-It relationships.

    H: Defining Interpersonal Communication, p. 13; C: conceptual; D: medium; L.O.: interpersonal communication needs

    Possible Answer: I-It suggests that communicators relate to one another as simple roles or objects, while in an I-Thou relationship, communication is based upon an understanding of each other as unique individuals.

97. What are the most basic needs defined by Maslow in his hierarchy of needs?

    H: Interpersonal Communication and Human Needs, p. 20; C: factual/definitional; D: easy; L.O.: interpersonal communication needs

    Possible Answer: Physical—such as food, water, and rest—and security—such as shelter and safety.

98. Identify the three goals of interpersonal communication.

    H: Interpersonal Communication and Specific Goals, p. 20; C: factual/definitional; D: easy; L.O.: interpersonal communication needs

    Possible Answer: Self-presentation goals, instrumental goals, and relationship goals.

99. Define meta-communication and provide an example.

    H: Interpersonal communication conveys both content and relationship information, p. 15; C: conceptual; D: medium; L.O.: interpersonal communication needs

    Possible Answer: Communication about communication, such as when one talks to one's partner about how they seem not to talk to each other as often or as personally as they used to.

100. How can communication be both intentional and unintentional?

    H: Interpersonal communication can be intentional and unintentional, p. 17; C: conceptual; D: medium; L.O.: interpersonal communication needs

    Possible Answer: Words tend to be intentional; nonverbal communication tends to be unintentional.

101. What is sexual orientation, and how can a continuum be used to describe it?

    H: Gender and Sexual Orientation, p. 25; C: conceptual; D: medium; L.O.: interpersonal communication needs

    Possible Answer: An enduring emotional, romantic, sexual, or affectionate attraction to another person. It is plotted on a continuum ranging from heterosexuality to homosexuality.

102. How can you increase communication competence and skills?

    H: Interpersonal Skills, p. 29; C: conceptual; D: medium; L.O.: elements of interpersonal communication

    Possible Answer: By communicating in appropriate, effective, and ethical ways, and by applying new behaviors that can impact your personal relationships.

103. Identify the text's five suggestions for making effective interpersonal communication choices.

    H: Making Relationship Choices, p. 30; C: conceptual; D: medium; L.O.: making relationship choices

    Answer: Reflect on yourself, reflect on your partners, identify optimal outcomes, locate roadblocks, chart your course.

Essay

Please respond to the following questions in paragraph form.

104. Identify the five features that characterize communication.

    H: Defining Communication, p. 6; C: conceptual; D: medium; L.O.: communication

    Possible Answer: It's a process; communicators use messages; communicators engage in a variety of contexts; people communicate through various channels; and communicators use a variety of media to transmit information.

105. Define interpersonal communication and its four characteristics.

    H: Defining Interpersonal Communication, p. 13; C: conceptual; D: medium; L.O.: interpersonal communication needs

    Possible Answer: A dynamic form of communication between two (or more) people in which the message exchanged significantly influences their thoughts, emotions, behaviors, and relationships. Dynamic: constantly in motion and changing over time. Transactional: simultaneous exchange between senders and receivers. Dyadic: involves two people. Changes: results in influence upon thoughts, emotions, behavior, and relationships.

106. Identify and explain Maslow's hierarchy of needs.

   H: Interpersonal Communication and Human Needs, p. 20; C: conceptual; D: medium;
   L.O.: interpersonal communication needs

   Possible Answer: We have basic needs that must be met before we can address higher-order needs. The hierarchy starts with physical needs such as food, water, and air; security needs, such as needs for safety and shelter; social needs, such as being loved and validated; ego needs, such as the needs for self-esteem and power; and finally, the apex of the needs, self-actualization needs, including the need for self-development and creativity.

107. What are the five principles of interpersonal communication?

   H: Principles of Interpersonal Communication, p. 15; C: conceptual; D: medium;
   L.O.: interpersonal communication needs

   Possible Answer: Interpersonal communication conveys both content and relationship information; interpersonal communication can be intentional or unintentional; interpersonal communication is irreversible; interpersonal communication is dynamic; interpersonal communication is intertwined with ethics.

108. Describe the five critical issues of study today in interpersonal communication.

   H: Issues in Interpersonal Communication, p. 24; C: conceptual; D: medium; L.O.: issues of interpersonal communication

   Possible Answer: Culture: a set of beliefs, attitudes, values, and practices shared by a group of people. Gender: social, psychological, and cultural distinctions between men and women. Sexual orientation: an enduring emotional, romantic, sexual, or affectionate attraction to another person, which can be plotted on a continuum ranging from heterosexuality to homosexuality. Online communication: interaction via e-mail, text or instant messaging, discussion boards, and so on. The dark side of relationships: problems of violence, pettiness, and vindictive behavior between relational partners.

Chapter 2: Considering Self

Matching

Match the concept, term, or theory with its correct response or definition.

A. attachment anxiety
B. attachment avoidance
C. autonomy
D. collectivistic culture
E. culture
F. dismissive attachment
G. embarrassment
H. face
I. fearful attachment
J. gender
K. individualistic culture
L. looking-glass self
M. mask

N. openness
O. preoccupied attachment
P. secure attachment
Q. self
R. self-awareness
S. self-concept
T. self-disclosure
U. self-discrepancy theory
V. self-esteem
W. self-fulfilling prophecies
X. social comparison
Y. social penetration theory

1. An individual's public self.
    H: Maintaining Your Public Self, p. 53; C: factual/definitional; D: easy; L.O.: presenting your self
    Answer: H. face

2. A component of self that refers to your ability to perceive yourself as a unique person and to reflect upon your own thoughts, feelings, and behaviors.
    H: Self-Awareness, p. 40; C: factual/definitional; D: easy; L.O.: components of self
    Answer: R. self-awareness

3. The degree to which a person fears rejection from their relational partner.
    H: Family and Self, p. 49; C: factual/definitional; D: easy; L.O.: sources of self
    Answer: A. attachment anxiety

4. The degree to which a person desires close interpersonal relationships.
   H: Family and Self, p. 49; C: factual/definitional; D: easy; L.O.: sources of self
   Answer: B. attachment avoidance

5. The process of observing and assigning meaning to others' behaviors and comparing them against your own.
   H: Self-Awareness, p. 40; C: factual/definitional; D: easy; L.O.: components of self
   Answer: X. social comparison

6. Style of a person having both high attachment and avoidance anxiety.
   H: Family and Self, p. 49; C: factual/definitional; D: easy; L.O.: sources of self
   Answer: I. fearful attachment

7. Tending to act in ways that ensure an interaction will occur as we believed and predicted it would.
   H: Self-Concept, p. 41; C: factual/definitional; D: easy; L.O.: components of self
   Answer: W. self-fulfilling prophecies

8. Your assessment and comparison of your ideal self with your ought self.
   H: Self-Esteem, p. 43; C: factual/definitional; D: easy; L.O.: components of self
   Answer: U. self-discrepancy theory

9. A composite of one's self-awareness, self-concept, and self-esteem.
   H: The Components of Self, p. 40; C: factual/definitional; D: easy; L.O.: components of self
   Answer: Q. self

10. A composite of social, psychological, and cultural characteristics that characterize you as male or female.
    H: Gender and Self, p. 47; C: factual/definitional; D: easy; L.O.: influences on self
    Answer: J. gender

11. Style of an individual who experiences both low anxiety and avoidance in relationships with others.
    H: Family and Self, p. 49; C: factual/definitional; D: easy; L.O.: sources of self
    Answer: P. secure attachment

12. A component of self that refers to how you perceive yourself.
    H: Self-Concept, p. 41; C: factual/definitional; D: easy; L.O.: components of self
    Answer: S. self-concept

13. Feelings of shame, humiliation, and sadness.
    H: Maintaining Your Public Self, p. 53; C: factual/definitional; D: easy; L.O.: presenting your self
    Answer: G. embarrassment

14. The overall evaluation of your self.
    H: Self-Esteem, p. 43; C: factual/definitional; D: easy; L.O.: components of self
    Answer: V. self-esteem

15. An established, coherent set of beliefs, attitudes, values, and practices shared by a large group of people.
    H: Culture and Self, p. 50; C: factual/definitional; D: easy; L.O.: influences on self
    Answer: E. culture

16. How you believe others perceive and evaluate you.
    H: Self-Concept, p. 41; C: factual/definitional; D: easy; L.O.: components of self
    Answer: L. looking-glass self

17. A culture that values individual over group or societal goals.
    H: Culture and Self, p. 50; C: factual/definitional; D: easy; L.O.: influences on self
    Answer: K. individualistic culture

18. A public self designed to hide your private self.
    H: Maintaining Your Public Self, p. 53; C: factual/definitional; D: easy; L.O.: presenting your self
    Answer: M. mask

19. A model of revealing your self in layers like those of an onion.
    H: Opening Your Self to Others, p. 60; C: factual/definitional; D: easy; L.O.: managing self in relationships
    Answer: Y. social penetration theory

20. The act of revealing personally private information about your self to others.
    H: Disclosing Your Self to Others, p. 64; C: factual/definitional; D: easy; L.O.: managing self in relationships
    Answer: T. self-disclosure

21. Style of individuals who are characterized as having high anxiety yet low avoidance of relationships.
    H: Family and Self, p. 49; C: factual/definitional; D: easy; L.O.: sources of self
    Answer: O. preoccupied attachment

22. Style of a person with low anxiety but high avoidance.
    H: Family and Self, p. 49; C: factual/definitional; D: easy; L.O.: sources of self
    Answer: F. dismissive attachment

23. A culture that values the group or society over individual goals.
    H: Culture and Self, p. 50; C: factual/definitional; D: easy; L.O.: influences on self
    Answer: D. collectivistic culture

True/False

Please select whether the following statements are true or false.

24. In the entire animal kingdom, only humans have been found to demonstrate a complex understanding of self-awareness.

    H: The Components of Self, p. 40; C: factual/definitional; D: easy; L.O.: components of self

    Answer: F

25. Your "face" is the part of you that you only show to yourself.

    H: Maintaining Your Public Self, p. 53; C: conceptual; D: medium; L.O.: presenting your self

    Answer: F

26. The process of social comparison can result in positive or negative self-esteem, depending on whether we compare favorably or unfavorably with others.

    H: Self-Awareness, p. 40; C: factual/definitional; D: easy; L.O.: components of self

    Answer: T

27. According to the Johari Window, the components of the self that are known to others but not to you are called the unknown area.

    H: Your Hidden and Revealed Self, p. 63; C: factual/definitional; D: easy; L.O.: managing self in relationships

    Answer: F

28. Social penetration refers to the gradual process of shedding the layers of the self and increasing the level of physical intimacy in our personal relationships.

    H: Opening Your Self to Others, p. 60; C: factual/definitional; D: easy; L.O.: managing self in relationships

    Answer: F

29. Our self-fulfilling prophecies can result in both positive and negative outcomes in our future behavior.

    H: Self-Concept, p. 41; C: factual/definitional; D: easy; L.O.: components of self

    Answer: T

30. If a caregiver and child have a close, affectionate, and secure relationship, the child is likely to learn a secure attachment style.

    H: Family and Self, p. 49; C: conceptual; D: medium; L.O.: influences on self

    Answer: T

31. People have a tendency to disclose more quickly, broadly, and deeply face-to-face than when interacting online.

    H: Disclosing Your Self to Others, p. 64; C: conceptual; D: medium; L.O.: managing self in relationships

    Answer: F

32. Our self is formed at infancy and remains fairly static over time and life experiences.

    H: The Components of Self, p. 40; C: factual/definitional; D: easy; L.O.: components of self

    Answer: F

33. According to self-discrepancy theory, the greater the discrepancy between your ideal self and your ought self, the higher your self-esteem.

    H: Measuring Up to Your Own Standards, p. 43; C: conceptual; D: medium; L.O.: components of self

    Answer: F

34. Gender is a set of behaviors learned through the process of socialization that begins at birth and continues with our families.

    H: Gender and Self, p. 47; C: factual/definitional; D: easy; L.O.: influences on self

    Answer: T

35. According to social penetration theory, breadth refers to how personally or deeply individuals disclose about themselves.

    H: Opening Your Self to Others, p. 60; C: factual/definitional; D: easy; L.O.: managing self in relationships

    Answer: F

36. Taiwan is viewed as an individualistic culture; the United States is viewed as a collectivistic culture.

    H: Culture and Self, p. 50; C: factual/definitional; D: easy; L.O.: influences on self

    Answer: F

37. Cooley's concept of the looking-glass self suggests that we form our self-concepts by closely examining and evaluating ourselves.

    H: Self-Concept, p. 41; C: conceptual; D: medium; L.O.: components of self

    Answer: F

38. Gender refers to the biological state of having either male or female sexual organs.

    H: Gender and Self, p. 47; C: factual/definitional; D: easy; L.O.: influences on self

    Answer: F

39. One's public self is synonymous with one's face.

    H: Maintaining Your Public Self, p. 53; C: factual/definitional; D: easy; L.O.: presenting your self

    Answer: T

40. If your ought self and ideal self are consistent, you are likely to experience higher levels of happiness and self-esteem.

    H: Measuring Up to Your Own Standards, p. 43; C: conceptual; D: medium; L.O.: components of self

    Answer: T

41. By wearing a mask, an individual is better able to keep his or her self private.

    H: Maintaining Your Public Self, p. 53; C: conceptual; D: medium; L.O.: presenting your self

    Answer: T

42. If a relational partner feels unlovable and unworthy of your love, he or she may be experiencing attachment anxiety.

    H: Family and Self, p. 49; C: conceptual; D: medium; L.O.: sources of self

    Answer: T

43. Your self-concept is based upon the sets of beliefs, attitudes, and values your significant others have about you.

    H: Self-Concept, p. 41; C: factual/definitional; D: easy; L.O.: components of self

    Answer: F

44. If one loses face, feelings of shame, humiliation, and embarrassment may result.

    H: Maintaining Your Public Self, p. 53; C: factual/definitional; D: easy; L.O.: presenting your self

    Answer: T

45. According to social penetration theory, depth refers to the possible range and number of categories of self a relational partner will disclose.

    H: Opening Your Self to Others, p. 60; C: factual/definitional; D: easy; L.O.: managing self in relationships

    Answer: F

46. Self-disclosure is a necessary condition for the initiation and development of our personal relationships.

    H: Disclosing Your Self to Others, p. 64; C: conceptual; D: medium; L.O.: managing self in relationships

    Answer: T

47. Self-awareness is a term that can be used synonymously with self-esteem.

    H: Self-Esteem, p. 43; C: conceptual; D: medium; L.O.: components of self

    Answer: F

48. Culture can be defined as a coherent set of attitudes, values, and practices held by an individual.

    H: Culture and Self, p. 50; C: factual/definitional; D: easy; L.O.: influences on self

    Answer: F

Multiple Choice

Please choose the correct response to the following statements.

49. What are a person's learned evaluative appraisals, ranging from positive to negative responses about themselves and others?
    A. attitudes
    B. values
    C. beliefs
    D. personal constructs
    E. reflected appraisals

    H: Self-Concept, p. 41; C: factual/definitional; D: easy; L.O.: components of self

    Answer: A

50. If Mark was raised by caregivers who fluctuated between caring and unresponsive or abusive care, what attachment style is he likely to exhibit?
    A. secure attachment style
    B. Linus's security blanket
    C. anxious attachment style
    D. avoidant attachment style
    E. high attachment style

    H: Family and Self, p. 49; C: application; D: difficult; L.O.: influences on self

    Answer: C

51. Thoughts and convictions that an individual holds to be true are called
    A. attitudes
    B. beliefs
    C. values
    D. personal constructs
    E. looking-glass self

    H: Self-Concept, p. 41; C: factual/definitional; D: easy; L.O.: components of self

    Answer: B

52. If you and your friend talk about many different topics but maintain a superficial level, your self-disclosure has
    A. minimal breadth and depth
    B. great breadth and depth
    C. great breadth but little depth
    D. great depth but little breadth
    E. none of the above

    H: Opening Your Self to Others, p. 60; C: application; D: medium; L.O.: managing self in relationships

    Answer: C

53. When you perceive that you are not good at giving speeches, and so you don't prepare and research your speech topic, this is an example of
    A. social comparison
    B. the looking-glass self

C. self-discrepancy theory

D. self-fulfilling prophecy

E. none of the above

H: Self-Concept, p. 41; C: application; D: difficult; L.O.: components of self

Answer: D

54. People who have high self-esteem exhibit which of the following behaviors?

A. experience greater satisfaction in their personal relationships

B. demonstrate greater leadership behaviors

C. have increased academic performance

D. show greater athleticism

E. all of the above

H: Self-Esteem, p. 43; C: conceptual; D: medium; L.O.: components of self

Answer: E

55. According to the Johari Window, what is the part of self that is known to others and known to self?

A. unknown area

B. known area

C. hidden area

D. public area

E. blind area

H: Your Hidden and Revealed Self, p. 63; C: conceptual; D: medium; L.O.: managing self in relationships

Answer: D

56. Our self-concept can be influenced and developed by

A. labeling

B. interacting with others

C. gender

D. family

E. all of the above

H: Self-Concept, p. 41; C: conceptual; D: medium; L.O.: influences on self

Answer: E

57. When you begin a new relationship, which of the following represents an appropriate amount of self-disclosure for this stage of the relationship?

A. little breadth and little depth

B. little breadth and great depth

C. great breadth and little depth

D. great breadth and great depth

E. none of the above

H: Opening Your Self to Others, p. 60; C: application; D: difficult; L.O.: managing self in relationships

Answer: A

58. Which of the following patterns of self-disclosure would characterize an intimate personal relationship of choice?
    A. little breadth and little depth
    B. little breadth and great depth
    C. great breadth and little depth
    D. great breadth and great depth
    E. none of the above

    H: Opening Your Self to Others, p. 60; C: application; D: difficult; L.O.: managing self in relationships

    Answer: D

59. Which of the following accurately describes our use of self-disclosure?
    A. men disclose more than women
    B. women disclose more than men
    C. women are more likely to be recipients of self-disclosure
    D. teenage girls disclose most to their boyfriends
    E. both b and c

    H: Differences in Disclosure, p. 65; C: conceptual; D: medium; L.O.: managing self in relationships

    Answer: E

60. Kyle engages in frequent casual sexual relationships. He seems avoidant of close, long-term relationships, yet exhibits little anxiety. What attachment style best describes him?
    A. secure attachment
    B. dismissive attachment
    C. preoccupied attachment
    D. fearful attachment
    E. none of the above

    H: Family and Self, p. 49; C: application; D: difficult; L.O.: sources of self

    Answer: B

61. According to the Johari Window, what is the part of the self that is known to others but not known to self?
    A. open area
    B. blind area
    C. hidden area
    D. closed area
    E. unknown area

    H: Your Hidden and Revealed Self, p. 63; C: conceptual; D: medium; L.O.: managing self in relationships

    Answer: B

62. Which of the following statements exemplifies the influence that the looking-glass self has upon our self-concept?
    A. Mom always tells me I am the best little boy in the world and I believe her.
    B. I am a son and a student.
    C. I think she's the smartest student in the class besides me.

D. I am an extroverted, people person.

E. none of the above

H: Self-Concept, p. 41; C: application; D: difficult; L.O.: components of self

Answer: A

63. Which of the following is NOT a part of a female's lifelong gender socialization process?

A. femininity

B. sensitivity

C. nurturance

D. independence

E. compassion

H: Gender and Self, p. 47; C: conceptual; D: medium; L.O.: influences on self

Answer: D

64. Which of the following is a risk of self-disclosure?

A. helps one manage personal stress and anxiety

B. irreversible

C. develops relationships

D. increased psychological health

E. none of the above

H: Disclosing Your Self to Others, p. 64; C: conceptual; D: medium; L.O.: managing self in relationships

Answer: B

65. According to self-discrepancy theory, we feel happiest when

A. our self-concept matches our ideal and ought selves

B. our self-concept exceeds our ideal and ought selves

C. there is a great discrepancy between our ideal and ought selves

D. we perceive our self-concept to be inferior to our ideal and ought selves

E. none of the above

H: Measuring Up to Your Own Standards, p. 43; C: conceptual; D: medium; L.O.: components of self

Answer: A

66. According to the Johari Window, what is the part of the self that is not known to others but is known to self?

A. open area

B. blind area

C. hidden area

D. closed area

E. unknown area

H: Your Hidden and Revealed Self, p. 63; C: conceptual; D: medium; L.O.: managing self in relationships

Answer: C

67. Enduring principles of what is good or bad and right or wrong are called

A. attitudes

B. values

C. beliefs

D. personal constructs

E. masks

H: Self-Concept, p. 41; C: factual/definitional; D: easy; L.O.: components of self

Answer: B

68. Which of the following characteristics are part of a male's lifelong gender socialization process?

A. independence

B. competitiveness

C. assertiveness

D. masculinity

E. all of the above

H: Gender and Self, p. 47; C: conceptual; D: medium; L.O.: influences on self

Answer: E

69. Jacqueline finds that she fears rejection and is anxious in her relationship with her boyfriend, who she believes will leave her. What attachment style is she experiencing?

A. fearful attachment

B. Linus's security blanket

C. dismissive attachment

D. preoccupied attachment

E. none of the above

H: Family and Self, p. 49; C: application; D: difficult; L.O.: sources of self

Answer: A

70. How would a culture that values mutual support and expects loyalty be classified according to Hofstede?

A. masculine

B. feminine

C. collectivistic

D. individualistic

E. none of the above

H: Culture and Self, p. 60; C: application; D: difficult; L.O.: influences on self

Answer: C

71. If a Hollywood actor is gay but not out of the closet to his fans, which strategy is he using to maintain his public self?

A. face

B. mask

C. hidden self

D. closed self

E. none of the above

H: Maintaining Your Public Self, p. 53; C: application; D: difficult; L.O.: influences on self

Answer: B

72. Which of the following is a strategy one can use to maintain or save face?
    A. use words and actions consistent with the face you are trying to use
    B. use communication that complements your face
    C. use communication consistent with other's perceptions of you
    D. use communication that is reinforced by objects or events of the context
    E. all of the above

    H: Maintaining Your Public Self, p. 53; C: conceptual; D: medium; L.O.: presenting your self

    Answer: E

73. Which of the following is true of women's online communication?
    A. women are more likely to adopt an "expert" mask
    B. women are more likely to "gender-swap"
    C. women are more likely to lose face
    D. women are more likely to express support and welcome others to a group
    E. women are more likely to lie

    H: Presenting the Self Online, p. 56; C: conceptual; D: medium; L.O.: presenting your self

    Answer: D

74. Which of the following vegetables serves as an effective metaphor for social penetration theory?
    A. broccoli
    B. asparagus
    C. carrot
    D. cucumber
    E. onion

    H: Opening Your Self to Others, p. 60; C: conceptual; D: medium; L.O.: managing self in relationships

    Answer: E

75. According to social penetration theory, what is the layer in which a person's attitudes, beliefs, and opinions are disclosed?
    A. peripheral layer
    B. intermediate layer
    C. central layers
    D. outer layer
    E. innermost layer

    H: Opening Your Self to Others, p. 60; C: conceptual; D: medium; L.O.: managing self in relationships

    Answer: B

76. According to social penetration theory, in which layer would a person's values, self-concept, and deep personality be?
    A. peripheral layer
    B. intermediate layer
    C. central layer

D. outer layer

E. innermost layer

H: Opening Your Self to Others, p. 60; C: conceptual; D: medium; L.O.: managing self in relationships

Answer: C

77. Mike will tell anybody who will listen intimate details about his personal relationship with his live-in girlfriend. According to the Johari Window, Mike has a relatively large

A. ego

B. blind area

C. hidden area

D. unknown area

E. public area

H: Your Hidden and Revealed Self, p. 63; C: application; D: difficult; L.O.: managing self in relationships

Answer: E

78. A relational partner with a preoccupied attachment style may be characterized by

A. high anxiety

B. low avoidance

C. desire for closeness

D. fear of rejection

E. all of the above

H: Family and Self, p. 49; C: conceptual; D: medium; L.O.: sources of self

Answer: E

79. According to the Johari Window, what is the part of the self that is not known to you or others?

A. open area

B. blind area

C. hidden area

D. closed area

E. unknown self

H: Your Hidden and Revealed Self, p. 63; C: conceptual; D: medium; L.O.: managing self in relationships

Answer: E

80. According to social penetration theory, if someone is comfortable disclosing only their favorite foods, restaurants, bands, or hobbies, which layer of the self is shared?

A. peripheral layer

B. intermediate layer

C. core layer

D. central layer

E. external layer

H: Opening Your Self to Others, p. 60; C: conceptual; D: medium; L.O.: managing self in relationships

Answer: B

81. Self-concept can best be characterized as
    A. perceptions we have about ourselves
    B. static, unchanging over time
    C. always positive
    D. always negative
    E. never seen through the roles you enact each day

    H: Self-Concept, p. 41; C: factual/definitional; D: easy; L.O.: components of self

    Answer: A

82. Which of the following statements is true about the self?
    A. continually changes over time
    B. based upon our life experiences
    C. composed of self-awareness
    D. composed of self-esteem
    E. all of the above

    H: The Components of Self, p. 40; C: conceptual; D: easy; L.O.: components of self

    Answer: E

83. Which of the following may help increase one's self-esteem?
    A. gaining more consistency between one's ought and ideal selves
    B. living in an appearance culture
    C. revising unrealistic standards for your self
    D. engaging in social comparison
    E. both A and C

    H: Improving Your Self-Esteem, p. 45; C: conceptual; D: medium; L.O.: components of self

    Answer: E

84. The chapter's opening anecdote about Eric Staib illustrates what aspect of self-concept?
    A. looking-glass self
    B. social comparison
    C. ideal self
    D. ought self
    E. none of the above

    H: Self-Concept, p. 41; C: application; D: difficult; L.O.: components of self

    Answer: A

85. Our self-esteem is likely to
    A. increase as we decrease differences between our ought and ideal selves
    B. decrease as we increase differences between ought and ideal selves
    C. stay the same as long as we align our ought and ideal selves
    D. increase once we find our ideal self
    E. increase only if we live in an appearance culture

    H: Improving Your Self-Esteem, p. 45; C: conceptual; D: medium; L.O.: components of self

    Answer: A

86. When singer Ashlee Simpson was caught lip-synching her song "Pieces of Me" on *Saturday Night Live* she experienced
    A. individualism
    B. losing face
    C. embarrassment
    D. both B and C
    E. none of the above
    H: Maintaining Your Public Self, p. 53; C: application; D: hard; L.O.: presenting your self
    Answer: D

87. According to social penetration theory, a person's age, sex, race, or ethnicity would be represented by
    A. the peripheral layer
    B. the intermediate layer
    C. the central layer
    D. the outer layer
    E. the innermost layer
    H: Opening Your Self to Others, p. 60; C: conceptual; D: medium; L.O.: managing self in relationships
    Answer: A

88. An appearance culture can cause us to
    A. think negatively about our selves
    B. think we are too fat
    C. crave unattainable perfection
    D. want to look like the perfected images portrayed by the media
    E. all of the above
    H: How Does the Media Shape Your Self-Esteem?, p. 45; C: conceptual; D: medium; L.O.: components of self
    Answer: E

89. Which of the following is NOT characteristic of online masks?
    A. men are more likely to present themselves as expert
    B. women are more likely to present themselves as expert
    C. women are more likely to offer supportive messages
    D. men are more likely to answer questions
    E. women are more likely to make others feel welcome
    H: Presenting the Self Online, p. 56; C: conceptual; D: medium; L.O.: presenting your self
    Answer: B

90. What does post-cyber-disclosure panic mean?
    A. we tend to disclose more online
    B. we tend to disclose too little online
    C. adolescents don't disclose enough to their parents
    D. we fear someone has discovered that our online persona is fake
    E. the realization that our personal e-mail disclosure may be read by others
    H: Differences in Disclosure, p. 65; C: conceptual; D: medium; L.O.: managing self in relationships
    Answer: E

91. What are some ways in which we can improve our self-disclosure?
    A. know our selves
    B. know others
    C. be sensitive to cultural differences
    D. go slowly and gradually disclose intermediate and central aspects of self
    E. all of the above

    H: Effectively Disclosing Your Self, p. 70; C: conceptual; D: medium; L.O.: managing self in relationships

    Answer: E

92. Which of the following are engaged in by users of online social networking and dating sites?
    A. selective self-presentation
    B. use of masks
    C. accentuating positive characteristics
    D. gender swapping
    E. all of the above

    H: Presenting the Self Online, p. 56; C: conceptual; D: medium; L.O.: presenting your self

    Answer: E

93. A self-fulfilling prophecy occurs when
    A. thinking and believing decreases the likelihood of an event
    B. predictions cause you to act in ways that help make the predictions come true
    C. we fail to live up to labels others have of us
    D. we fail to act as others expect
    E. none of the above

    H: Self-Concept, p. 41; C: conceptual; D: easy; L.O.: components of self

    Answer: B

94. People with large hidden areas as depicted in the Johari Window
    A. fear rejection
    B. do not want to know much about the people with whom they relate
    C. expect acceptance
    D. do not try to avoid becoming known
    E. none of the above

    H: Your Hidden and Revealed Self, p. 63; C: application; D: difficult; L.O.: managing self in relationships

    Answer: A

95. Which of the following statements reflects the notion that our self-concept is influenced by the labels others apply to us?
    A. my father always said I was the black sheep of the family
    B. I see myself as a student, worker, and son
    C. I am happy with myself
    D. I am an extroverted person
    E. none of the above

    H: Self-Concept, p. 41; C: application; D: difficult; L.O.: influences on self

    Answer: A

96. Which of the following is NOT considered to be a source of influence upon self?
    A. face
    B. culture
    C. family
    D. gender
    E. none of the above
    H: The Sources of Self, p. 47; C: factual/definitional; D: easy; L.O.: sources of self
    Answer: A

97. Which of the following is NOT true of self-disclosure?
    A. people tend to disclose more quickly online than in face-to-face interaction
    B. self-disclosure increases our mental health and relieves stress
    C. Euro-Americans tend to disclose less than Hispanics
    D. women disclose more than men
    E. keeping problems to yourself can cause problems
    H: Differences in Disclosure, p. 65; C: conceptual; D: medium; L.O.: managing self in relationships
    Answer: C

98. Which of the following is a guideline for increasing the effectiveness of your self-disclosure?
    A. know your self
    B. know your audience
    C. be sensitive to cultural differences
    D. don't presume gender differences
    E. all of the above
    H: Effectively Disclosing Your Self, p. 70; C: conceptual; D: medium; L.O.: managing self in relationships
    Answer: E

99. Which of the following is true about self-concept?
    A. difficult to change
    B. composed of attitudes
    C. composed of beliefs
    D. composed of values
    E. all of the above
    H: Self-Concept, p. 41; C: conceptual; D: easy; L.O.: components of self
    Answer: E

100. Culture can include
    A. age
    B. gender
    C. sexual orientation
    D. religion
    E. all of the above
    H: Culture and Self, p. 50; C: conceptual; D: medium; L.O.: culture and self
    Answer: E

101. If you have a secure attachment style, you are more likely
    A. to develop stable relationships
    B. to be in the majority
    C. to be more trusting
    D. to have high self-esteem
    E. all of the above

    H: Family and Self, p. 49; C: conceptual; D: medium; L.O.: influences on self in relationships

    Answer: E

102. If your friend made the statement, "Dishonoring and disrespecting your mother is just plain wrong," this would be an example of
    A. an attitude
    B. a belief
    C. a value
    D. a personal construct
    E. the looking-glass self

    H: Self-Concept, p. 41; C: application; D: difficult; L.O.: components of self

    Answer: C

Short Answer

Briefly respond to the following questions in full sentences.

103. How does interacting with others impact or help shape our self-concept?

    H: Self-Concept, p. 41; C: conceptual; D: medium; L.O.: components of self

    Possible Answer: We tend to see ourselves through other's perceptions, a concept known as the looking-glass self.

104. How does one's self-esteem impact interpersonal communication?

    H: Self-Esteem, p. 43; C: conceptual; D: medium; L.O.: components of self

    Possible Answer: Low self-esteem may result in negative interactions with others; high self-esteem may result in positive interactions with others.

105. Explain the difference between self-esteem and self-concept.

    H: Self-Esteem, p. 43; C: conceptual; D: medium; L.O.: components of self

    Possible Answer: Self-esteem is how we evaluate our self-concept; self-concept is how we perceive ourselves.

106. Identify benefits or rewards of self-disclosure.

    H: Disclosing Your Self to Others, p. 64; C: conceptual; D: medium; L.O.: managing self in relationships

    Possible Answer: Self-disclosure can increase intimacy in relationships and promote the mental health and decrease the stress of the discloser.

107. Identify risks or costs of self-disclosure.

H: Disclosing Your Self to Others, p. 64; C: conceptual; D: medium; L.O.: managing self in relationships

Possible Answer: Disclosing information can hurt one's self, an other, or a relationship, and/or make the receiver feel uncomfortable.

108. What are the three components of self?

H: The Components of Self, p. 40; C: factual/definitional; D: easy; L.O.: components of self

Possible Answer: Self-awareness, self-concept, and self-esteem.

109. Our self-esteem is composed of what two mental standards?

H: Measuring Up to Your Own Standards, p. 43; C: factual/definitional; D: easy; L.O.: components of self

Possible Answer: Ideal self and ought self.

110. Identify the two primary components of social penetration theory.

H: Opening Your Self to Others, p. 60; C: factual/definitional; D: easy; L.O.: managing self in relationships

Possible Answer: Depth and breadth of self-disclosure.

111. Identify a country that has an individualistic culture and one that has a collectivistic culture.

H: Culture and Self, p. 50; C: conceptual; D: easy; L.O.: influences on self

Possible Answer: The United States is individualistic; Taiwan is collectivistic.

112. What is gender?

H: Gender and Self, p. 47; C: conceptual; D: medium; L.O.: influences on self

Possible Answer: Gender is the understanding of what it means to be male or female, learned through socialization.

113. Explain how the self-fulfilling prophecy works and how it may impact or relate to your performance in this course thus far.

H: Self-Concept, p. 41; C: application; D: medium; L.O.: components of self

Possible Answer: Our thoughts and beliefs can help bring about those very beliefs; in short, if we think we will do well in this course, we probably will (the opposite is also true).

114. What are some ways we can improve our self-esteem?

H: Improving Your Self-Esteem, p. 45; C: conceptual; D: medium; L.O.: managing self in relationships

Possible Answer: Think positively, associate with confirming significant others, reduce discrepancy between ideal and ought selves, set reasonable standards for yourself.

115. Explain how low self-esteem can be a vicious cycle.

H: Self-Esteem, p. 43; C: conceptual; D: medium; L.O.: components of self

Possible Answer: Reference Figure 2.1 on page 43 of the text and explain how negative beliefs lead to low self-esteem, which further fuels initial negative beliefs.

116. Explain how warranting value is used to assess a person's online persona.

H: Presenting the Self Online, p. 56; C: conceptual; D: medium; L.O.: presenting your self

Possible Answer: It is used to determine the degree to which information presented about someone is corroborated by other people and outside evidence.

Essay

Please respond to the following questions in paragraph form.

117. Explain social penetration theory and how it relates to and impacts our use of self-disclosure by providing an example of a personal relationship.

H: Opening Your Self to Others, p. 60; C: application; D: difficult; L.O.: managing self in relationships

Possible Answer: Using the metaphor of the onion, disclosure occurs incrementally, penetrating more deeply into the layers toward intimacy, and includes peripheral, intermediate, and central layers of self. Self-disclosure increases in both depth and breadth.

118. Describe the Johari Window, making sure to identify and give an example of each quadrant by citing examples of significant others in your own life.

H: Your Hidden and Revealed Self, p. 63; C: application; D: difficult; L.O.: managing self in relationships

Possible Answer: The Johari Window defines four quadrants: public area, known to you and others; blind area, known to others but not to you; hidden area, known to you but hidden from others; and unknown area, unknown both to you and to others.

119. Differentiate between an online description that has low warranting value and one that has high warranting value.

H: Presenting the Self Online, p. 56; C: conceptual; D: medium; L.O.: presenting your self

Possible Answer: Information has low warranting value when it isn't supported by others and can't be verified offline. It may only be presented by the author. Information has high warranting value when it is authored by others and can be verified by off- and online sources. This information may also be presented by the author, but is consistent with other sources.

120. Discuss your opinion of the overall value of self-disclosure to your personal relationships. Compare and contrast the benefits as well as the risks of engaging in self-disclosure.

H: Disclosing Your Self to Others, p. 64; C: application; D: difficult; L.O.: managing self in relationships

Possible Answer: Benefits: increased mental health and stability, closeness to others, and increased relational intimacy; risks: information can hurt or be used against you.

121. Explain attachment theory. Be sure to identify and give examples of the four attachment styles.

H: Family and Self, p. 49; C: application; D: difficult; L.O.: sources of self

Possible Answer: Attachment theory is based on two dimensions, attachment anxiety and attachment avoidance. Attachment anxiety is the amount of fear of rejection a person experiences in relationships with others. Attachment avoidance is how much one desires close interpersonal relationships. There are four attachment styles. Secure attachment involves low anxiety and avoidance. People with this style seek close intimate relationships with others. Preoccupied attachment has a high level of anxiety and a low level of avoidance. Those with the dismissive attachment style show low anxiety, yet high avoidance. The fearful attachment style involves both high anxiety and avoidance.

Chapter 3: Perceiving Others

Matching

Match the concept, term, or theory with its correct response or definition.

A. actor-observer effect
B. algebraic impressions
C. attributions
D. conscientiousness
E. empathy
F. extraversion
G. fundamental attribution error
H. Gestalt
I. halo effect
J. horn effect
K. implicit personality theories
L. interpretation
M. negativity effect

N. openness
O. organization
P. perception
Q. personality
R. positivity bias
S. punctuation
T. salience
U. schemata
V. selection
W. self-serving bias
X. stereotyping
Y. Uncertainty Reduction Theory

1. Our tendency to interpret information in a positive way if it concerns someone for whom we have established a positive Gestalt.
   H: Halos and Horns, p. 99; C: factual/definitional; D: easy; L.O.: forming impressions
   Answer: I. halo effect

2. The human tendency to attribute internal causes, rather than external or environmental causes, to others' behaviors.
   H: Creating Explanations, p. 82; C: factual/definitional; D: easy; L.O.: perception process
   Answer: G. fundamental attribution error

3. Focusing our attention on specific stimuli found in our environment.
   H: Selecting Information, p. 78; C: factual/definitional; D: easy; L.O.: perception process
   Answer: V. selection

4. A personality trait of individuals who are organized and persistent in achieving their goals.
   H: Personality, p. 91; C: factual/definitional; D: easy; L.O.: influences on perception
   Answer: D. conscientiousness

5. A phase of the perception process in which we structure information and stimuli into coherent, meaningful patterns.
   H: Organizing the Information You've Selected, p. 79; C: factual/definitional; D: easy; L.O.: perception process
   Answer: O. organization

6. The tendency to make internal attributions about one's own successful behaviors.
   H: Creating Explanations, p. 82; C: factual/definitional; D: easy; L.O.: perception process
   Answer: W. self-serving bias

7. A personality trait of an individual who seeks out new ideas and experiences.
   H: Personality, p. 91; C: factual/definitional; D: easy; L.O.: influences on perception
   Answer: N. openness

8. Mental structures containing information that defines the characteristics and interrelationships of various concepts.
   H: Using Familiar Information, p. 81; C: factual/definitional; D: easy; L.O.: perception process
   Answer: U. schemata

9. Explanations for comments and behaviors of others.
   H: Creating Explanations, p. 82; C: factual/definitional; D: easy; L.O.: perception process
   Answer: C. attributions

10. The tendency to negatively interpret the communication and behaviors of people for whom we have negative Gestalts.
    H: Halos and Horns, p. 99; C: factual/definitional; D: easy; L.O.: forming impressions
    Answer: J. horn effect

11. The process of making sense of our world.
    H: Perception as a Process, p. 78; C: factual/definitional; D: easy; L.O.: perception process
    Answer: P. perception

12. The tendency to assign external causes to one's own behavior.
    H: Creating Explanations, p. 82; C: factual/definitional; D: easy; L.O.: perception process
    Answer: A. actor-observer effect

13. The tendency toward forming positive Gestalts.
    H: The Positivity Bias, p. 98; C: factual/definitional; D: easy; L.O.: forming impressions
    Answer: R. positivity bias

14. According to this theory, our primary goal during initial interactions is to reduce the feeling of uncertainty about our conversation partners.

    H: Experiencing Uncertainty, p. 84; C: factual/definitional; D: easy; L.O.: perception process

    Answer: Y. Uncertainty Reduction Theory

15. Impressions of others formed through a process of comparing and assessing positive and negative characteristics.

    H: Calculating Algebraic Impressions, p. 99; C: factual/definitional; D: easy; L.O.: forming impressions

    Answer: B. algebraic impressions

16. A personality trait of an individual who is motivated by and seeks out interaction with others.

    H: Personality, p. 91; C: factual/definitional; D: easy; L.O.: influences on perception

    Answer: F. extraversion

17. Personal beliefs about different personalities and the ways traits cluster together.

    H: Generalizing from the Traits We Know, p. 95; C: factual/definitional; D: easy; L.O.: influences on perception

    Answer: K. implicit personality theories

18. The process of assigning meaning to information we have selected.

    H: Interpreting the Information, p. 81; C: factual/definitional; D: easy; L.O.: perception process

    Answer: L. interpretation

19. The way in which humans categorize others as a group based upon mental schemata.

    H: Using Stereotypes, p. 100; C: factual/definitional; D: easy; L.O.: forming impressions

    Answer: X. stereotyping

20. A general sense of a person that is either positive or negative.

    H: Constructing Gestalts, p. 97; C: factual/definitional; D: easy; L.O.: forming impressions

    Answer: H. Gestalt

21. The degree to which different stimuli attract our attention.

    H: Selecting Information, p. 78; C: factual/definitional; D: easy; L.O.: perception process

    Answer: T. salience

22. The human tendency to perceive negative perceptions or information as more salient.

    H: The Negativity Effect, p. 98; C: factual/definitional; D: easy; L.O.: forming impressions

    Answer: M. negativity effect

23. An individual's characteristic way of thinking, feeling, and acting, based on his or her traits.

    H: Personality, p. 91; C: factual/definitional; D: easy; L.O.: influences on perception

    Answer: Q. personality

24. A process of organizing information and stimuli using a chronological sequence.
    H: Organizing the Information You've Selected, p. 79; C: factual/definitional; D: easy;
    L.O.: perception process
    Answer: S. punctuation

25. The process of trying to feel and experience the thoughts and emotions of others.
    H: Offering Empathy, p. 104; C: factual/definitional; D: easy; L.O.: improving perception
    Answer: E. empathy

True/False

Please select whether the following statements are true or false.

26. As we perceive others, we are more influenced by negative characteristics than positive characteristics.
    H: The Negativity Effect, p. 98; C: factual/definitional; D: easy; L.O.: forming impressions
    Answer: T

27. If a person is able to see from another's perspective, he or she is offering empathy.
    H: Offering Empathy, p. 104; C: application; D: difficult; L.O.: improving perception
    Answer: F

28. If Jolene attributes negative outcomes to external sources while simultaneously attributing positive outcomes to internal or personal characteristics, she is demonstrating a self-serving bias.
    H: Creating Explanations, p. 82; C: application; D: difficult; L.O.: forming impressions
    Answer: T

29. The three stages of the interpersonal perception process are salience, organization, and interpretation.
    H: Perception as a Process, p. 78; C: factual/definitional; D: easy; L.O.: perception process
    Answer: F

30. During the organization phase of perception, we engage in punctuation, where we tend to make internal attributions, crediting ourselves for our own behavior.
    H: Organizing the Information You've Selected, p. 79; C: factual/definitional; D: easy;
    L.O.: perception process
    Answer: F

31. When we pay attention to specific stimuli or information in our environments while simultaneously ignoring other stimuli, we are engaging in the selection process of perception.
    H: Selecting Information, p. 78; C: factual/definitional; D: easy; L.O.: perception process
    Answer: T

32. Implicit personality theories operate similarly to stereotyping.
H: Generalizing from the Traits We Know, p. 95; C: conceptual; D: medium; L.O.: forming impressions
Answer: T

33. The Gestalts we form of other people may be either positive or negative impressions.
H: Constructing Gestalts, p. 97; C: conceptual; D: medium; L.O.: forming impressions
Answer: T

34. A halo effect may occur when we attribute positive motives to someone's actions without having actually observed those particular qualities.
H: Halos and Horns, p. 99; C: conceptual; D: medium; L.O.: forming impressions
Answer: T

35. If you ignore the positive or good in someone that you do not like, you are demonstrating the horn effect.
H: Halos and Horns, p. 99; C: factual/definitional; D: easy; L.O.: forming impressions
Answer: T

36. Culture, gender, and personality are three examples of filters that influence the way we perceive people and events in our lives.
H: Influences on Perception, p. 86; C: conceptual; D: medium; L.O.: influences on perception
Answer: T

37. We tend to pay more attention to positive than to negative characteristics of others.
H: The Negativity Effect, p. 98; C: conceptual; D: medium; L.O.: forming impressions
Answer: F

38. Stereotyping automatically leads to negative generalizations about other people, cultures, and genders.
H: Using Stereotypes, p. 100; C: conceptual; D: medium; L.O.: forming impressions
Answer: F

39. People who share fundamentally similar attitudes, values, and beliefs with you are considered ingroupers.
H: Perception and Culture, p. 86; C: conceptual; D: medium; L.O.: perception process
Answer: T

40. We form algebraic impressions as a result of forming quick first impressions of others.
H: Calculating Algebraic Impressions, p. 99; C: conceptual; D: medium; L.O.: forming impressions
Answer: F

41. Gestalts are formed as the result of a specific positive or negative observation we have of another person.
H: Constructing Gestalts, p. 97; C: conceptual; D: medium; L.O.: forming impressions
Answer: F

42. Perception is a sense-making process in which individuals actively manage information and stimuli by selecting, organizing, and interpreting information from their environment.
H: Perception as a Process, p. 78; C: factual/definitional; D: easy; L.O.: perception process
Answer: T

43. We engage in the selection process of perception by focusing our attention on specific stimuli while ignoring others because of human limitations on processing information.
H: Selecting Information, p. 78; C: conceptual; D: medium; L.O.: perception process
Answer: T

44. Salience relates to the importance you place on the attributes you perceive in others.
H: Selecting Information, p. 78; C: conceptual; D: medium; L.O.: perception process
Answer: F

45. Punctuation occurs in the organization stage of perception and refers to structuring information and events in chronological order.
H: Organizing the Information You've Selected, p. 79; C: conceptual; D: medium; L.O.: perception process
Answer: T

46. The fundamental attribution error results from attributing others' behaviors to social or environmental, rather than internal or personal, causes.
H: Creating Explanations, p. 82; C: conceptual; D: medium; L.O.: perception process
Answer: F

47. An attribution is our way of explaining other people's responses and behaviors toward us.
H: Creating Explanations, p. 82; C: conceptual; D: easy; L.O.: perception process
Answer: T

48. The actor-observer effect results from the innate human tendency to make internal or dispositional attributions concerning one's own behavior.
H: Creating Explanations, p. 82; C: conceptual; D: medium; L.O.: perception process
Answer: F

49. The human tendency to credit ourselves, not the environment or external causes, for our successful behavior is called a self-serving bias.
H: Creating Explanations, p. 82; C: factual/definitional; D: easy; L.O.: perception process
Answer: T

50. According to the Uncertainty Reduction Theory, people have a basic need to reduce uncertainty in initial interactions, and to increase their ability to explain and predict the behavior of others.

H: Experiencing Uncertainty, p. 84; C: factual/definitional; D: easy; L.O.: perception process

Answer: T

Multiple Choice

Please choose the correct response to the following statements.

51. Chris's friend Beth has had a miscarriage, so he rushes over to her apartment to see how he can comfort or console her. Chris is displaying:
    A. empathy
    B. supportiveness
    C. self-serving bias
    D. selflessness
    E. none of the above

    H: Offering Empathy, p. 104; C: application; D: difficult; L.O.: improving perception

    Answer: A

52. Individuals tend to judge and perceive themselves
    A. more honestly than others
    B. more positively than others
    C. about the same as others
    D. more critically than others
    E. less frequently as they mature

    H: Creating Explanations, p. 82; C: conceptual; D: medium; L.O.: perception process

    Answer: B

53. Which of the following is NOT one of the major influences on the perception process?
    A. culture
    B. gender
    C. personality
    D. negativity effect
    E. none of the above

    H: Influences on Perception, p. 86; C: conceptual; D: medium; L.O.: influences on perception

    Answer: D

54. What process is involved when we direct our attention to specific stimuli while ignoring other stimuli?
    A. perception
    B. perceptual loss
    C. selection
    D. punctuation
    E. organization

    H: Selecting Information, p. 78; C: conceptual; D: medium; L.O.: perception process

    Answer: C

55. Which of the following processes is involved in the human perception process?
    A. selection
    B. organization
    C. interpretation
    D. response
    E. all of the above

    H: Perception as a Process, p. 78; C: factual/definitional; D: difficult; L.O.: perception process

    Answer: E

56. Which of the following judgments are we most likely to make when deciding whether someone is an ingrouper or an outgrouper?
    A. how similar the person is to us
    B. how dissimilar the person is to us
    C. how positive our impressions of the person are
    D. how negative our impressions of the person are
    E. all of the above

    H: Perception and Culture, p. 86; C: conceptual; D: medium; L.O.: perception process

    Answer: E

57. Many factors influence the selection stage of the perception process. Which of the following is NOT one of these factors?
    A. salience
    B. communication that deviates from our expectations
    C. communication that is viewed as important
    D. communication that is stimulating
    E. punctuation

    H: Selecting Information, p. 78; C: conceptual; D: medium; L.O.: perception process

    Answer: E

58. In interpreting information, we form attributions, which are defined as
    A. explanations for others' behaviors and comments
    B. mental structures that define concept characteristics
    C. stimuli that attract our attention
    D. judgments about the characteristics of other people
    E. none of the above

    H: Creating Explanations, p. 82; C: conceptual; D: medium; L.O.: perception process

    Answer: A

59. Which of the following factors influences the interpretation stage of the perception process?
    A. schemata
    B. internal attributions
    C. external attributions
    D. fundamental attribution error
    E. all of the above

    H: Interpreting the Information, p. 81; C: conceptual; D: medium; L.O.: perception process

    Answer: E

60. When we perceive and judge our own behavior, we often use the
    A. fundamental attribution error
    B. actor-observer effect
    C. self-serving bias
    D. both B and C
    E. both A and B

    H: Creating Explanations, p. 82; C: conceptual; D: difficult; L.O.: perception process

    Answer: D

61. If you overate at a dinner buffet and later explained that everyone overeats at buffets, what perceptual error are you exhibiting?
    A. fundamental attribution error
    B. salience
    C. internal attribution
    D. actor-observer effect
    E. none of the above

    H: Creating Explanations, p. 82; C: application; D: difficult; L.O.: perception process

    Answer: D

62. At a party your friend got drunk. You later explained that he or she was stressed out from a recent breakup. What type of attribution are you making?
    A. fundamental attribution error
    B. faulty attribution
    C. internal attribution
    D. external attribution
    E. none of the above

    H: Creating Explanations, p. 82; C: application; D: difficult; L.O.: perception process

    Answer: D

63. When you are winning at poker and explain to others at the table that you are good at cards and tend to have good luck, what type of attribution error are you making?
    A. self-serving bias
    B. fundamental attribution error
    C. actor-observer effect
    D. external attribution
    E. none of the above

    H: Creating Explanations, p. 82; C: application; D: difficult; L.O.: perception process

    Answer: A

64. A husband and wife are having dinner at a restaurant when the wife accuses her husband of paying too much attention to their server. The husband claims he was just returning her eye contact and engaging smile. Which process in the organizational stage of perception have the husband and wife engaged in differently?
    A. salience
    B. punctuation
    C. selection
    D. uncertainty reduction
    E. none of the above

H: Organizing the Information You've Selected, p. 79; C: application; D: difficult; L.O.: perception process

Answer: B

65. When we categorize people as a group based upon our own schemata while simultaneously ignoring individual differences, what perceptual process are we illustrating?
   A. self-serving bias
   B. punctuation
   C. stereotyping
   D. algebraic impressions
   E. none of the above

   H: Using Stereotypes, p. 100; C: conceptual; D: medium; L.O.: forming impressions

   Answer: C

66. If your girlfriend says she goes to the gym after work because you are never home, but you always go out for drinks after work because she is working out, then your difference in perception is due to
   A. punctuation
   B. stereotyping
   C. fundamental attribution error
   D. negativity effect
   E. self-serving bias

   H: Organizing the Information You've Selected, p. 79; C: application; D: difficult; L.O.: forming impressions

   Answer: A

67. Which of the following does NOT influence the interpretation stage of perception?
   A. schemata
   B. attributions
   C. actor-observer effect
   D. punctuation
   E. none of the above

   H: Interpreting the Information, p. 81; C: conceptual; D: medium; L.O.: perception process

   Answer: D

68. Which of the following play(s) an important role in forming our Gestalts?
   A. schemata
   B. attributions
   C. salience
   D. punctuation
   E. none of the above

   H: Using Familiar Information, p. 81; C: conceptual; D: medium; L.O.: perception process

   Answer: A

69. Which of the following is (are) used in the punctuation process during the organization stage of perception?
   A. cause-effect
   B. related events

C. schemata

D. chronological sequence

E. none of the above

H: Organizing the Information You've Selected, p. 79; C: conceptual; D: medium;

L.O.: perception process

Answer: D

70. If the chairperson of the Federal Reserve predicted that inflation would continue, you would be likely to interpret this prediction as credible and accurate. This is an example of which influence on interpreting information?

A. interpretation

B. attribution

C. punctuation

D. salience

E. schemata

H: Using Familiar Information, p. 81; C: application; D: difficult; L.O.: perception process

Answer: E

71. If your romantic partner does not respond to your instant message while you are both online and you assume he or she is losing interest in you, what kind of attribution are you making?

A. internal attribution

B. external attribution

C. true perception

D. actor-observer effect

E. none of the above

H: Creating Explanations, p. 82; C: application; D: difficult; L.O.: perception process

Answer: A

72. When we perceive and judge others we commonly

A. form a negative Gestalt

B. feel secure in our initial interactions

C. attribute their behavior to internal, personal causes

D. judge them more positively than we do ourselves

E. none of the above

H: Creating Explanations, p. 82; C: conceptual; D: medium; L.O.: perception process

Answer: C

73. If you yell at your roommate and later explain that your reaction was related to stress at work, what type of error are you making?

A. fundamental attribution error

B. internal attribution

C. self-serving bias

D. actor-observer effect

E. none of the above

H: Creating Explanations, p. 82; C: application; D: difficult; L.O.: perception process

Answer: D

74. If Paulo won a bet by guessing correctly who would win the basketball championship and later claimed it was because of his understanding of probability and statistics, what attribution is he making?
    A. fundamental attribution error
    B. external attribution
    C. self-serving bias
    D. actor-observer effect
    E. none of the above

    H: Creating Explanations, p. 82; C: application; D: difficult; L.O.: perception process

    Answer: C

75. According to Uncertainty Reduction Theory, which of the following is a primary goal of initial interaction?
    A. reduce uncertainty
    B. explain behavior
    C. predict behavior
    D. help anticipate how others will respond to us
    E. all of the above

    H: Experiencing Uncertainty, p. 84; C: conceptual; D: medium; L.O.: perception process

    Answer: E

76. Which of the following is an active strategy for reducing uncertainty regarding a person's behavior?
    A. observing the person
    B. asking questions of the person
    C. disclosing personal information to the person
    D. stalking the person
    E. third-person questioning

    H: Experiencing Uncertainty, p. 84; C: conceptual; D: medium; L.O.: perception process

    Answer: E

77. Which of the following are methods used for reducing uncertainty in our initial interactions with others?
    A. passive strategies
    B. active strategies
    C. interactive strategies
    D. observing and learning about how someone acts in social settings
    E. all of the above

    H: Experiencing Uncertainty, p. 84; C: conceptual; D: medium; L.O.: perception process

    Answer: E

78. Which of the following is NOT a characteristic of salient communication?
    A. it is visually and audibly stimulating
    B. it is consistent with our goals and is seen as important
    C. it deviates from our expectations
    D. it is predictable
    E. all of the above

    H: Selecting Information, p. 78; C: conceptual; D: medium; L.O.: perception process

    Answer: D

79. Which of the following is (are) characteristic of an ingrouper?
    A. someone who shares similar values
    B. someone who shares similar attitudes
    C. someone who shares similar beliefs
    D. someone whom you perceive as similar to you
    E. all of the above

    H: Perception and Culture, p. 86; C: conceptual; D: medium; L.O.: influences on perception

    Answer: E

80. Which of the following conclusions can be made about gender differences?
    A. women and men are substantially similar
    B. women and men are substantially dissimilar
    C. women and men are essentially similar and respond similarly
    D. women use indirect language, whereas men use direct language
    E. none of the above

    H: Perception and Gender, p. 88; C: conceptual; D: medium; L.O.: influences on perception

    Answer: C

81. Characteristic ways of thinking, feeling, and acting constitute
    A. an interpersonal impression
    B. implicit personality theory
    C. an algebraic impression
    D. schemata
    E. personality

    H: Personality, p. 91; C: factual/definitional; D: easy; L.O.: influences on perception

    Answer: E

82. Psychologists suggest that there are five primary personality traits. Which of the following is NOT part of the Big Five?
    A. agreeableness
    B. openness
    C. extraversion
    D. introversion
    E. neuroticism

    H: Personality, p. 91; C: factual/definitional; D: easy; L.O.: influences on perception

    Answer: D

83. Tomas is often on an emotional roller coaster and his partner is never sure what mood he is going to be in. Tomas is both insecure and overly emotional. What personality trait does Tomas display a high level of?
    A. openness
    B. neuroticism
    C. conscientiousness
    D. agreeableness
    E. extraversion

    H: Personality, p. 91; C: application; D: difficult; L.O.: influences on perception

    Answer: B

84. Wade is highly organized at work and keeps detailed to-do lists on his Blackberry. He is never late. What personality trait does Wade display a high level of?
    A. neuroticism
    B. extraversion
    C. conscientiousness
    D. openness
    E. agreeableness

    H: Personality, p. 91; C: application; D: difficult; L.O.: influences on perception

    Answer: C

85. Celeste is gregarious and is often found talking with her colleagues at the office kitchen. What personality trait does Celeste display a high level of?
    A. openness
    B. neuroticism
    C. agreeableness
    D. conscientiousness
    E. extraversion

    H: Personality, p. 91; C: application; D: difficult; L.O.: influences on perception

    Answer: E

86. Which of the following is not part of the interpretation phase of the perception process?
    A. salience
    B. schemata
    C. attributions
    D. self-serving bias
    E. actor-observer effect

    H: Interpreting the Information, p. 81; C: conceptual; D: medium; L.O.: perception process

    Answer: A

87. Leslie likes Josh because he has an extraverted, engaging, and humorous personality. When Sarah tells Leslie that Josh can be very impatient and demonstrates road rage on a daily basis, Leslie refuses to believe her. What perceptual problem is Leslie having?
    A. fundamental attribution error
    B. self-serving bias
    C. actor-observer effect
    D. horn effect
    E. halo effect

    H: Halos and Horns, p. 99; C: application; D: difficult; L.O.: forming impressions

    Answer: E

88. Paul thinks that Professor Lee is a poor instructor because he finds her class too challenging. After she spends a half-hour helping him with his paper, he tells his friend that her class requires too much of his time. What perceptual process is affecting Paul?
    A. horn effect
    B. halo effect
    C. actor-observer effect
    D. consistency effect
    E. self-serving bias

H: Halos and Horns, p. 99; C: application; D: difficult; L.O.: forming impressions

Answer: A

89. Ellen communicates well with her partner Carmen. When they experience miscommunication, Ellen feels able to ask her partner questions to clarify her understanding. Ellen is demonstrating what perceptual skill in her relationship?
    A. positivity bias
    B. salience
    C. halo effect
    D. empathy
    E. perception-checking

    H: Checking Your Perception, p. 105; C: application; D: difficult; L.O.: improving perception

    Answer: E

90. Which of the following is involved in the perception-checking process?
    A. checking your punctuation
    B. checking your attributions
    C. checking your perceptual influences
    D. checking your impressions
    E. all of the above

    H: Checking Your Perception, p. 105; C: conceptual; D: medium; L.O.: improving perception

    Answer: E

Short Answer

Briefly respond to the following questions in full sentences.

91. Define perception and identify the three stages of the process.

    H: Perception as a Process, p. 78; C: factual/definitional; D: easy; L.O.: perception process

    Possible Answer: Using their senses, humans select, organize, and interpret information from their environment.

92. Define and give an example of how implicit personality theories work.

    H: Generalizing from the Traits We Know, p. 95; C: conceptual; D: medium; L.O.: influences on perception

    Possible Answer: Personal beliefs we have about types of personalities and how traits cluster together. If you meet someone and see her as open-minded, you might also assume she is liberal and democratic.

93. What are the three strategies for reducing uncertainty? Give an example of each strategy.

    H: Experiencing Uncertainty, p. 84; C: conceptual; D: medium; L.O.: perception process

    Possible Answer: Passive, Active, Interactive. Observing a person in social settings, asking a person's friends about the person, directly asking the person questions.

94. Explain the difference between the halo effect and the horn effect.

    H: Halos and Horns, p. 99; C: factual/definitional; D: easy; L.O.: forming impressions

    Possible Answer: The halo effect occurs when we positively interpret behaviors of people for whom we have positive Gestalts; the horn effect occurs when our negative Gestalts result in negative interpretations of others' behaviors and comments.

95. Define empathy and its two components.

    H: Offering Empathy, p. 104; C: conceptual; D: medium; L.O.: improving perception

    Possible Answer: "Feeling into" others' thoughts and emotions and identifying with them. Components: 1) perspective-taking: the ability to see things from another's perspective; 2) empathic concern.

96. Explain the difference between the cultural concepts of ingroupers and outgroupers.

    H: Perception and Culture, p. 86; C: conceptual; D: medium; L.O.: influences on perception

    Possible Answer: Ingroupers are those we perceive to be similar to us; outgroupers are those we perceive to be dissimilar to us.

97. Define the negativity effect and explain its role in how you perceive others.

    H: The Negativity Effect, p. 98; C: factual/definitional; D: easy; L.O.: forming impressions

    Possible Answer: The negativity effect is when we believe someone's "true character" is based more on the negative information we learn about them than the positive. While a negative Gestalt can be true, it is important to always carefully and critically assess all information we learn about others.

98. How does punctuation impact the organization stage of the perception process?

    H: Organizing the Information You've Selected, p. 79; C: conceptual; D: medium; L.O.: perception process

    Possible Answer: During the organization stage of perception, we punctuate by structuring information according to chronological order.

99. How does salience impact the selection stage of the perception process?

    H: Selecting Information, p. 78; C: conceptual; D: medium; L.O.: perception process

    Possible Answer: In the first stage of perception, selection, we use salience to decide what stimuli to either focus on or ignore.

100. How do attributions play a role in the interpretation stage of the perception process?

    H: Creating Explanations, p. 82; C: conceptual; D: medium; L.O.: perception process

    Possible Answer: We form attributions to create explanations for information we've perceived.

101. What's the difference between an internal attribution and an external attribution?

    H: Creating Explanations, p. 82; C: conceptual; D: medium; L.O.: improving perception

    Possible Answer: An internal attribution assumes that a person's behavior stems from internal, or personal, causes. An external attribution assumes that a person's behavior stems from outside factors unrelated to their character or personality.

102. Explain what the fundamental attribution error is and why it is so common.

   H: Creating Explanations, p. 82; C: conceptual; D: medium; L.O.: perception process

   Possible Answer: The common tendency for humans to attribute others' behaviors to internal or dispositional causes. It is common because our focus is the person, not his or her environment.

103. Explain why we often make the perceptual error of self-serving bias.

   H: Creating Explanations, p. 82; C: conceptual; D: medium; L.O.: perception process

   Possible Answer: We don't always make external attributions regarding our own behavior; when it is to our advantage we may make internal attributions, thereby taking credit for our own success.

104. Identify two interactive strategies for reducing uncertainty.

   H: Experiencing Uncertainty, p. 84; C: conceptual; D: medium; L.O.: perception process

   Possible Answer: Asking questions and self-disclosure.

105. How do algebraic impressions impact how we form interpersonal impressions of others?

   H: Calculating Algebraic Impressions, p. 99; C: conceptual; D: medium; L.O.: forming impressions

   Possible Answer: Instead of forming simple, generalized impressions of others, we develop more complex impressions by considering both positive and negative attributes of a person.

Essay

Please respond to the following questions in paragraph form.

106. Discuss the relationship between gender and perception. What are some common misconceptions about the ways in which women and men communicate differently?

   H: Perception and Gender, p. 88; C: application; D: difficult; L.O.: influences on perception

   Possible Answer: Brain functioning and development are different in women and men. Women are more skilled at spatial relationships, emotions, and language. Men think more linearly and focus on problem solving. People perceive that women talk more about emotions and gossip more than men do; in reality, however, men and women tend to talk in much the same way.

107. Identify and explain the Big Five personality traits.

   H: Personality, p. 91; C: conceptual; D: medium; L.O.: influences on perception

   Possible Answer: Extraversion, agreeableness, conscientiousness, neuroticism, and openness.

108. Explain how we form impressions using stereotypes. Is stereotyping always negative? Provide an example.

   H: Using Stereotypes, p. 100; C: application; D: difficult; L.O.: forming impressions

   Possible Answer: We form impressions by mentally sorting people into our pre-existing categories, ignoring individual differences. Stereotypes can be either positive or negative. Example: We might stereotype Asian students as excelling in math and the sciences.

109. How can offering empathy be used to improve the accuracy of our perceptions?

H: Offering Empathy, p. 104; C: conceptual; D: medium; L.O.: improving perception

Possible Answer: We first engage in perspective-taking to see things from someone else's perspective by trying to "feel into" and identify with another. Then we demonstrate empathic concern by trying to experience the emotions of others.

110. Explain the five-step process of perception-checking.

H: Checking Your Perception, p. 105; C: conceptual; D: medium; L.O.: improving perception

Possible Answer: Check your punctuation, knowledge, attributions, perceptual influences, and impressions.

Chapter 4: Experiencing and Expressing Emotions

Matching

Match the concept, term, or theory with its correct response or definition.

A. anger
B. blended emotions
C. catharsis
D. chronic hostility
E. deactivation
F. display rules
G. emoticon
H. emotion
I. emotion management
J. emotion-sharing
K. emotional contagion
L. emotional intelligence
M. encounter avoidance

N. encounter structuring
O. feelings
P. grief
Q. Jefferson strategy
R. moods
S. neuroticism
T. primary emotions
U. Rational Emotive Behavior Therapy
V. reappraisal
W. supportive communication
X. suppression
Y. venting

1. A form of communication in which we tell others about emotional experiences.
   H: Defining Emotion, p. 118; C: factual/definitional; D: easy; L.O.: basics of emotion
   Answer: J. emotion-sharing

2. A therapeutic method for helping patients systemically purge themselves of self-defeating beliefs.
   H: Personality, p. 126; C: factual/definitional; D: easy; L.O.: managing emotion
   Answer: U. Rational Emotive Behavior Therapy

3. Short-term emotional reactions generating only limited arousal.
   H: Feelings and Moods, p. 119; C: factual/definitional; D: easy; L.O.: basics of emotion
   Answer: O. feelings

4. Low-intensity states lasting longer than feelings or emotions.

   H: Feelings and Moods, p. 119; C: factual/definitional; D: easy; L.O.: basics of emotion

   Answer: R. moods

5. The ability to interpret and effectively manage emotion.

   H: Managing Your Emotional Experience and Expression, p. 127; C: factual/definitional; D: easy; L.O.: influences on emotion

   Answer: L. emotional intelligence

6. Attempts to influence which emotions you feel and how and when you experience them.

   H: Managing Your Emotional Experience and Expression, p. 127; C: factual/definitional; D: easy; L.O.: influences on emotion

   Answer: I. emotion management

7. Allowing emotions to dominate our thoughts and explosively expressing them.

   H: Managing Your Emotions After They Occur, p. 129; C: factual/definitional; D: easy; L.O.: managing emotion

   Answer: Y. venting

8. The tendency to shy away from people, places, or activities that provoke unwanted emotions.

   H: Preventing Emotions, p. 130; C: factual/definitional; D: easy; L.O.: managing emotion

   Answer: M. encounter avoidance

9. An intense sadness following a substantial loss.

   H: Grief, p. 139; C: factual/definitional; D: easy; L.O.: manage challenging emotions

   Answer: P. grief

10. Intentional avoidance of specific topics that provoke unwanted emotions.

    H: Preventing Emotions, p. 130; C: factual/definitional; D: easy; L.O.: managing emotion

    Answer: N. encounter structuring

11. Emotions that involve unique and consistent displays across cultures.

    H: Types of Emotions, p. 121; C: factual/definitional; D: easy; L.O.: basics of emotion

    Answer: T. primary emotions

12. The process of systemically desensitizing oneself to emotional experiences.

    H: Preventing Emotions, p. 130; C: factual/definitional; D: easy; L.O.: managing emotion

    Answer: E. deactivation

13. An active process of changing how you think about the meaning of emotional situations to alter their emotional impact.

    H: Reappraising Your Emotions, p. 131; C: factual/definitional; D: easy; L.O.: managing emotion

    Answer: V. reappraisal

14. An intense human reaction to an event, involving interpretation, physiological arousal, and communication.

    H: Defining Emotion, p. 117; C: factual/definitional; D: easy; L.O.: basics of emotion

    Answer: H. emotion

15. The tendency to think negative thoughts about oneself.

    H: Personality, p. 126; C: factual/definitional; D: easy; L.O.: nature of emotion

    Answer: S. neuroticism

16. A negative primary emotion that occurs when you are interrupted or blocked from achieving your goal by the improper action of an external agent.

    H: Anger, p. 134; C: factual/definitional; D: easy; L.O.: manage challenging emotions

    Answer: A. anger

17. When emotion-sharing rapidly spreads an emotion from one person to another.

    H: Defining Emotion, p. 117; C: factual/definitional; D: easy; L.O.: basics of emotion

    Answer: K. emotional contagion

18. A near-constant state of arousal and negative thinking.

    H: Anger, p. 134; C: factual/definitional; D: easy; L.O.: manage challenging emotions

    Answer: D. chronic hostility

19. The purging of negative emotions by expressing them openly.

    H: Anger, p. 134; C: factual/definitional; D: easy; L.O.: manage challenging emotions

    Answer: C. catharsis

20. The sharing of messages that express emotional support or offer personal assistance.

    H: Helping Others Manage Their Grief, p. 140; C: factual/definitional; D: easy;
    L.O.: manage challenging emotions

    Answer: W. supportive communication

21. A culture's agreement on which forms of emotion management and communication are considered socially desirable and appropriate.

    H: Culture, p. 123; C: factual/definitional; D: easy; L.O.: basics of emotion

    Answer: F. display rules

22. A simultaneous experience of two or more primary emotions.

    H: Types of Emotions, p. 121; C: factual/definitional; D: easy; L.O.: basics of emotion

    Answer: B. blended emotions

23. An approach to managing emotions in which one counts before acting or speaking.

    H: Anger, p. 134; C: factual/definitional; D: easy; L.O.: manage challenging emotions

    Answer: Q. Jefferson strategy

24. An individual's attempt to inhibit thoughts, arousal, and outward behavioral displays of unwanted emotion.

    H: Managing Your Emotions After They Occur, p. 129; C: factual/definitional; D: easy; L.O.: managing emotion

    Answer: X. suppression

25. A symbol that represents emotional expression.

    H: Defining Emotion, p. 117; C: factual/definitional; D: easy; L.O.: nature of emotion

    Answer: G. emoticon

True/False

Please select whether the following statements are true or false.

26. The two most common strategies for managing emotions after they occur are suppression and repression.

    H: Managing Your Emotions After They Occur, p. 129; C: factual/definitional; D: easy; L.O.: managing emotion

    Answer: F

27. Rational Emotive Behavior Therapy is a method for helping patients systematically purge themselves of self-defeating beliefs.

    H: Personality, p. 126; C: factual/definitional; D: easy; L.O.: managing emotion

    Answer: T

28. Mexican culture's display rules encourage the open expression of emotions and feelings.

    H: Culture, p. 123; C: application; D: difficult; L.O.: influences on emotion

    Answer: T

29. High-extraversion people seem to experience positive emotions less often than do low-extraversion people.

    H: Personality, p. 126; C: conceptual; D: medium; L.O.: influences on emotion

    Answer: F

30. The six primary emotions exist only in Western cultures.

    H: Types of Emotions, p. 121; C: conceptual; D: medium; L.O.: basics of emotion

    Answer: F

31. Women seem more likely to experience and express emotions that support relationships while simultaneously repressing those emotions that assert their self-interests over others.

    H: Gender, p. 125; C: conceptual; D: medium; L.O.: influences on emotion

    Answer: T

32. In traditional Chinese culture, shame and sad love are considered primary emotions.

    H: Types of Emotions, p. 121; C: factual/definitional; D: easy; L.O.: basics of emotion

    Answer: T

33. Emotional contagion only occurs when negative emotions spread from one person to another.
    H: Defining Emotion, p. 117; C: factual/definitional; D: easy; L.O.: basics of emotion
    Answer: F

34. According to the text, emotions, feelings, and moods refer to the same human experiences.
    H: Feelings and Moods, p. 119; C: conceptual; D: medium; L.O.: basics of emotion
    Answer: F

35. Display rules governing emotion are fairly consistent across cultures.
    H: Culture, p. 123; C: factual/definitional; D: easy; L.O.: influences on emotion
    Answer: F

36. The display rules of Chinese culture suggest that emotions and feelings need to be controlled and restrained.
    H: Culture, p. 123; C: application; D: difficult; L.O.: influences on emotion
    Answer: T

37. Emotions are often triggered by our perception of outside events.
    H: Defining Emotion, p. 117; C: conceptual; D: easy; L.O.: basics of emotion
    Answer: T

38. According to your text, emotional intelligence cannot be accurately measured using self-report tests.
    H: Managing Your Emotional Experience and Expression, p. 127; C: factual/definitional; D: easy; L.O.: influences on emotion
    Answer: T

39. Irrespective of culture, women experience more feelings of anger and men experience more feelings of guilt.
    H: Gender, p. 125; C: application; D: difficult; L.O.: influences on emotion
    Answer: F

40. Although it is difficult to practice, reappraisal is the most effective strategy for managing emotion.
    H: Reappraising Your Emotions, p. 131; C: conceptual; D: medium; L.O.: managing emotion
    Answer: T

41. A blended emotion occurs when you experience a primary emotion followed subsequently by a second one.
    H: Types of Emotions, p. 121; C: conceptual; D: easy; L.O.: basics of emotion
    Answer: F

42. Research suggests that when it comes to the impact of gender on emotion, women seem to experience emotion with greater intensity than do men.

H: Gender, p. 125; C: conceptual; D: medium; L.O.: influences on emotion

Answer: F

43. By using the process of deactivation, one is able to manage emotion by systematically desensitizing oneself to emotional experience.

H: Preventing Emotions, p. 130; C: factual/definitional; D: easy; L.O.: managing emotion

Answer: T

44. High-extraversion people report being better able to manage their emotional communication than do low-extraversion people.

H: Personality, p. 126; C: conceptual; D: medium; L.O.: influences on emotion

Answer: T

45. Some of the six primary emotions are linked to distinct patterns of internal physiological arousal.

H: Types of Emotions, p. 121; C: conceptual; D: medium; L.O.: basics of emotion

Answer: T

46. People who demonstrate high agreeableness are better able to manage their emotions and report being happier than those who demonstrate low agreeableness.

H: Personality, p. 126; C: conceptual; D: medium; L.O.: influences on emotion

Answer: T

47. Reappraisal is effective because it is employed before a large emotional reaction occurs.

H: Reappraising Your Emotions, p. 131; C: conceptual; D: medium; L.O.: managing emotion

Answer: T

48. Feedback allows us to experience empathy and gauge appropriateness of emotional expression.

H: Online Communication and Empathy Deficits, p. 132; C: factual/definitional; D: easy; L.O.: emotional challenges

Answer: T

49. Euro-American cultures have display rules that encourage more open expression of emotions and feelings than Chinese culture, but less than Mexican culture.

H: Culture, p. 123; C: application; D: difficult; L.O.: influences on emotion

Answer: T

50. By engaging in encounter structuring, one is able to prevent emotion by avoiding encounters with others.

H: Preventing Emotions, p. 130; C: factual/definitional; D: easy; L.O.: managing emotion

Answer: F

Multiple Choice

Please choose the correct response to the following statements.

51. Which of the following emotions results from the blocking of one's goals?
    A. anger
    B. surprise
    C. sadness
    D. fear
    E. none of the above

    H: Anger, p. 134; C: conceptual; D: medium; L.O.: manage challenging emotions

    Answer: A

52. What strategy did the character Marianne from Jane Austen's novel *Sense and Sensibility* use when she openly expressed emotion?
    A. suppression
    B. encounter avoidance
    C. reappraisal
    D. venting
    E. encounter structuring

    H: Managing Your Emotions After They Occur, p. 129; C: application; D: medium; L.O.: managing emotion

    Answer: D

53. The primary emotion of fear is associated with what high-intensity counterpart?
    A. rage
    B. loathing
    C. terror
    D. grief
    E. none of the above

    H: Types of Emotions, p. 121; C: conceptual; D: medium; L.O.: basics of emotion

    Answer: C

54. Jealousy is a blended emotion of
    A. anger and grief
    B. fear and sadness
    C. sadness and fear
    D. anger, sadness, and fear
    E. none of the above

    H: Types of Emotions, p. 121; C: conceptual; D: medium; L.O.: basics of emotion

    Answer: D

55. Which of the following is considered a mood?
    A. boredom
    B. contentment
    C. grouchiness
    D. serenity
    E. all of the above

Answer: E

56. Which of the following has a measurable influence on one's happiness?
    A. social or economic class
    B. age
    C. gender or biological sex
    D. population density
    E. physical exercise

    H: Types of Emotions, p. 121; C: conceptual; D: medium; L.O.: basics of emotion
    Answer: E

57. The Jefferson strategy is best used
    A. before someone upsets you
    B. while someone is upsetting you
    C. after someone upsets you
    D. if you have been a president
    E. after other strategies have failed

    H: Anger, p. 134; C: conceptual; D: medium; L.O.: influences on emotion
    Answer: C

58. If Mark exhibits high extraversion, he is likely to
    A. cope successfully with stress and his emotions
    B. have a hard time managing his emotions
    C. focus his attention on negative events
    D. be less skilled at communication
    E. none of the above

    H: Personality, p. 126; C: conceptual; D: medium; L.O.: influences on emotion
    Answer: A

59. Which of the following is NOT true regarding culture's influence on display rules?
    A. Mexican cultures discourage the outward display or expression of emotion
    B. Chinese cultures discourage the outward display or expression of emotion
    C. Euro-American cultures encourage the outward display or expression of emotion
    D. culture determines display rules
    E. none of the above

    H: Culture, p. 123; C: conceptual; D: medium; L.O.: influences on emotion
    Answer: A

60. What does "jumped the couch" mean?
    A. able to jump over a couch
    B. able to handle difficult tasks
    C. can manage one's emotions
    D. in love
    E. has lost control and is unable to manage one's emotions

    H: Managing Your Emotional Experience and Expression, p. 127; C: conceptual;
    D: medium; L.O.: influences on emotion
    Answer: E

61. We can manage our emotions
    A. after they occur
    B. before they occur
    C. by reappraisal
    D. all of the above
    E. none of the above

    H: Managing Your Emotional Experience and Expression, p. 127; C: conceptual; D: easy; L.O.: managing emotion

    Answer: D

62. What strategy for managing emotion did Tom Cruise use when he disclosed his love for Katie Holmes on the *Oprah* show?
    A. denial
    B. suppression
    C. encounter avoidance
    D. venting
    E. reappraisal

    H: Managing Your Emotions After They Occur, p. 129; C: application; D: difficult; L.O.: managing emotion

    Answer: D

63. The primary emotion of joy is associated with what high-intensity counterpart?
    A. amazement
    B. surprise
    C. ecstasy
    D. terror
    E. none of the above

    H: Types of Emotions, p. 121; C: conceptual; D: medium; L.O.: basics of emotion

    Answer: C

64. Emotion-sharing
    A. can help manage grief
    B. allows you to talk with others who have experienced similar loss and grief
    C. can occur in a face-to-face support group
    D. can take place online
    E. all of the above

    H: Managing Your Grief, p. 139; C: conceptual; D: medium; L.O.: manage challenging emotion

    Answer: E

65. What strategy did the character Elinor, the older sister of Marianne from Jane Austen's novel *Sense and Sensibility*, use by remaining silent when it came to expressing emotion?
    A. suppression
    B. encounter avoidance
    C. reappraisal
    D. venting
    E. encounter structuring

H: Managing Your Emotions After They Occur, p. 129; C: application; D: medium;
L.O.: managing emotion
Answer: A

66. After Charley goes through a painful breakup with Tom he finds himself trying to avoid Tom. Charley no longer goes to the same bars, restaurants, or gym they frequented when they were together. What emotional management strategy is Charley demonstrating?
    A. suppression
    B. encounter avoidance
    C. reappraisal
    D. venting
    E. encounter structuring
    H: Preventing Emotions, p. 130; C: application; D: difficult; L.O.: managing emotion
    Answer: B

67. A student arrives on the first day of her interpersonal communication class and observes that the instructor makes wild gestures while lecturing. If the student chooses to focus only upon the content while trying to ignore the body language, what strategy is she employing?
    A. suppression
    B. attention focus
    C. reappraisal
    D. venting
    E. encounter structuring
    H: Preventing Emotions, p. 130; C: application; D: difficult; L.O.: managing emotion
    Answer: B

68. If you have a phobia of riding elevators after being trapped in one, but choose to confront and overcome your fear by entering a stationary elevator while the door remains open, what emotional management strategy are you using?
    A. deactivation
    B. encounter avoidance
    C. reappraisal
    D. venting
    E. encounter structuring
    H: Preventing Emotions, p. 130; C: application; D: difficult; L.O.: managing emotion
    Answer: A

69. Your girlfriend receives a flirty e-mail from her ex, but tells you it means nothing to her; however, you feel upset. If you choose to rethink why you are upset and why you feel threatened by your girlfriend's ex, what emotional management strategy are you using?
    A. suppression
    B. encounter avoidance
    C. reappraisal
    D. venting
    E. encounter structuring
    H: Reappraising Your Emotions, p. 131; C: application; D: difficult; L.O.: managing emotion
    Answer: C

70. Which of the following is true regarding the use of reappraisal as an emotional management strategy?
    A. it is the most fruitful way to deal with difficult emotions
    B. it is used before an emotional outburst occurs
    C. it is a primary strategy used by those who are most effective at managing their emotions
    D. it requires users to accept responsibility for the way they think and feel
    E. all of the above
    H: Reappraising Your Emotions, p. 131; C: conceptual; D: medium; L.O.: managing emotion
    Answer: E

71. Passion is
    A. a blended emotion
    B. composed of surprise and joy
    C. includes positive feelings of excitement and amazement
    D. includes feelings of sexual attraction
    E. all of the above
    H: Passion, p. 137; C: conceptual; D: medium; L.O.: managing emotion
    Answer: E

72. Romantic partners are more likely to experience passion during the early stages of a relationship rather than during the later stages because
    A. passion is primarily based upon fear
    B. passion cannot exist in long-term relationships
    C. later communication tends to be more positive
    D. passion relies more on fantasy than reality
    E. none of the above
    H: Passion, p. 137; C: conceptual; D: medium; L.O.: managing emotion
    Answer: E

73. What is the most commonly used emotional management strategy for managing unwanted emotions?
    A. suppression
    B. repression
    C. venting
    D. reappraisal
    E. none of the above
    H: Reappraising Your Emotions; p. 131; C: conceptual; D: medium; L.O.: managing emotion
    Answer: A

74. Which of the following is not considered a primary emotion?
    A. anger
    B. jealousy
    C. sadness
    D. surprise
    E. fear
    H: Types of Emotions, p. 121; C: factual/definitional; D: easy; L.O.: basics of emotion
    Answer: B

75. Which of the following is true about suppression as an emotional management strategy?
    A. widely used and practiced strategy
    B. only marginally effective
    C. users of this strategy have lower levels of well-being
    D. users rate their personal relationships as less positive
    E. all of the above

    H: Reappraising Your Emotions, p. 131; C: conceptual; D: medium; L.O.: managing emotion

    Answer: E

76. Which of the following is NOT true about venting as an emotional management strategy?
    A. can include expressing positive emotion
    B. is the inverse of suppression
    C. used to manage emotions after they occur
    D. is only about expressing negative emotions
    E. all of the above are true

    H: Managing Your Emotions After They Occur, p. 129; C: conceptual; D: medium; L.O.: managing emotion

    Answer: D

77. Suppression is most commonly used to manage which emotions?
    A. joy and fear
    B. happiness and disgust
    C. anger and sadness
    D. surprise and jealousy
    E. none of the above

    H: Managing Your Emotions After They Occur, p. 129; C: conceptual; D: medium; L.O.: managing emotion

    Answer: C

78. Which of the following strategies is used to prevent undesired emotions before they occur?
    A. encounter avoidance
    B. encounter structuring
    C. attention focus
    D. deactivation
    E. all of the above

    H: Preventing Emotions, p. 130; C: conceptual; D: medium; L.O.: managing emotion

    Answer: E

79. Emotion management includes attempts to
    A. control which emotions you experience
    B. control when you experience an emotion
    C. control how you experience an emotion
    D. control how you express an emotion
    E. all of the above

    H: Managing Your Emotional Experience and Expression, p. 127; C: conceptual; D: easy; L.O.: managing emotion

    Answer: E

80. Emotional intelligence refers to
    A. the ability to suppress emotion
    B. the ability to vent emotion
    C. the ability to mask an emotion
    D. the ability to accurately perceive and interpret emotions
    E. none of the above

    H: Managing Your Emotional Experience and Expression, p. 127; C: conceptual;
    D: medium; L.O.: managing emotion

    Answer: D

81. Which of the following does NOT influence how you manage emotion?
    A. extraversion
    B. neuroticism
    C. agreeableness
    D. sexual orientation
    E. none of the above

    H: Personality, p. 126; C: conceptual; D: medium; L.O.: influences on emotion

    Answer: D

82. Women are more likely than men to report which emotion(s)?
    A. guilt
    B. shame
    C. fear
    D. sadness
    E. all of the above

    H: Gender, p. 125; C: conceptual; D: medium; L.O.: influences on emotion

    Answer: E

83. In terms of the impact of gender upon emotion, which of the following is true?
    A. women and men experience emotion with similar levels of intensity
    B. women seem to experience higher levels of anger
    C. men seem to experience higher levels of guilt
    D. men seem to experience higher levels of sadness
    E. none of the above

    H: Gender, p. 125; C: conceptual; D: medium; L.O.: influences on emotion

    Answer: A

84. Each Thanksgiving Sarah and Darcie visit Darcie's family. However, each holiday is a painful reminder of their diametrically opposed political differences. Sarah is a Democrat; Darcie and her family are staunch Republicans. This year Sarah chooses not to discuss political topics or issues. What emotional management strategy is she using?
    A. suppression
    B. encounter avoidance
    C. reappraisal
    D. venting
    E. encounter structuring

    H: Preventing Emotions, p. 130; C: application; D: difficult; L.O.: managing emotion

    Answer: E

85. Which of the following is not one of the five primary personality traits?
    A. agreeableness
    B. openness
    C. introversion
    D. extraversion
    E. neuroticism

    H: Personality, p. 126; C: conceptual; D: easy; L.O.: influences on emotion

    Answer: C

86. Americanized Chinese Americans are likely to
    A. use suppression more than traditional Chinese Americans
    B. display negative emotions less often than traditional Chinese Americans
    C. display negative emotions more often than traditional Chinese Americans
    D. display very different emotions from traditional Chinese Americans
    E. none of the above

    H: Culture, p. 123; C: application; D: difficult; L.O.: influences on emotion

    Answer: C

87. When a given culture socializes its members to communicate their emotions in ways that are socially desirable and appropriate, these norms are called
    A. display rules
    B. cultural values
    C. emotion management
    D. attention focus
    E. emotional intelligence

    H: Culture, p. 123; C: conceptual; D: easy; L.O.: influences on emotion

    Answer: A

88. According to research, by engaging in catharsis
    A. one's anger is vented
    B. one's anger actually increases
    C. one's anger decreases
    D. one's anger stays the same
    E. one's anger is not affected

    H: Anger, p. 134; C: conceptual; D: medium; L.O.: influences on emotion

    Answer: B

89. An intense sadness that usually results from the loss of a loved one is called
    A. grief
    B. sadness
    C. anger
    D. ambivalence
    E. depressions

    H: Grief, p. 139; C: conceptual; D: easy; L.O.: influences on emotion

    Answer: A

Short Answer

Briefly respond to the following questions in full sentences.

90. Define emotional intelligence and explain why it is difficult to measure.

    H: Managing Your Emotional Experience and Expression, p. 127; C: conceptual; D: medium; L.O.: managing emotion

    Possible Answer: Ability to effectively interpret your own and others' emotional messages. Existing measurements can't measure emotion, only personality traits.

91. Identify the five key elements of emotion.

    H: Defining Emotion, p. 117; C: conceptual; D: easy; L.O.: basics of emotion

    Possible Answer: Intense reaction to an interpretation of event, physiological arousal, labeling, management of the reaction, and communicating it.

92. Identify the three most important personality traits that influence the experience and communication of emotion.

    H: Personality, p. 126; C: conceptual; D: medium; L.O.: nature of emotion

    Possible Answer: Extraversion, outgoing and sociable; agreeableness, trusting and friendly; neuroticism, negative thoughts about oneself.

93. Describe what primary emotions are and name them.

    H: Types of Emotions, p. 121; C: factual/definitional; D: easy; L.O.: basics of emotion

    Possible Answer: Six primary emotions have been defined and are displayed consistently across cultures: surprise, joy, disgust, anger, fear, and sadness.

94. What's the difference between feelings and moods?

    H: Feelings and Moods, p. 119; C: conceptual; D: medium; L.O.: basics of emotion

    Possible Answer: Feelings are short-term reactions that generate only limited arousal, whereas moods also provoke limited arousal but are longer lasting.

95. Explain how online communication can foster inappropriate expression of emotion.

    H: Online Communication and Empathy Deficits, p. 132; C: conceptual; D: medium; L.O.: managing emotion

    Possible Answer: Due to the asynchronous nature and delayed response of online communication, we are likely to express emotions inappropriately. Since we don't share physical interaction with others online, and lack feedback, we may feel safer and be less likely to express empathy.

96. In what ways do men and women experience emotion differently?

    H: Gender, p. 125; C: conceptual; D: medium; L.O.: influences on emotion

    Possible Answer: Women experience more sadness, fear, shame, and guilt, whereas men feel more anger and other hostile emotions. Both men and women experience emotions with the same intensity.

97. How does the personality trait of extraversion impact emotion?

    H: Personality, p. 126; C: conceptual; D: medium; L.O.: influences on emotion

    Possible Answer: High extraversion is associated with experiencing more positive emotions such as happiness and better management of emotional experience than low extraversion.

98. Identify and define the two strategies for managing emotion after they occur.

    H: Managing Your Emotions After They Occur, p. 129; C: conceptual; D: easy; L.O.: managing emotion

    Possible Answer: Suppression, or inhibiting manifest displays of emotion, and venting, or openly expressing emotion.

99. Identify two out of four strategies for managing emotions before they occur.

    H: Preventing Emotions, p. 130; C: conceptual; D: easy; L.O.: managing emotion

    Possible Answer: Encounter avoidance, encounter structuring, attention focus, or deactivation.

100. Identify and define the three most challenging emotions we must manage in our personal relationships.

    H: Emotional Challenges, p. 132; C: conceptual; D: medium; L.O.: manage challenging emotions

    Possible Answer: Passion, a blended emotion of surprise and joy; anger, a primary emotion resulting from the blocking of one's goal; and grief, an intense emotion resulting from loss.

101. Explain how the Jefferson strategy can be used to manage emotions after they occur.

    H: Anger, p. 134; C: conceptual; D: medium; L.O.: manage challenging emotions

    Possible Answer: After you begin to feel angry, slowly count to 10 before reacting.

102. What are a benefit and a cost of using venting?

    H: Anger, p. 134; C: conceptual; D: medium; L.O.: manage challenging emotions

    Possible Answer: Benefit: catharsis or openly venting emotions rids ourselves of anger. Cost: by venting or openly expressing emotions, our anger may actually increase.

103. Explain why chronic hostility can be destructive.

    H: Anger, p. 134; C: conceptual; D: medium; L.O.: manage challenging emotions

    Possible Answer: While in a constant state of suppressed rage we are stressed, negative, and narcissistic.

104. Why is it so difficult to manage grief?

    H: Grief, p. 139; C: conceptual; D: medium; L.O.: manage challenging emotions

    Possible Answer: Grief is more painful because of the significant loss involved, because it is enduring, and because it is repeatedly triggered through experiences associated with the loved one.

Essay

Please respond to the following questions in paragraph form.

105. Compare and contrast the advantages and disadvantages of online versus face-to-face support groups.

    H: Managing Your Grief, p. 139; C: conceptual; D: medium; L.O.: managing emotion

    Possible Answer: Online groups overcome barriers of distance and provide a degree of anonymity; however, the online medium prevents the use of nonverbal communication and poses the risk of flaming. Face-to-face communication allows physical contact, nonverbal communication, and the immediacy of feedback.

106. How can those who suffer from neuroticism manage their negative thoughts?

    H: Personality, p. 126; C: conceptual; D: medium; L.O.: nature of emotion

    Possible Answer: Identify situations that upset you; identify irrational beliefs; consider negative outcomes you wish to change; challenge beliefs; identify realistic beliefs.

107. How can we demonstrate supportive communication?

    H: Helping Others Manage Their Grief, p. 140; C: conceptual; D: medium; L.O.: manage challenging emotions

    Possible Answer: By expressing sympathy, giving and offering support, and encouraging emotional expression from others. For example, "I am sorry for your loss," "You are always in my thoughts and in my prayers," and "I am always here for you."

108. In the example from Jane Austen's *Sense and Sensibility*, the two main characters exhibit two different emotional management styles. Identify the two styles and compare and contrast them.

    H: Managing Your Emotions After They Occur, p. 129; C: application; D: difficult; L.O.: managing emotion

    Possible Answer: Venting and suppression. Venting can get emotions off your chest; however, this strategy can backfire and fuel further negative emotional experience. Suppression, depending upon the context, may be appropriate. However, this strategy could result in chronic hostility.

Chapter 5: Listening Actively

Matching

Match the concept, term, or theory with its correct response or definition.

A. action-oriented listeners
B. aggressive listening
C. attending
D. back-channel cues
E. bizarreness effect
F. content-oriented listeners
G. eavesdropping
H. feedback
I. hearing
J. hearing impairment
K. listening
L. mental bracketing
M. mnemonics

N. narcissistic listening
O. noise pollution
P. paraphrasing
Q. people-oriented listeners
R. provocateurs
S. pseudo-listening
T. recalling
U. receiving
V. responding
W. selective listening
X. time-oriented listeners
Y. understanding

1. Those who act like effective listeners even when they are not engaging in effective listening.
   H: Pseudo-Listening, p. 170; C: factual/definitional; D: easy; L.O.: ineffective listening
   Answer: S. pseudo-listening

2. Listeners who prefer brief, concise encounters and follow strict schedules.
   H: Four Listening Styles, p. 164; C: factual/definitional; D: easy; L.O.: listening styles
   Answer: X. time-oriented listeners

3. The second step in the listening process, in which one pays attention to information.
   H: Attending, p. 153; C: factual/definitional; D: easy; L.O.: listening process
   Answer: C. attending

4. Devices that aid memory during the listening process.
   H: Recalling, p. 158; C: factual/definitional; D: easy; L.O.: listening process
   Answer: M. mnemonics

5. The fourth step in the listening process, in which one communicates one's understanding back to the speaker.
   H: Responding, p. 155; C: factual/definitional; D: easy; L.O.: listening process
   Answer: V. responding

6. The fifth step in the listening process, in which one remembers information.
   H: Recalling, p. 158; C: factual/definitional; D: easy; L.O.: listening process
   Answer: T. recalling

7. Summarizing others' comments after they have finished speaking.
   H: Paraphrasing and Clarifying, p. 158; C: factual/definitional; D: easy; L.O.: listening process
   Answer: P. paraphrasing

8. The use of verbal and nonverbal communication to signal attention and understanding.
   H: Positive Feedback, p. 156; C: factual/definitional; D: easy; L.O.: listening process
   Answer: H. feedback

9. Verbal and nonverbal messages, such as nodding your head and saying "yes."
   H: Positive Feedback, p. 156; C: factual/definitional; D: easy; L.O.: listening process
   Answer: D. back-channel cues

10. The process of receiving, attending to, understanding, responding to, and recalling information from an interpersonal encounter.
    H: Listening: A Five-Step Process, p. 152; C: factual/definitional; D: easy; L.O.: listening process
    Answer: K. listening

11. The tendency to remember unusual information more readily than commonplace information.
    H: Recalling, p. 158; C: factual/definitional; D: easy; L.O.: listening process
    Answer: E. bizarreness effect

12. Sound in the environment that detracts our attention away from auditory input.
    H: Receiving, p. 152; C: factual/definitional; D: easy; L.O.: listening process
    Answer: O. noise pollution

13. Those who participate only in conversations that revolve around them are engaging in this.
    H: Narcissistic Listening, p. 174; C: factual/definitional; D: easy; L.O.: ineffective listening
    Answer: N. narcissistic listening

14. Those who attend to what others say only to attack or ambush them are engaging in this.
    H: Aggressive Listening, p. 171; C: factual/definitional; D: easy; L.O.: ineffective listening
    Answer: B. aggressive listening

15. The restricted ability to receive sound input across the humanly audible frequency range.
    H: Receiving, p. 152; C: factual/definitional; D: easy; L.O.: listening process
    Answer: J. hearing impairment

16. Listeners who prefer brief, accurate messages from others.
    H: Four Listening Styles, p. 164; C: factual/definitional; D: easy; L.O.: listening styles
    Answer: A. action-oriented listeners

17. Listeners who prefer to be intellectually challenged or stimulated by messages.
    H: Four Listening Styles, p. 164; C: factual/definitional; D: easy; L.O.: listening styles
    Answer: F. content-oriented listeners

18. The first step in the listening process, in which one sees and hears.
    H: Receiving, p. 152; C: factual/definitional; D: easy; L.O.: listening process
    Answer: U. receiving

19. A form of listening in which the listener only takes in salient bits of information.
    H: Selective Listening, p. 169; C: factual/definitional; D: easy; L.O.: ineffective listening
    Answer: W. selective listening

20. The action of intentionally and systematically setting up situations so that a person can listen to private conversations.
    H: Eavesdropping, p. 169; C: factual/definitional; D: easy; L.O.: ineffective listening
    Answer: G. eavesdropping

21. The third step in the listening process, in which one interprets the meaning of information communicated.
    H: Understanding, p. 154; C: factual/definitional; D: easy; L.O.: listening process
    Answer: Y. understanding

22. Online listeners who post messages designed solely to annoy others.
    H: Aggressive Listening, p. 171; C: factual/definitional; D: easy; L.O.: ineffective listening
    Answer: R. provocateurs

23. The process in which vibrations travel along acoustic nerves to one's brain.
    H: Receiving, p. 152; C: factual/definitional; D: easy; L.O.: listening process
    Answer: I. hearing

24. The systematic process of putting aside irrelevant thoughts while listening.
    H: Attending, p. 153; C: factual/definitional; D: easy; L.O.: listening process
    Answer: L. mental bracketing

25. Listeners whose goal is to establish connection and commonality with others.
    H: Four Listening Styles, p. 164; C: factual/definitional; D: easy; L.O.: listening styles
    Answer: Q. people-oriented listeners

True/False

26. According to the text, the greatest challenge to active listening is selective listening.
    H: Selective Listening, p. 169; C: conceptual; D: medium; L.O.: ineffective listening
    Answer: T

27. A listener can improve the salience of communication by reminding him- or herself of the importance of the exchange.
    H: Attending, p. 153; C: conceptual; D: medium; L.O.: listening process
    Answer: T

28. If you misunderstand information when you first receive and attend to it, you will likely make flawed decisions and communications based on it when you recall it.
    H: Recalling, p. 158; C: factual/definitional; D: easy; L.O.: listening process
    Answer: T

29. Listening is considered to be our most primal and primary communication skill.
    H: Chapter introduction, p. 151; C: conceptual; D: medium; L.O.: listening process
    Answer: T

30. In a collectivistic culture, people-oriented and content-oriented listening styles are valued and practiced.
    H: Culture and Listening Styles, p. 167; C: application; D: medium; L.O.: listening styles
    Answer: T

31. Listening is a process that involves both auditory and visual cues.
    H: Listening: A Five-Step Process, p. 152; C: conceptual; D: easy; L.O.: listening process
    Answer: T

32. Long-term memory is used in the receiving stage of the listening process.
    H: Understanding, p. 154; C: conceptual; D: medium; L.O.: listening process
    Answer: F

33. Both seeing and hearing constitute receiving, the first step of the listening process.
    H: Receiving, p. 152; C: factual/definitional; D: easy; L.O.: listening process
    Answer: T

34. Noise pollution has caused hearing loss or impairment in more than 75 percent of college students.
    H: Receiving, p. 152; C: factual/definitional; D: easy; L.O.: listening process
    Answer: F

35. Both internal and external factors can impact one's attention level for listening.
    H: Receiving, p. 152; C: conceptual; D: easy; L.O.: listening process
    Answer: T

36. We should attempt to avoid mental bracketing because we can easily fall prey to our wandering attentions.

    H: Attending, p. 153; C: conceptual; D: medium; L.O.: listening process

    Answer: F

37. In the movie *Memento*, Leonard Shelby has problems forming new memories, which is an integral component of the understanding step of the listening process.

    H: Understanding, p. 154; C: application; D: medium; L.O.: listening process

    Answer: T

38. Back-channel cues are an effective method for offering negative feedback to a speaker.

    H: Positive Feedback, p. 156; C: conceptual; D: medium; L.O.: listening process

    Answer: F

39. Responding with "amen" or "hallelujah" during a Catholic priest's sermon would be considered an appropriate use of positive feedback.

    H: Positive Feedback, p. 156; C: application; D: difficult; L.O.: listening process

    Answer: F

40. Recalling, the fifth step of listening, is crucial because we judge others' listening skills by their ability to recall what we said.

    H: Recalling, p. 158; C: conceptual; D: medium; L.O.: listening process

    Answer: T

41. When communicating with a man, you should assume that he will use a people-oriented or content-oriented listening style.

    H: Gender Differences in Listening Styles, p. 166; C: conceptual; D: difficult; L.O.: listening styles

    Answer: F

42. In recalling information, we tend to remember our own behavior as more positive and constructive than the behavior of others.

    H: Recalling, p. 158; C: conceptual; D: medium; L.O.: listening process

    Answer: T

43. One simple method for bolstering memory is to incorporate as many of the five senses as possible.

    H: Recalling, p. 158; C: conceptual; D: easy; L.O.: listening process

    Answer: T

44. Mr. Rogers demonstrated a people-oriented listening style.

    H: Four Listening Styles, p. 164; C: application; D: difficult; L.O.: listening styles

    Answer: T

45. Those with an action-oriented listening style prefer brief, to-the-point communication and become impatient when communicating with those who are long-winded.

H: Four Listening Styles, p. 164; C: application; D: difficult; L.O.: listening styles

Answer: T

46. If your partner has trouble focusing upon your conversations and seems easily distracted, he or she may be having trouble practicing mental bracketing.

H: Attending, p. 153; C: application; D: difficult; L.O.: listening process

Answer: T

47. Women are more likely to use time-oriented and action-oriented listening styles.

H: Gender Differences in Listening Styles, p. 166; C: conceptual; D: medium; L.O.: listening styles

Answer: F

48. In an individualistic culture such as in the United States, time-oriented and action-oriented listening styles are valued and practiced.

H: Culture and Listening Styles, p. 167; C: application; D: medium; L.O.: listening styles

Answer: T

49. The bizarreness effect suggests that it is easier to recall basic, common information than highly unusual information.

H: Recalling, p. 158; C: conceptual; D: medium; L.O.: listening process

Answer: F

Multiple Choice

Please choose the correct response to the following statements.

50. Unlike hearing, listening
    A. is automatic
    B. is a physiological process
    C. requires no conscious effort
    D. is merely an external process
    E. involves conscious, deliberate thought and effort

    H: Listening: A Five-Step Process, p. 152; C: conceptual; D: medium; L.O.: listening process

    Answer: E

51. Hearing impairment is a problem with
    A. seeing
    B. receiving
    C. attending
    D. understanding
    E. none of the above

    H: Receiving, p. 152; C: conceptual; D: medium; L.O.: listening process

    Answer: B

52. If Laila purposefully moves her seat at the cafe to get closer to a couple who is gossiping about a friend of hers, she is engaged in
   A. narcissistic listening
   B. eavesdropping
   C. pseudo-listening
   D. aggressive listening
   E. selective listening

   H: Eavesdropping, p. 169; C: application; D: difficult; L.O.: ineffective listening

   Answer: B

53. If your colleague begins a conversation by saying, "We only have ten minutes to talk," she is displaying
   A. time-oriented listening
   B. empathic listening
   C. action-oriented listening
   D. people-oriented listening
   E. passive listening

   H: Four Listening Styles, p. 164; C: application; D: difficult; L.O.: listening styles

   Answer: A

54. If you have a tendency primarily to recall the most unusual events in your life, you are experiencing
   A. back-channel cues
   B. hearing
   C. short-term memory
   D. recalling
   E. bizarreness effect

   H: Recalling, p. 158; C: application; D: difficult; L.O.: listening process

   Answer: E

55. If Vic, who is concerned his girlfriend might still be angry with him after a recent fight, carefully listens not only to the words she is saying but how they are said, he is
   A. listening to support
   B. listening to appreciate
   C. listening to discern
   D. listening to comprehend
   E. listening to analyze

   H: Listening to Discern, p. 164; C: application; D: difficult; L.O.: listening purposes

   Answer: C

56. If Jules, when listening to his interpersonal communication professor lecture, actively seeks to interpret and understand the information, he is
   A. listening to discern
   B. listening to appreciate
   C. listening to support
   D. listening to analyze
   E. listening to comprehend

   H: Listening to Comprehend, p. 162; C: application; D: medium; L.O.: listening purposes

   Answer: E

57. If your friend Brian spends time posting messages on online discussion boards baiting readers' responses so he can attack them, he is acting as
    A. a provocateur
    B. an action-oriented listener
    C. an eavesdropper
    D. a pseudo-listener
    E. a narcissistic listener

    H: Aggressive Listening, p. 171; C: application; D: difficult; L.O.: ineffective listening

    Answer: A

58. Which of the following is NOT true of feedback?
    A. can be positive
    B. can be negative
    C. occurs while others are speaking
    D. occurs after others speak
    E. none of the above

    H: Positive Feedback, p. 156; C: conceptual; D: medium; L.O.: listening process

    Answer: E

59. On *American Idol,* Simon Cowell, who serves as a judge, listens to evaluate and judge performances. Which listening function is he demonstrating?
    A. listening to discern
    B. listening to appreciate
    C. listening to support
    D. listening to analyze
    E. listening to comprehend

    H: Listening to Analyze, p. 163; C: application; D: medium; L.O.: listening purposes

    Answer: D

60. You go to your coworker's tuba recital because you enjoy music and think it might be interesting. What listening function are you demonstrating?
    A. listening to discern
    B. listening to appreciate
    C. listening to support
    D. listening to analyze
    E. listening to comprehend

    H: Listening to Appreciate, p. 163; C: application; D: difficult; L.O.: listening purposes

    Answer: B

61. In a situation in which a friend or family member turns to you for comfort, the best listening style to apply would be
    A. selective listening
    B. time-oriented listening
    C. people-oriented listening
    D. content-oriented listening
    E. passive listening

    H: Four Listening Styles, p. 164; C: application; D: medium; L.O.: listening styles

    Answer: C

62. Active listening involves
    A. controlling factors that impede attention
    B. providing clear, timely feedback
    C. devoting effort to improve recall
    D. developing awareness of listening functions and styles
    E. all of the above

    H: Listening: A Five-Step Process, p. 152; C: factual/definitional; D: easy; L.O.: ineffective listening

    Answer: E

63. John comes home and says, "I am so upset! I can't believe I was fired today." If his roommate Amir responds, "Wow, it sounds like you are bummed out about losing your job," he is using
    A. mental-bracketing
    B. passive listening
    C. paraphrasing
    D. pseudo-listening
    E. narcissistic listening

    H: Paraphrasing and Clarifying, p. 158; C: application; D: difficult; L.O.: listening process
    Answer: C

64. In class you sit up front, maintain eye contact with the instructor, and nod in agreement; however, your mind is far away and not focused on the lecture. This is an example of
    A. passive listening
    B. active listening
    C. selective listening
    D. narcissistic listening
    E. pseudo-listening

    H: Pseudo-Listening, p. 170; C: application; D: difficult; L.O.: ineffective listening
    Answer: E

65. People who consistently use aggressive listening may also
    A. engage in eavesdropping
    B. think less favorably of themselves
    C. experience less violence in their relationships
    D. achieve more success in their personal goals
    E. none of the above

    H: Aggressive Listening, p. 171; C: application; D: difficult; L.O.: ineffective listening
    Answer: B

66. Your friend Lonie tends to talk a lot, often ignoring what you have to say; in fact, she often focuses the conversation on her issues, problems, and interests. What type of listening is she displaying?
    A. pseudo-listening
    B. passive listening
    C. narcissistic listening
    D. active listening
    E. action-oriented listening

H: Narcissistic Listening, p. 174; C: application; D: difficult; L.O.: ineffective listening

Answer: C

67. Mr. Rogers, who was cited in the chapter's opening anecdote and postscript, demonstrated which listening style?
    A. selective listening
    B. action-oriented listening
    C. content-oriented listening
    D. time-oriented listening
    E. people-oriented listening

    H: Four Listening Styles, p. 164; C: application; D: difficult; L.O.: listening styles

    Answer: E

68. Which of the following is not an example of noise pollution?
    A. thoughts
    B. music
    C. construction
    D. crowds
    E. road and air traffic

    H: Receiving, p. 152; C: conceptual; D: medium; L.O.: listening process

    Answer: A

69. On *American Idol,* Paula Abdul, who serves as a judge, listens and responds by offering praise and support while withholding judgment. What listening function is she demonstrating?
    A. listening to discern
    B. listening to appreciate
    C. listening to support
    D. listening to analyze
    E. listening to comprehend

    H: Listening to Support, p. 162; C: application; D: medium; L.O.: listening purposes

    Answer: C

70. Who or what has primary control of the salience of a message?
    A. listener
    B. speaker
    C. context
    D. environment
    E. none of the above

    H: Attending, p. 153; C: conceptual; D: medium; L.O.: listening process

    Answer: B

71. Which of the following is an example of an internal factor that can impact one's attention level?
    A. illness
    B. stress
    C. fatigue

D. hunger

E. all of the above

H: Receiving, p. 152; C: conceptual; D: medium; L.O.: listening process

Answer: E

72. What listening strategy would you recommend to your friend Ron, who says he can't seem to pay attention in his interpersonal communication class because his mind often wanders?

A. eavesdropping

B. pseudo-listening

C. bizarreness effect

D. mental bracketing

E. back-channel cues

H: Attending, p. 153; C: application; D: difficult; L.O.: listening process

Answer: D

73. Which of the following is true of long-term memory?

A. it is a temporary storage place for information

B. it's the place where new information is stored

C. it plays a minimal role in the understanding stage of listening

D. it is devoted to permanent information storage

E. none of the above

H: Understanding, p. 154; C: conceptual; D: medium; L.O.: listening process

Answer: D

74. Your friend Sheila is a very animated communicator and active listener. When she listens to you recount the events of your day, she often responds with nonverbal and verbal cues including "uh-huh," "yes," and "okay." What listening strategy is Sheila using?

A. feedback

B. mental bracketing

C. back-channel cues

D. paraphrasing

E. mnemonics

H: Positive Feedback, p. 156; C: application; D: difficult; L.O.: listening process

Answer: C

75. To use positive feedback effectively, one should make it

A. obvious

B. appropriate

C. clear

D. immediate

E. all of the above

H: Positive Feedback, p. 156; C: conceptual; D: medium; L.O.: listening process

Answer: E

76. If you overhear that you are expected to remove your shoes at your Japanese friend's house and do so the next time you are there, what rule of giving positive feedback are you displaying?

A. negativity

B. obviousness

C. immediacy

D. appropriateness

E. clarity

H: Positive Feedback, p. 156; C: application; D: difficult; L.O.: listening process

Answer: D

77. What is one primary difference between feedback and paraphrasing?
    A. paraphrasing summarizes others' comments after they talk
    B. feedback is a way to summarize the speaker's thoughts
    C. paraphrasing is done while someone is speaking
    D. feedback is done after others talk
    E. none of the above

    H: Paraphrasing and Clarifying, p. 158; C: conceptual; D: medium; L.O.: listening process

    Answer: A

78. Using paraphrasing as a listening strategy can be problematic when
    A. the receiver feels it is contrived
    B. the receiver feels it is overused
    C. it leads to conversational lapses
    D. it doesn't allow the conversational topic to advance
    E. all of the above

    H: Paraphrasing and Clarifying, p. 158; C: conceptual; D: medium; L.O.: listening process

    Answer: E

79. Our ability and accuracy in recalling information are usually
    A. lower with simple rote memorization
    B. higher with simple rote memorization
    C. higher with more complex activities
    D. unaffected by the type of information
    E. none of the above

    H: Recalling, p. 158; C: conceptual; D: medium; L.O.: listening process

    Answer: B

80. Studies suggest that people will perceive you as more sensitive if you adopt which listening style?
    A. content-oriented
    B. other-oriented
    C. people-oriented
    D. time-oriented
    E. sexual-oriented

    H: Four Listening Styles, p. 164; C: conceptual; D: medium; L.O.: listening styles

    Answer: C

81. Your friend Michael is a news junkie; however, when you ask him about today's current events he seems to recall only the unusual, news of the weird. What listening recall issue is he experiencing?
    A. mnemonics
    B. primacy effect

C. bizarreness effect

D. mental bracketing

E. none of the above

H: Recalling, p. 158; C: application; D: difficult; L.O: listening process

Answer: C

82. Which listening function would be most appropriate for you to practice if your shyest friend decided to sing a song at your local karaoke bar?

A. listening to discern

B. listening to analyze

C. narcissistic listening

D. listening to support

E. listening to comprehend

H: Listening to Support, p. 162; C: application; D: difficult; LO.: listening purposes

Answer: D

83. In individualistic cultures such as the United States, listening can be characterized as

A. people-oriented

B. content-oriented

C. other-oriented

D. time-oriented

E. none of the above

H: Four Listening Styles, p. 164; C: application; D: difficult; L.O.: culture and listening styles

Answer: D

84. If someone views listening as an opportunity to establish commonalities with others, which listening style does he or she exemplify?

A. action-oriented listening

B. time-oriented listening

C. people-oriented listening

D. content-oriented listening

E. none of the above

H: Four Listening Styles, p. 164; C: application; D: medium; L.O.: listening styles

Answer: C

85. Men tend to practice

A. action-oriented listening

B. people-oriented listening

C. content-oriented listening

D. listening for support

E. listening as an emotional and relational activity

H: Gender Differences in Listening Styles, p. 166; C: conceptual; D: medium; L.O.: listening styles

Answer: A

86. In many collectivistic cultures, Confucian teachings emphasize that listening is
    A. people-oriented
    B. content-oriented
    C. sensitive to other's feelings
    D. all of the above
    E. none of the above

    H: Culture and Listening Styles, p. 167; C: conceptual; D: medium; L.O.: listening styles

    Answer: D

87. Which of the following is considered ineffective?
    A. seeing
    B. receiving
    C. selective listening
    D. attending
    E. mental bracketing

    H: Selective Listening, p. 169; C: conceptual; D: medium; L.O.: ineffective listening

    Answer: C

88. Eavesdropping is
    A. inappropriate
    B. unethical
    C. intentional
    D. personally damaging
    E. all of the above

    H: Eavesdropping, p. 169; C: conceptual; D: medium; L.O.: ineffective listening

    Answer: E

89. Your text suggests that pseudo-listening is
    A. effective
    B. appropriate
    C. active
    D. deceptive
    E. none of the above

    H: Pseudo-Listening, p. 170; C: conceptual; D: medium; L.O.: ineffective listening

    Answer: D

Short Answer

Briefly respond to the following questions in full sentences.

90. Identify the five steps in the process of listening.

    H: Listening: A Five-Step Process, p. 152; C: factual/definitional; D: easy; L.O.: listening process

    Possible Answer: Receiving, attending, understanding, responding, and recalling.

91. Identify the first step of the listening process, along with its two components.

    H: Receiving, p. 152; C: factual/definitional; D: easy; L.O.: listening process

    Possible Answer: Receiving: seeing and hearing.

92. If Charles is having relationship problems, what listening function and style would you recommend his friend Christina engage in when communicating with him about his problems?

    H: Listening to Support, p. 162, and Four Listening Styles, p. 164; C: application; D: difficult; L.O.: listening purposes and styles

    Possible Answer: Listening to support and people-oriented listening.

93. If Sharon is not listening carefully to Marie recount her recent trip to Italy because she is more interested in talking about her own recent trip to France, what form of ineffective listening is Sharon engaged in? What could Sharon do to manage this problem?

    H: Narcissistic Listening, p. 174; C: application; D: difficult; L.O.: ineffective listening

    Possible Answer: Narcissistic listening; allow conversation to focus on topics outside of herself, and offer positive feedback to others.

94. What is the difference between positive and negative feedback?

    H: Positive Feedback, p. 156; C: conceptual; D: medium; L.O.: listening process

    Possible Answer: Positive feedback involves using nonverbal behavior, such as eye contact, aligning body with speaker, and smiling; and verbal behavior, such as back-channel cues, to show that you are interested and listening. Negative feedback is the avoidance of such verbal and nonverbal behaviors to indicate that you are uninterested, not listening, or displeased.

95. Identify factors that influence the attending step of the listening process.

    H: Attending, p. 153; C: conceptual; D: medium; L.O.: listening process

    Possible Answer: Salience of information and various internal and external factors that control attention span, such as noise, stress, hunger, illness, or fatigue.

96. What is the value of empathy in listening?

    H: Listening to Support, p. 162; C: conceptual; D: medium; L.O.: listening purposes

    Possible Answer: By listening to support, we can offer a speaker compassion and kindness, making the speaker feel understood.

97. List and explain two challenges or barriers to effective listening.

    H: Preventing Ineffective Listening, p. 168; C: conceptual; D: medium; L.O.: ineffective listening

    Possible Answer: Selective listening, a natural tendency to take in only information that has salience. Pseudo-listening, in which you behave as an effective listener even though you are not really listening. Aggressive listening, narcissistic listening, and eavesdropping are other possible answers.

98. Explain two strategies for improving recall and memory.

    H: Recalling, p. 158; C: conceptual; D: medium; L.O.: listening process

    Possible Answer: Use mnemonics, devices used by listeners to aid memory. Use all five senses. Break down complex ideas into simpler ones. Remember your emotional reaction.

99. Identify the five functions of listening.

H: The Five Functions of Listening, p. 161; C: factual/definitional; D: easy; L.O.: listening purposes

Possible Answer: Listening to comprehend, listening to support, listening to analyze, listening to appreciate, and listening to discern.

100. Identify the four listening styles.

H: Four Listening Styles, p. 164; C: factual/definitional; D: easy; L.O.: listening styles

Possible Answer: People-, action-, content-, and time-oriented listening.

101. What are two ways to demonstrate active listening after one's conversational partner has finished speaking?

H: Paraphrasing and Clarifying, p. 158; C: factual/definitional; D: easy; L.O.: listening process

Possible Answer: Paraphrasing and clarifying.

102. What are two ways to demonstrate active listening while a conversational partner is speaking?

H: Positive Feedback, p. 156; C: factual/definitional; D: easy; L.O.: listening process

Possible Answer: Using positive feedback and back-channel cues.

103. How can aggressive listening occur online?

H: Aggressive Listening, p. 171; C: conceptual; D: medium; L.O.: ineffective listening

Possible Answer: Provocateurs post annoying messages in hopes of provoking a response they can attack.

104. Define narcissistic listening and give an example of how a narcissistic listener might behave in conversation.

H: Narcissistic Listening, p. 174; C: factual/definitional; D: easy; L.O.: ineffective listening

Possible Answer: Narcissistic listening occurs when one ignores what others have to say and directs the conversation back to one's own self-interests. Narcissistic listeners will refuse to give feedback on information that doesn't focus on them or might even create a disturbance if the focus shifts from them.

Essay

Please respond to the following questions in paragraph form.

105. Compare and contrast listening styles of women and men.

H: Gender Differences in Listening Styles, p. 166; C: conceptual; D: medium; L.O.: listening styles

Possible Answer: Women tend to use people-oriented and content-oriented listening styles; men are more likely to use time-oriented and action-oriented styles. Women view listening as an emotional, relational activity; men see it as a task that needs to be completed in a timely manner.

106. What are some ways to enhance memory and recall? Give an example of each.

H: Recalling, p. 158; C: conceptual; D: medium; L.O.: listening process

Possible Answer: Use mnemonics, engage as many of the five senses as possible, break complex ideas down into simple phrases or symbols in your head, use repetition, write detailed notes or draw diagrams.

107. Identify and explain the four styles of listening. Give an example of each.

H: Four Listening Styles, p. 164; C: conceptual; D: medium; L.O.: listening styles

Possible Answer: Action-oriented listeners want brief, accurate messages that can be used to make decisions; for example, a professional football coach during a game. Time-oriented listeners want brief, concise messages for those concerned with schedules; for example, a busy CEO. People-oriented listeners focus on connecting with people and their emotions; for example, Mr. Rogers. Content-oriented listeners prefer messages that challenge them intellectually; for example, a graduate student working toward an advanced degree.

108. How does culture impact listening styles?

H: Culture and Listening Styles, p. 167; C: conceptual; D: medium; L.O.: listening styles

Possible Answer: Americans are viewed as less patient and less willing to spend time listening. People from other parts of the world value and focus more upon people-oriented listening rather than the time-oriented and action-oriented listening found in Western cultures. Individualistic cultures focus on time- and action-oriented listening; collectivistic cultures value people- and content-oriented listening.

109. Discuss problems associated with online listening.

H: Aggressive Listening, p. 171; C: conceptual; D: medium; L.O.: ineffective listening

Possible Answer: Aggressive listening is more likely to occur online because of the anonymity associated with online communication. Provocateurs intentionally post inflammatory rhetoric and responses designed to upset others. In the absence of nonverbal behavior, users may misunderstand messages and have to rely upon emoticons.

Chapter 6: Communicating Verbally

Matching

Match the concept, term, or theory with its correct response or definition.

A. commissive
B. communication accommodation theory
C. concealment
D. connotative meaning
E. constitutive rules
F. Cooperative Principle
G. cooperative verbal communication
H. deception
I. denotative meaning
J. dialects
K. directive
L. high-context cultures
M. "I" language

N. linguistic determinism
O. linguistic relativity
P. low-context cultures
Q. misunderstanding
R. naming
S. personal idioms
T. regulative rules
U. speech acts
V. symbols
W. verbal communication
X. "we" language
Y. "you" language

1. The exchange of spoken language with others during interaction.

   H: Characteristics of Verbal Communication, p. 182; C: factual/definitional; D: easy; L.O.: characteristics of language

   Answer: W. verbal communication

2. Rules that tell us which words represent which objects.

   H: Language Is Governed by Rules, p. 182; C: factual/definitional; D: easy; L.O.: characteristics of language

   Answer: E. constitutive rules

3. Making conversation informative, honest, relevant, and clear.

   H: Understandable Messages, p. 199; C: factual/definitional; D: easy; L.O.: cooperative verbal communication

   Answer: F. Cooperative Principle

4. Words and phrases that have unique meaning for people within their relationship.
   H: Language Is Flexible, p. 183; C: factual/definitional; D: easy; L.O.: characteristics of language
   Answer: S. personal idioms

5. Items we use to represent other people, objects, events, and ideas.
   H: Language Is Symbolic, p. 182; C: factual/definitional; D: easy; L.O.: characteristics of language
   Answer: V. symbols

6. Intentionally using language to mislead others.
   H: Deception, p. 205; C: factual/definitional; D: easy; L.O.: miscommunication
   Answer: H. deception

7. A group of people who assume listeners don't share their beliefs and who use direct and clear language to express their viewpoints.
   H: Language Is Cultural, p. 184; C: factual/definitional; D: easy; L.O.: characteristics of language
   Answer: P. low-context cultures

8. A word's literal, dictionary meaning.
   H: Sharing Meaning, p. 189; C: factual/definitional; D: easy; L.O.: functions of verbal communication
   Answer: I. denotative meaning

9. Failing to actively listen and misperceiving another's thoughts, beliefs, or feelings.
   H: Misunderstanding, p. 207; C: factual/definitional; D: easy; L.O.: barriers to verbal communication
   Answer: Q. misunderstanding

10. A word's implied meaning.
    H: Sharing Meaning, p. 189; C: factual/definitional; D: easy; L.O.: functions of verbal communication
    Answer: D. connotative meaning

11. The creation of linguistic symbols for objects.
    H: Naming, p. 192; C: factual/definitional; D: easy; L.O.: functions of verbal communication
    Answer: R. naming

12. The idea that language determines thought.
    H: Shaping Thought, p. 191; C: factual/definitional; D: easy; L.O.: functions of verbal communication
    Answer: N. linguistic determinism

13. Variations on language rules shared by large groups of people.

    H: Language Is Flexible, p. 183; C: factual/definitional; D: easy; L.O.: characteristics of language

    Answer: J. dialects

14. A speech act that attempts to get the listener to do things.

    H: Table 6.1: Types of Speech Acts, p. 195; C: factual/definitional; D: easy; L.O.: functions of verbal communication

    Answer: K. directive

15. Rules that govern how language is used in verbal communication.

    H: Language Is Governed by Rules, p. 182; C: factual/definitional; D: easy; L.O.: characteristics of language

    Answer: T. regulative rules

16. Messages that are easily understood use "I" language and make others feel included.

    H: Cooperative Verbal Communication, p. 198; C: factual/definitional; D: easy; L.O.: verbal communication principles

    Answer: G. cooperative verbal communication

17. A group of people that assumes listeners share its beliefs, uses language indirectly, and relies upon implicit understanding.

    H: Language Is Cultural, p. 184; C: factual/definitional; D: easy; L.O.: characteristics of language

    Answer: L. high-context cultures

18. Language that focuses attention on and blames others.

    H: Using "I" Language, p. 201; C: factual/definitional; D: easy; L.O.: verbal communication principles

    Answer: Y. "you" language

19. Phrases and language that emphasize one's own beliefs, feelings, and opinions.

    H: Using "I" Language, p. 201; C: factual/definitional; D: easy; L.O.: cooperative verbal communication

    Answer: M. "I" language

20. Language of inclusion that expresses connection with others.

    H: Using "We" Language, p. 201; C: factual/definitional; D: easy; L.O.: verbal communication principles

    Answer: X. "we" language

21. The idea that people from different cultures perceive and think about the world in different ways because of language.

    H: Shaping Thought, p. 191; C: factual/definitional; D: easy; L.O.: functions of verbal communication

    Answer: O. linguistic relativity

22. The adaptation of language to facilitate relationships with others.

    H: Culture and Cooperative Verbal Communication, p. 204; C: factual/definitional; D: easy; L.O.: verbal communication principles

    Answer: B. communication accommodation theory

23. The most common form of deception.

    H: Deception, p. 205; C: factual/definitional; D: easy; L.O.: barriers to verbal communication

    Answer: C. concealment

24. A type of speech act that commits the speaker to future action.

    H: Table 6.1: Types of Speech Acts, p. 195; C: factual/definitional; D: easy; L.O.: functions of verbal communication

    Answer: A. commissive

25. The actions that we perform with language.

    H: Performing Actions, p. 194; C: factual/definitional; D: easy; L.O.: functions of verbal communication

    Answer: U. speech acts

True/False

Please select whether the following statements are true or false.

26. The United States is a high-context culture.

    H: Language Is Cultural, p. 184; C: conceptual; D: medium; L.O.: characteristics of language

    Answer: F

27. Dialects do not include differences in accents.

    H: Language Is Flexible, p. 183; C: conceptual; D: medium; L.O.: characteristics of language

    Answer: F

28. Symbols can have multiple meanings, which can lead to misunderstanding.

    H: Language Is Symbolic, p. 182; C: conceptual; D: easy; L.O.: characteristics of language

    Answer: T

29. Regulative rules only apply to speaking.

    H: Language Is Governed by Rules, p. 182; C: conceptual; D: medium; L.O.: characteristics of language

    Answer: F

30. When a couple uses nicknames for each other, they are using personal idioms.

    H: Language Is Flexible, p. 183; C: conceptual; D: medium; L.O.: characteristics of language

    Answer: T

31. Individuals with chronic hostility are unlikely to experience intentional misunderstanding.

    H: Misunderstanding, p. 207; C: conceptual; D: medium; L.O.: barriers to verbal communication

    Answer: F

32. Although a language's constitutive rules may change, regulative rules are constant.

    H: Language Evolves, p. 186; C: conceptual; D: medium; L.O.: characteristics of language

    Answer: F

33. Research suggests that we seem to prefer and rate more favorably those who use a dialect similar to our own.

    H: Language Is Flexible, p. 183; C: conceptual; D: medium; L.O.: characteristics of language

    Answer: T

34. Being honest means sharing information even if you're not certain of its reliability.

    H: Being Honest, p. 200; C: conceptual; D: medium; L.O.: characteristics of language

    Answer: F

35. Members of high-context cultures need explicit information to understand one another.

    H: Language Is Cultural, p. 184; C: conceptual; D: medium; L.O.: characteristics of language

    Answer: F

36. A lobbying group that advocates that English be used as the primary language would be likely to support the exclusive use of Standard English in the public schools.

    H: Language Is Cultural, p. 184; C: application; D: difficult; L.O.: characteristics of language

    Answer: T

37. The influx of new terms such as "Wi-Fi hotspot" and "Twitter" demonstrates the characteristic that language evolves.

    H: Language Evolves, p. 186; C: application; D: difficult; L.O.: characteristics of language

    Answer: T

38. In the film *High Fidelity,* Laura's use of "not yet" to mean "but I really want to" is an example of the denotative meaning of language.

    H: Sharing Meaning, p. 189; C: application; D: medium; L.O.: functions of verbal communication

    Answer: F

39. Regulative rules tell us which words represent which objects.

    H: Language Is Governed by Rules, p. 182; C: conceptual; D: medium; L.O.: characteristics of language

    Answer: F

40. If, in the film *High Fidelity,* Rob looked up "not yet" and found "not up to the time specified," this definition would be an example of the connotative meaning of language.

    H: Sharing Meaning, p. 189; C: application; D: medium; L.O.: functions of verbal communication

    Answer: F

41. Constitutive rules govern how we use language to communicate nonverbally.

    H: Language Is Governed by Rules, p. 182; C: factual/definitional; D: easy; L.O.: characteristics of language

    Answer: F

42. Members of low-context cultures assume that listeners share similar attitudes, values, and beliefs.

    H: Language Is Cultural, p. 184; C: conceptual; D: medium; L.O.: characteristics of language

    Answer: F

43. Research confirms the fact that men interrupt more than women.

    H: Gender and Cooperative Verbal Communication, p. 202; C: factual/definitional; D: easy; L.O.: cooperative verbal communication

    Answer: F

44. If your girlfriend calls you at work and says she wants to "light the candle tonight," and you understand that she wants to be intimate, she is using a personal idiom.

    H: Language Is Flexible, p. 183; C: application; D: difficult; L.O.: characteristics of language

    Answer: T

45. If your interpersonal communication professor seems to tailor his lectures and examples to students in his class, he is demonstrating the Cooperative Principle.

    H: Understandable Messages, p. 199; C: application; D: difficult; L.O.: functions of verbal communication

    Answer: T

46. Linguistic determinism suggests that there is little relationship between language and thought.

    H: Shaping Thought, p. 191; C: conceptual; D: medium; L.O.: functions of verbal communication

    Answer: F

47. According to linguistic relativity, people who speak a language that uses masculine and feminine articles may perceive and understand their world differently than people who use a language without them.

    H: Shaping Thought, p. 191; C: application; D: difficult; L.O.: functions of verbal communication

    Answer: T

48. Communicators in high-context cultures tend to rely upon indirect, ambiguous language and silence when they communicate with one another.

H: Language Is Cultural, p. 184; C: conceptual; D: medium; L.O.: characteristics of language

Answer: T

49. Because gays and lesbians continue to face cultural prejudice and struggle with identity terms, they find the naming function of verbal communication to be a potent issue.

H: Naming, p. 192; C: application; D: medium; L.O.: functions of verbal communication

Answer: T

50. Commissive speech acts tend to commit the speaker to future action.

H: Table 6.1: Types of Speech Acts, p. 195; C: conceptual; D: medium; L.O.: functions of verbal communication

Answer: T

Multiple Choice

Please choose the correct response to the following statements.

51. As opposed to denotative meaning, connotative meaning is
    A. more literal
    B. more permanent
    C. more effective in intimate relationships
    D. probably found on dictionary.com
    E. less emotional and personal

    H: Sharing Meaning, p. 189; C: conceptual; D: medium; L.O.: functions of verbal communication

    Answer: C

52. When words are used as symbols, they represent
    A. people
    B. places
    C. objects
    D. ideas
    E. all of the above

    H: Language Is Symbolic, p. 182; C: conceptual; D: medium; L.O.: characteristics of verbal communication

    Answer: E

53. According to the text, which of the following are considered to be symbols?
    A. thoughts
    B. words
    C. attitudes
    D. values
    E. beliefs

H: Language Is Symbolic, p. 182; C: conceptual; D: easy; L.O.: functions of verbal communication

Answer: B

54. Mark has a short temper and always screams, "You are so dumb!" at his younger brother. What strategy of cooperative verbal communication is he violating?
    A. be easy to understand
    B. adapt messages to the context
    C. take ownership of one's own thoughts and feelings
    D. be honest
    E. none of the above

H: Using "I" Language, p. 201; C: application; D: difficult; L.O.: verbal communication principles

Answer: C

55. In the Focus on Culture box in the text, "Names and Prejudice," four college students discuss their thoughts on how to describe sexual orientation. These students are addressing what function of language?
    A. linguistic relativity
    B. naming
    C. linguistic determinism
    D. sharing meaning
    E. none of the above

H: Focus on Culture: Names and Prejudice, p. 193; C: application; D: difficult; L.O.: functions of verbal communication

Answer: B

56. The theory that suggests our ability to shape language shapes our relationships with others is called
    A. regulative rules
    B. communication accommodation theory
    C. Cooperative Principle
    D. linguistic determinism
    E. linguistic relativity

H: Shaping Thought, p. 191; C: conceptual; D: medium; L.O.: functions of verbal communication

Answer: D

57. When someone from the North says she is going "tanning," whereas someone from the South says he is going to "lay out," what characteristic of language is being illustrated?
    A. naming
    B. denotation
    C. dialect
    D. connotation
    E. linguistic relativity

H: Language Is Flexible, p. 183; C: application; D: difficult; L.O.: characteristics of language

Answer: C

58. You and your sister are discussing the nuances of an abstract word such as "white." She types in the word on dictionary.com, only to find many different definitions. What has she found?
   A. connotative meanings
   B. denotative meanings
   C. contextual meanings
   D. names
   E. symbols

   H: Sharing Meaning, p. 189; C: application; D: difficult; L.O.: functions of verbal communication

   Answer: B

59. According to research by Grice, you must do what in order to be informative?
   A. present all relevant information
   B. present information that is appropriate
   C. be ethical
   D. all of the above
   E. only A and B

   H: Being Informative, p. 200; C: conceptual; D: difficult; L.O.: verbal communication principles

   Answer: E

60. What is considered to be the most important characteristic of cooperative verbal communication?
   A. relationship
   B. timing
   C. context
   D. honesty
   E. ethics

   H: Being Honest, p. 200; C: factual/definitional; D: easy; L.O.: verbal communication principles

   Answer: D

61. According to research by Kellermann, a critical aspect of constructing conversations is the need to adhere to and follow
   A. speech acts
   B. constitutive rules
   C. regulative rules
   D. conversational scripts
   E. communication accommodation theory

   H: Crafting Conversations, p. 195; C: conceptual; D: medium; L.O.: functions of verbal communication

   Answer: D

62. When President Clinton reported to the public, "I did not have sexual relations with that woman," he was engaging in
   A. concealment
   B. misunderstanding

C. deception

D. paraphrasing

E. mnemonics

H: Deception, p. 205; C: application; D: medium; L.O.: miscommunication

Answer: C

63. What is a characteristic fundamental to conversation?
    A. it is interactive
    B. it is locally managed
    C. it is universal
    D. it uses scripts
    E. all of the above

    H: Crafting Conversations, p. 195; C: conceptual; D: medium; L.O.: functions of verbal communication

    Answer: E

64. The textbook suggests using which strategy to achieve cooperative verbal communication?
    A. decreasing use of "I" language
    B. increasing use of "we" language
    C. increasing use of "you" language
    D. avoiding use of "we" language
    E. watching the film *Yours, Mine, and Ours*

    H: Using "We" Language, p. 201; C: conceptual; D: medium; L.O.: verbal communication principles

    Answer: B

65. If Mark and Eddie self-select who goes next in their conversation, they are demonstrating which characteristic of conversation?
    A. local management
    B. using scripts
    C. universality
    D. interactivity
    E. none of the above

    H: Crafting Conversations, p. 195; C: application; D: difficult; L.O.: functions of verbal communication

    Answer: A

66. In comparing competitive encounters to collaborative encounters, research suggests
    A. men use clearer, more concise language than women in competitive encounters
    B. women use wordier, more flowery language in competitive encounters
    C. women and men tend to use the same language, irrespective of whether the encounter is competitive or collaborative
    D. both women and men adjust their language, depending upon whether the encounter is competitive or collaborative
    E. none of the above

    H: Gender and Cooperative Verbal Communication, p. 202; C: conceptual; D: medium; L.O.: verbal communication principles

    Answer: D

67. "We should definitely adopt your course of action" is an example of what type of speech act?
    A. directive
    B. representative
    C. commissive
    D. expressive
    E. declarative

    H: Table 6.1: Types of Speech Acts, p. 195; C: application; D: difficult; L.O.: functions of verbal communication

    Answer: C

68. In comparing gender and culture and their impact on verbal communication, we can conclude
    A. both gender and culture strongly impact verbal communication
    B. gender has a greater impact than culture on verbal communication
    C. culture has a greater impact than gender on verbal communication
    D. gender and culture have little impact on verbal communication
    E. none of the above

    H: Culture and Cooperative Verbal Communication, p. 204; C: conceptual; D: medium; L.O.: verbal communication principles

    Answer: C

69. According to communication accommodation theory, we are more likely to
    A. adapt language when seeking social approval
    B. adapt language when establishing relationships with others
    C. adapt language when we perceive others' usage as appropriate
    D. accentuate language differences to distance ourselves from others
    E. all of the above

    H: Culture and Cooperative Verbal Communication, p. 204; C: conceptual; D: medium; L.O.: verbal communication principles

    Answer: E

70. If Cadence wants to become closer to Ravi, according to communication accommodation theory she can
    A. decrease speech rate
    B. take longer turns
    C. use ambiguous wording
    D. adapt her language to Ravi's
    E. all of the above

    H: Culture and Cooperative Verbal Communication, p. 204; C: application; D: difficult; L.O.: verbal communication principles

    Answer: D

71. According to research on verbal communication accommodation, you would be advised to do which of the following if you were traveling abroad?
    A. match the host culture's language use
    B. moderately adjust your language to match the host culture's language use
    C. don't adjust your language at all to match the host culture's language use

D. try to match the host culture's dialect

E. try to match the host culture's word usage

H: Culture and Cooperative Verbal Communication, p. 204; C: application; D: difficult; L.O.: verbal communication principles

Answer: B

72. "I hope I did not hurt your feelings" is an example of what type of speech act?

A. representative

B. directive

C. declarative

D. expressive

E. commissive

H: Table 6.1: Types of Speech Acts, p. 195; C: application; D: difficult; L.O.: functions of verbal communication

Answer: D

73. "Get out of my house" is an example of what type of speech act?

A. representative

B. declarative

C. directive

D. commissive

E. expressive

H: Table 6.1: Types of Speech Acts, p. 195; C: application; D: difficult; L.O.: functions of verbal communication

Answer: C

74. The idea that we cannot conceive of anything that we lack a vocabulary for is called

A. Sapir-Whorf Hypothesis

B. linguistic relativity

C. naming

D. representative speech acts

E. none of the above

H: Shaping Thought, p. 191; C: factual/definitional; D: medium; L.O.: functions of verbal communication

Answer: A

75. What can someone do to understand the meaning of what a speaker is referring to?

A. use constitutive rules

B. use context

C. use regulative rules

D. use personal idioms

E. use naming

H: Language Is Symbolic, p. 182; C: conceptual; D: medium; L.O.: characteristics of language

Answer: B

76. What is the most frequent form of deception?
    A. naming
    B. misunderstanding
    C. flaming
    D. concealment
    E. none of the above

    H: Deception, p. 205; C: factual/definitional; D: easy; L.O.: miscommunication

    Answer: D

77. The language style of men has been stereotypically associated with
    A. passive verbs
    B. politeness
    C. directness
    D. wordiness
    E. all of the above

    H: Gender and Cooperative Verbal Communication, p. 202; C: conceptual; D: medium; L.O.: verbal communication principles

    Answer: C

78. Which of the following is NOT true of misunderstanding?
    A. can be intentional
    B. can be unintentional
    C. often caused by failure to use active listening
    D. cannot be intentional
    E. can be caused by relationship intimacy

    H: Misunderstanding, p. 207; C: conceptual; D: medium; L.O.: miscommunication

    Answer: D

79. A culture that values straight, direct talk could be described as
    A. no context
    B. ethical
    C. empathic
    D. low-context
    E. high-context

    H: Language Is Cultural, p. 184; C: conceptual; D: medium; L.O.: characteristics of language communication

    Answer: D

80. The theory that people from different cultures perceive the world differently because of language is called
    A. linguistic relativity
    B. linguistic determinism
    C. low-context culture
    D. high-context culture
    E. none of the above

    H: Shaping Thought, p. 191; C: conceptual; D: medium; L.O.: functions of verbal communication

    Answer: A

81. When the speaker and context influence a word's meaning, what type of meaning is affected?
    A. denotative meaning
    B. connotative meaning
    C. contextual meaning
    D. intentional meaning
    E. unintentional meaning

    H: Sharing Meaning, p. 189; C: conceptual; D: medium; L.O.: functions of verbal communication

    Answer: B

82. "If you don't take out the trash, you will not get your allowance" is an example of what type of speech act?
    A. representative
    B. directive
    C. declarative
    D. commissive
    E. expressive

    H: Table 6.1: Types of Speech Acts, p. 195; C: application; D: difficult; L.O.: functions of verbal communication

    Answer: B

83. If your girlfriend calls you "lover" and you call her "honeybun" these are examples of
    A. personal idioms
    B. dialect
    C. naming
    D. speech act
    E. symbols

    H: Language Is Flexible, p. 183; C: application; D: difficult; L.O.: characteristics of language

    Answer: A

84. What is a cause or origin of unintentional misunderstandings?
    A. failure to use active listening
    B. omitting pertinent information
    C. misinterpreting other's messages
    D. both A and B
    E. both A and C

    H: Misunderstanding, p. 207; C: conceptual; D: medium; L.O.: miscommunication

    Answer: E

85. Which of the following is NOT true about gender's effect on communication?
    A. women are more likely to talk about their feelings
    B. women disclose more during same-gender conversations
    C. men and women both use clearer, more concise language in competitive encounters
    D. men do not use vaguer and wordier communication than women
    E. women and men interrupt in equal numbers

H: Gender and Cooperative Verbal Communication, p. 202; C: conceptual; D: medium; L.O.: verbal communication principles

Answer: A

86. According to communication accommodation theory, we tend
    A. not to change our language
    B. to change our language if we dislike the receiver
    C. not to change our language if we like the receiver
    D. to adapt our language when seeking to establish relationships with others
    E. none of the above

H: Culture and Cooperative Verbal Communication, p. 204; C: conceptual; D: medium; L.O.: verbal communication principles

Answer: D

87. "Until you do the right thing by me, everything you touch will crumble" is an example of what type of speech act?
    A. expressive
    B. commissive
    C. directive
    D. representative
    E. declarative

H: Table 6.1: Types of Speech Acts, p. 195; C: application; D: difficult; L.O.: functions of verbal communication

Answer: E

88. Which of the following would NOT be considered an example of conversation?
    A. instant messaging
    B. real-time Internet chatroom
    C. business meeting
    D. a moderated debate
    E. all of the above

H: Crafting Conversations, p. 195; C: conceptual; D: medium; L.O.: functions of verbal communication

Answer: D

89. In a high-context culture, communicators
    A. presume listeners share extensive knowledge with them
    B. do not feel a need to provide explicit information to listeners
    C. rely more on indirect and ambiguous language to create meaning
    D. all of the above
    E. none of the above

H: Language Is Cultural, p. 184; C: application; D: easy; L.O.: characteristics of language communication

Answer: D

Short Answer

Briefly respond to the following questions in full sentences.

90. Identify five fundamental characteristics of language.

    H: Characteristics of Verbal Communication, p. 182; C: factual/definitional; D: easy; L.O.: characteristics of language

    Possible Answer: It is symbolic, has rules, is flexible, is cultural, and evolves.

91. Identify four out of six functions of verbal communication.

    H: Functions of Verbal Communication, p. 188; C: factual/definitional; D: easy; L.O.: functions of verbal communication

    Possible Answer: Sharing meaning, shaping thought, naming, performing actions, crafting conversations, and managing relationships.

92. Identify two types of cooperative language.

    H: Using "I" Language, p. 201; C: factual/definitional; D: easy; L.O.: verbal communication principles

    Possible Answer: "I" and "we" language.

93. Describe how to facilitate communication across cultures.

    H: Culture and Cooperative Verbal Communication, p. 204; C: conceptual; D: medium; L.O.: verbal communication principles

    Possible Answer: Adjust your language moderately to reflect that of others: match the other person's speech rate, his or her use of indirect or direct language, and turn lengths.

94. Explain why connotative meanings can vary for different people.

    H: Sharing Meaning, p. 189; C: conceptual; D: medium; L.O.: functions of verbal communication

    Possible Answer: Connotative meanings are based on shared knowledge, personal meanings, and context.

95. Define linguistic relativity.

    H: Shaping Thought, p. 191; C: conceptual; D: medium; L.O.: functions of verbal communication

    Possible Answer: Because people from different cultures speak different languages, they perceive and experience the world differently.

96. Describe what linguistic determinism means.

    H: Shaping Thought, p. 191; C: conceptual; D: medium; L.O.: functions of verbal communication

    Possible Answer: The language we know determines how we perceive and understand our world.

97. Discuss the inherent danger of emphasizing gender's impact on language.

    H: Gender and Cooperative Verbal Communication, p. 202; C: conceptual; D: medium; L.O.: verbal communication principles

Possible Answer: Powerful, pervasive stereotypes seem to exaggerate the differences between the ways in which women and men use language, when in fact the differences are negligible.

98. How do differences in dialect affect perception?

    H: Language Is Flexible, p. 183; C: conceptual; D: medium; L.O.: characteristics of language

    Possible Answer: Listeners tend to perceive those who use similar dialects to themselves more positively than those who use dissimilar ones.

99. Explain the different ways romantic partners may use personal idioms.

    H: Language Is Flexible, p. 183; C: conceptual; D: medium; L.O.: characteristics of language

    Possible Answer: On average, romantic partners create at least six personal idioms, including nicknames, teasing insults, and sexual invitations.

100. Identify the responsibilities faced by those committed to using cooperative verbal communication.

    H: Cooperative Verbal Communication, p. 198; C: conceptual; D: medium; L.O.: verbal communication principles

    Possible Answer: To produce messages that are easily understood, to take ownership of what you say, and to be inclusive, not exclusive.

101. What is the difference between concealment and deception?

    H: Deception, p. 205; C: conceptual; D: medium; L.O.: verbal communication principles

    Possible Answer: Deception involves using uninformative, untruthful, irrelevant, or vague language to purposely mislead others, while concealment is when people deliberately leave out important information from a message.

102. Convert the following "you" language statements into "I" language: "You hurt my feelings." "You never listen to me." "You totally ruined the game for us."

    H: Using "I" Language, p. 201; C: application; D: difficult; L.O.: verbal communication principles

    Possible Answer: YOU: You hurt my feelings. I: I feel hurt. YOU: You never listen to me. I: I feel like you are not listening to me. YOU: You totally ruined the game for us. I: I'm disappointed in how the game turned out.

103. Identify one key mistake often made in cross-cultural communication.

    H: Culture and Cooperative Verbal Communication, p. 204; C: factual/definitional; D: easy L.O.: verbal communication principles

    Possible Answer: We often try too hard to match another person's dialect and/or word choice. This can be perceived as inappropriate and insulting.

104. Name one challenge we face when trying to communicate cooperatively online.

    H: Misunderstanding, p. 207; C: factual/definitional; D: easy; L.O.: verbal communication principles

    Possible Answer: Using e-mail frequently results in miscommunication of content or intent, due to the absence of nonverbal cues.

Essay

Please respond to the following questions in paragraph form.

105. Explain the five fundamental characteristics of language.

    H: Characteristics of Verbal Communication, p. 182; C: conceptual; D: medium;
    L.O.: characteristics of language

    Possible Answer: Symbolic: Words are used to represent people, object, events, and ideas;
    Rules: Govern meanings, structure, and order of words; Flexible: Allows for rules to change;
    Cultural: Different cultures use different languages to perpetuate culture; Evolves: Language
    and its symbols are constantly changing.

106. Explain the six functions of verbal communication.

    H: Functions of Verbal Communication, p. 188; C: conceptual; D: medium; L.O.: functions
    of verbal communication

    Possible Answer: Sharing meaning: By using denotative and connotative meanings we can
    use symbols to share meaning. Shaping thought: Language influences the way we think and
    the way we perceive our world. Naming: We name things in our world by using symbols.
    Performing actions: Using speech acts to influence others' behaviors and to meet our goals.
    Managing relationships: Using language to initiate, maintain, and end relationships. Crafting
    conversations: Allows us to control verbal interactions with local management and scripts.

107. How can you use verbal communication more cooperatively?

    H: Cooperative Verbal Communication, p. 198; C: conceptual; D: medium; L.O.: verbal
    communication principles

    Possible Answer: Avoid the use of "you" and instead use "I" and "we." Communication
    needs to be clear, easy to understand, and to make people feel included. Information must be
    relevant, appropriate, honest, and ethical.

108. Identify and explain two barriers to cooperative verbal communication.

    H: Barriers to Cooperative Verbal Communication, p. 204; C: conceptual; D: medium;
    L.O.: miscommunication

    Possible Answer: Deception occurs when an individual tries to deliberately mislead others
    by using uninformative, untruthful, irrelevant, or vague language. Misunderstanding is often
    the result of someone failing to actively listen to another. If someone does not listen actively,
    the messages he or she receives can be easily confused.

109. Explain culture's impact on verbal communication by discussing the differences between
    low-context and high-context cultures.

    H: Language Is Cultural, p. 184; C: conceptual; D: medium; L.O.: characteristics of verbal
    communication

    Possible Answer: Low-context cultures tend to assume dissimilarity to others and therefore
    rely more upon the explicit, direct, clear use of verbal communication; high-context cultures
    assume a higher degree of similarity and rely less upon direct, explicit communication and
    more upon implicit, implied, and indirect communication.

Chapter 7: Communicating Nonverbally

Matching

Match the concept, term, or theory with its correct response or definition.

A. adaptors
B. affect displays
C. artifacts
D. chronemics
E. dominance
F. emblems
G. environment
H. facial symmetry
I. friendship-warmth touch
J. functional-professional touch
K. haptics
L. illustrators
M. immediacy

N. intimacy
O. kinesics
P. love-intimacy touch
Q. nonverbal communication
R. nonverbal communication codes
S. power
T. proxemics
U. regulators
V. social-polite touch
W. submissiveness
X. territoriality
Y. vocalics

1. The tendency to claim physical space as your own.

   H: Communicating through Personal Space, p. 232; C: factual/definitional; D: easy; L.O.: nonverbal codes

   Answer: X. territoriality

2. The different means used for transmitting information nonverbally.

   H: Nonverbal Communication Codes, p. 223; C: factual/definitional; D: easy; L.O.: nonverbal communication codes

   Answer: R. nonverbal communication codes

3. Types of gesture that have specific verbal meaning.

   H: Gestures, p. 227; C: factual/definitional; D: easy; L.O.: nonverbal codes

   Answer: F. emblems

4. Intentional or unintentional nonverbal behaviors that display emotion.
   H: Expressing Emotion, p. 240; C: factual/definitional; D: easy; L.O.: nonverbal functions
   Answer: B. affect displays

5. The degree to which we find someone interesting and attractive.
   H: Posture, p. 227; C: factual/definitional; D: easy; L.O.: nonverbal codes
   Answer: M. immediacy

6. The ability to influence or control other people or events.
   H: Posture, p. 227; C: factual/definitional; D: easy; L.O.: nonverbal codes
   Answer: S. power

7. Behaviors used to exert power and influence over others.
   H: Dominance and Submissiveness, p. 243; C: factual/definitional; D: easy; L.O.: manage nonverbal communication
   Answer: E. dominance

8. Vocal characteristics, such as pitch and tone, used to communicate.
   H: Communicating through Voice, p. 228; C: factual/definitional; D: easy; L.O.: nonverbal codes
   Answer: Y. vocalics

9. The nonverbal communication code of touch.
   H: Communicating through Touch, p. 230; C: factual/definitional; D: easy; L.O.: nonverbal codes
   Answer: K. haptics

10. Touch used to accomplish a task.
    H: Communicating through Touch, p. 230; C: factual/definitional; D: easy; L.O.: nonverbal codes
    Answer: J. functional-professional touch

11. Intentional or unintentional transmission of meaning through an individual's nonspoken physical and behavioral cues.
    H: Principles of Nonverbal Communication, p. 218; C: factual/definitional; D: easy; L.O.: nonverbal basics
    Answer: Q. nonverbal communication

12. Touch used to convey deep emotional feeling.
    H: Communicating through Touch, p. 230; C: factual/definitional; D: easy; L.O.: nonverbal codes
    Answer: P. love-intimacy touch

13. Types of gesture that serve a psychological or physical purpose.
    H: Gestures, p. 227; C: factual/definitional; D: easy; L.O.: nonverbal codes
    Answer: A. adaptors

14. Communication through the use of physical distance.

    H: Communicating through Personal Space, p. 232; C: factual/definitional; D: easy; L.O.: nonverbal codes

    Answer: T. proxemics

15. Touch used to express liking of another person.

    H: Communicating through Touch, p. 230; C: factual/definitional; D: easy; L.O.: nonverbal codes

    Answer: I. friendship-warmth touch

16. Nonverbal communication through time and organization.

    H: Communicating through Time, p. 233; C: factual/definitional; D: easy; L.O.: nonverbal codes

    Answer: D. chronemics

17. A type of nonverbal code made up of visible body movements.

    H: Communicating through Body Movements, p. 224; C: factual/definitional; D: easy; L.O.: nonverbal codes

    Answer: O. kinesics

18. The degree to which each side of your face matches the other.

    H: Communicating through Physical Appearance, p. 236; C: factual/ definitional; D: easy; L.O.: nonverbal communication codes

    Answer: H. facial symmetry

19. The willingness to allow others to exert influence or power over us.

    H: Dominance and Submissiveness, p. 243; C: factual/definitional; D: easy; L.O.: functions of nonverbal communication

    Answer: W. submissiveness

20. Things we possess that communicate our identity to others.

    H: Communicating through Objects, p. 238; C: factual/definitional; D: easy; L.O.: nonverbal codes

    Answer: C. artifacts

21. Types of gesture that accent or illustrate a verbal message.

    H: Gestures, p. 227; C: factual/definitional; D: easy; L.O.: nonverbal codes

    Answer: L. illustrators

22. The physical features of our surroundings.

    H: Communicating through the Environment, p. 239; C: factual/definitional; D: easy; L.O.: nonverbal codes

    Answer: G. environment

23. Touch based upon social norms.

H: Communicating through Touch, p. 230; C: factual/definitional; D: easy; L.O.: nonverbal codes

Answer: V. social-polite touch

24. Feeling of emotional bonding or union between ourselves and others.

H: Intimacy, p. 242; C: factual/definitional; D: easy; L.O.: manage nonverbal communication

Answer: N. intimacy

25. Types of gesture that control turn-taking in conversation.

H: Gestures, p. 227; C: factual/definitional; D: easy; L.O.: nonverbal codes

Answer: U. regulators

True/False

Please select whether the following statements are true or false.

26. Verbal communication tends to be more credible or believable than nonverbal communication.

H: Nonverbal Communication Has More Meaning, p. 219; C: conceptual; D: medium; L.O.: nonverbal basics

Answer: F

27. If, while driving, you are cut off by another driver and "flip" him "the bird," you are using a gesture called an illustrator.

H: Gestures, p. 227; C: application; D: difficult; L.O.: nonverbal codes

Answer: F

28. Nonverbal communication tends to be more ambiguous than verbal communication.

H: Nonverbal Communication Is More Ambiguous, p. 218; C: conceptual; D: medium; L.O.: nonverbal basics

Answer: T

29. The Noh mask effect suggests that we have a tendency to create different impressions by wearing different masks and using different facial cues.

H: Facial Expression, p. 225; C: conceptual; D: medium; L.O.: nonverbal codes

Answer: F

30. The majority of meaning in an interpersonal encounter is communicated nonverbally.

H: Nonverbal Communication Has More Meaning, p. 219; C: conceptual; D: medium; L.O.: principles of nonverbal communication

Answer: T

31. Research suggests that women are more territorial than men.

    H: Nonverbal Communication Is Influenced by Gender, p. 220; C: conceptual; D: medium; L.O.: nonverbal basics

    Answer: F

32. In examining gender differences and nonverbal communication, it seems that men are better at using and understanding nonverbal communication.

    H: Nonverbal Communication Is Influenced by Gender, p. 220; C: conceptual; D: medium; L.O.: nonverbal basics

    Answer: F

33. Speech rate and volume are elements of vocalics.

    H: Communicating through Voice, p. 228; C: factual/definitional; D: easy; L.O.: nonverbal codes

    Answer: T

34. Physical appearance plays a minimal role in nonverbal communication.

    H: Communicating through Physical Appearance, p. 236; C: factual/definitional; D: easy; L.O.: nonverbal codes

    Answer: F

35. During initial interaction, nonverbal communication is more important than verbal communication in terms of our overall impressions of others.

    H: Nonverbal Communication Has More Meaning, p. 219; C: conceptual; D: medium; L.O.: nonverbal basics

    Answer: T

36. Men seem to smile more than women.

    H: Nonverbal Communication Is Influenced by Gender, p. 220; C: factual/definitional; D: easy; L.O.: nonverbal basics

    Answer: F

37. We express and experience verbal and nonverbal communication separately.

    H: Nonverbal and Verbal Combine to Create Communication, p. 223; C: conceptual; D: medium; L.O.: nonverbal basics

    Answer: F

38. Silence can be used to signal dominance over someone else.

    H: Dominance and Submissiveness, p. 243; C: factual/definitional; D: easy; L.O.: manage nonverbal communication

    Answer: T

39. Nonverbal communication can be either intentional or unintentional.

    H: Principles of Nonverbal Communication, p. 218; C: conceptual; D: medium; L.O.: nonverbal basics

    Answer: T

40. The American version of Sinéad O'Connor's album cover depicted a demure gaze rather than a screaming face because of American culture's norms about the ways that are appropriate for women and men to communicate.

    H: Nonverbal Communication Is Influenced by Gender, p. 220; C: application; D: difficult; L.O.: nonverbal basics

    Answer: T

41. The higher a couple's level of nonverbal involvement across all communication codes, the healthier their relationship is.

    H: Intimacy, p. 242; C: conceptual; D: medium; L.O.: nonverbal basics

    Answer: T

42. Women seem to gaze more at others during interaction than men do.

    H: Nonverbal Communication Is Influenced by Gender, p. 220; C: conceptual; D: medium; L.O.: nonverbal basics

    Answer: T

43. Nonverbal communication tends to be multichanneled, whereas verbal communication tends to be single-channeled.

    H: Nonverbal Communication Uses Multiple Channels, p. 218; C: conceptual; D: medium; L.O.: nonverbal basics

    Answer: T

44. Research suggests that men maintain more physical space than women.

    H: Nonverbal Communication Is Influenced by Gender, p. 220; C: conceptual; D: medium; L.O.: nonverbal basics

    Answer: T

45. According to research, if you post attractive friends' photos on your Facebook page, others are more likely to perceive you as physically and socially attractive.

    H: Communicating through Physical Appearance, p. 236; C: conceptual; D: medium; L.O.: nonverbal communication codes

    Answer: T

46. People with asymmetrical faces are judged as more attractive than people with symmetrical faces.

    H: Communicating through Physical Appearance, p. 236; C: conceptual; D: medium; L.O.: nonverbal communication codes

    Answer: F

47. Vocalics is considered to be the most powerful code of nonverbal communication in terms of communicating meaning.

    H: Communicating through Body Movements, p. 224; C: conceptual; D: medium; L.O.: nonverbal codes

    Answer: F

48. Prolonged staring is considered to be one of the most aggressive codes of nonverbal communication.

H: Eye Contact, p. 226; C: conceptual; D: medium; L.O.: nonverbal codes

Answer: T

49. Nonverbal communication is more ambiguous because it is governed by fewer rules.

H: Nonverbal Communication Has Fewer Rules, p. 219; C: conceptual; D: medium; L.O.: nonverbal basics

Answer: T

50. Some scholars argue that facial cues are the most important form of communication for forming impressions.

H: Facial Expression, p. 225; C: conceptual; D: medium; L.O.: nonverbal codes

Answer: T

Multiple Choice

Please choose the correct response to the following statements.

51. Nonverbal communication can be used to do all of the following EXCEPT
    A. communicate meaning
    B. repress emotion
    C. present self
    D. manage interaction
    E. none of the above

H: Functions of Nonverbal Communication, p. 239; C: conceptual; D: medium; L.O.: nonverbal functions

Answer: B

52. Compared to verbal communication, nonverbal communication is
    A. clearer
    B. single-channeled
    C. more intentional
    D. less credible
    E. more ambiguous

H: Nonverbal Communication Is More Ambiguous, p. 218; C: conceptual; D: medium; L.O.: nonverbal basics

Answer: E

53. Nonverbal communication can be used to convey meaning by
    A. reiterating
    B. contradicting
    C. replacing
    D. enhancing
    E. all of the above

Answer: E

54. The online use of emoticons emulates what type of nonverbal communication code?
    A. kinesics
    B. haptics
    C. chronemics
    D. physical appearance
    E. vocalics

    H: Facial Expression, p. 225; C: conceptual; D: difficult; L.O.: nonverbal basics
    Answer: A

55. Which of the following is true of women's use of nonverbal communication?
    A. women are better at sending and receiving nonverbal messages
    B. women smile more
    C. women gaze more
    D. women are more facially expressive
    E. all of the above

    H: Nonverbal Communication Is Influenced by Gender, p. 220; C: conceptual; D: medium; L.O.: nonverbal basics
    Answer: E

56. The handshake is considered what type of touch?
    A. sexual-arousal touch
    B. functional-professional touch
    C. social-polite touch
    D. friendship-warmth touch
    E. love-intimacy touch

    H: Communicating through Touch, p. 230; C: conceptual; D: medium; L.O.: nonverbal codes
    Answer: C

57. While at your workplace, what type of proxemics are you likely to communicate?
    A. intimate space
    B. personal space
    C. social space
    D. public space
    E. none of the above

    H: Communicating through Personal Space, p. 232; C: application; D: difficult; L.O.: nonverbal codes
    Answer: C

58. Most Americans are comfortable with a "wingspan distance" for which of the following proxemics?
    A. personal space
    B. social space
    C. intimate space
    D. public space
    E. none of the above

H: Communicating through Personal Space, p. 232; C: conceptual; D: medium; L.O.: nonverbal communication codes

Answer: A

59. Hispanics are more likely than Euro-Americans to use which form of touch?
    A. sexual-arousal touch
    B. love-intimacy touch
    C. social-polite touch
    D. functional-professional touch
    E. friendship-warmth touch

    H: Communicating through Touch, p. 230; C: application; D: difficult; L.O.: nonverbal communication codes

    Answer: E

60. Which location is named by the text as displaying the most frequent use of touch?
    A. United States
    B. Switzerland
    C. Norway
    D. England
    E. Puerto Rico

    H: Communicating through Touch, p. 230; C: factual/definitional; D: easy; L.O.: nonverbal codes

    Answer: E

61. People who have M-time orientation are
    A. careful about scheduling of time
    B. relaxed about their use of time
    C. rarely worried about wasting time
    D. patient waiting for others
    E. often from Latin American or African countries

    H: Communicating through Time, p. 233; C: conceptual; D: medium; L.O.: nonverbal codes

    Answer: A

62. When disciplining your two-year-old son, you raise your voice to emphasize the first word of the command "STOP throwing your bottle." What function of nonverbal communication are you using?
    A. reiteration
    B. contradiction
    C. spotlight
    D. replacement
    E. enhancement

    H: Conveying Meanings, p. 240; C: application; D: difficult; L.O.: nonverbal functions

    Answer: C

63. The Noh mask effect suggests that which aspect of facial expression should be considered?
    A. specific facial features
    B. angle of the eyebrows

C. curve of the mouth

D. width of the eyes

E. all of the above

H: Facial Expression, p. 225; C: conceptual; D: medium; L.O.: nonverbal codes

Answer: E

64. Amber notices her coworker hunched over her workstation holding her head in her hands and asks her, "Are you okay? You look upset." Her coworker responds, "I'm fine, just tired." This illustrates what principle of nonverbal communication?

A. nonverbal messages are less credible than verbal messages

B. nonverbal messages can be ambiguous

C. nonverbal messages are single-channeled

D. nonverbal messages are cultural

E. none of the above

H: Nonverbal Communication Is More Ambiguous, p. 218; C: application; D: difficult; L.O.: nonverbal basics

Answer: B

65. What is the study of human movement, gestures, and facial expression called?

A. kinesics

B. chronemics

C. proxemics

D. low context

E. vocalics

H: Communicating through Body Movements, p. 224; C: factual/definitional; D: easy; L.O.: nonverbal codes

Answer: A

66. If your track coach wraps your ankle with an ace bandage after you sprain it, what type of touch is your coach using?

A. sexual-arousal touch

B. functional-professional touch

C. social-polite touch

D. friendship-warmth touch

E. love-intimacy touch

H: Communicating through Touch, p. 230; C: application; D: difficult; L.O.: nonverbal codes

Answer: B

67. When the text suggests that nonverbal communication is ambiguous, it means

A. little work is needed to understand and interpret nonverbal behavior

B. nonverbal communication is less credible than verbal communication

C. we cannot assume that nonverbal communication has only one meaning

D. nonverbal communication is learned

E. it is difficult to misunderstand or misinterpret nonverbal behavior

H: Nonverbal Communication Is More Ambiguous, p. 218; C: conceptual; D: medium; L.O.: nonverbal basics

Answer: C

68. When Tony departs for a long business trip, he says "I love you" to his girlfriend Melinda, makes direct eye contact, and hugs her. What function of nonverbal communication is he using?
    A. reiterating
    B. contradicting
    C. spotlighting
    D. replacing
    E. enhancing

    H: Conveying Meanings, p. 240; C: application; D: difficult; L.O.: nonverbal functions

    Answer: E

69. If you and your partner engage in public displays of affection such as holding hands and hugging, you are displaying what type of touch?
    A. sexual-arousal touch
    B. functional-professional touch
    C. social-polite touch
    D. friendship-warmth touch
    E. love-intimacy touch

    H: Communicating through Touch, p. 230; C: application; D: difficult; L.O.: nonverbal codes

    Answer: E

70. If you ask your spouse if he is angry and he shouts, "No, I'm not angry," what function of nonverbal communication is he using?
    A. reiterating
    B. contradicting
    C. spotlighting
    D. replacing
    E. enhancing

    H: Conveying Meanings, p. 240; C: application; D: difficult; L.O.: nonverbal functions

    Answer: B

71. Which of the following distances do you typically maintain when talking with one of your close yet platonic friends?
    A. intimate space
    B. personal space
    C. social space
    D. public space
    E. none of the above

    H: Communicating through Personal Space, p. 232; C: application; D: difficult; L.O.: nonverbal codes

    Answer: B

72. Affect displays are primarily displayed through the
    A. head and eyes
    B. hands and eyes
    C. eyes and hands
    D. face and voice
    E. none of the above

H: Expressing Emotion, p. 240; C: factual/definitional; D: medium; L.O.: nonverbal functions

Answer: D

73. During Malik's presentation to the class, he constantly scratches his head and adjusts his tie. What type of gesture is he relying upon?
    A. illustrator
    B. regulator
    C. adaptor
    D. kinesics
    E. emblem

H: Gestures, p. 227; C: application; D: difficult; L.O.: nonverbal codes

Answer: C

74. To indicate the end of your part of the conversation, you probably will NOT
    A. decrease your pitch
    B. cease any gestures
    C. increase your volume
    D. focus your gaze on the other person
    E. none of the above

H: Managing Interactions, p. 241; C: factual/definitional; D: easy; L.O.: manage nonverbal communication

Answer: C

75. When your friend is talking to you, you typically look at him or her about
    A. 10% of the time
    B. 25% of the time
    C. 50% of the time
    D. 75% of the time
    E. 100% of the time

H: Managing Interactions, p. 241; C: factual/definitional; D: easy; L.O.: manage nonverbal communication

Answer: E

76. Studies have suggested that, to demonstrate that we like someone, we can
    A. increase distance
    B. decrease vocal expressiveness
    C. sit up straighter
    D. gaze
    E. decrease eye contact

H: Intimacy, p. 242; C: conceptual; D: medium; L.O.: manage nonverbal communication

Answer: D

77. Dominance can be demonstrated by
    A. using larger amounts of personal space
    B. direct gazing
    C. frowning

D. silence

E. all of the above

H: Dominance and Submissiveness, p. 243; C: conceptual; D: medium; L.O.: manage nonverbal communication

Answer: E

78. Which of the following does NOT communicate submissiveness?
    A. taking up less space
    B. letting others control time
    C. smiling less
    D. letting others control space
    E. permitting others to interrupt us

H: Dominance and Submissiveness, p. 243; C: conceptual; D: medium; L.O.: manage nonverbal communication

Answer: C

79. Research suggests that
    A. our nonverbal communication contains more meaning than our verbal messages
    B. we spend less time communicating nonverbally than verbally
    C. verbal messages are more cultural than nonverbal
    D. verbal communication is more ambiguous than nonverbal communication
    E. our verbal communication contains more meaning than our nonverbal messages

H: Nonverbal Communication Has More Meaning, p. 219; C: conceptual; D: medium; L.O.: nonverbal basics

Answer: A

80. While driving, Amy gets cut off and, instead of yelling out the window, she "flips" the other driver "the bird." What function of nonverbal communication is she using?
    A. reiterating
    B. contradicting
    C. spotlighting
    D. replacing
    E. enhancing

H: Conveying Meanings, p. 240; C: application; D: difficult; L.O.: nonverbal functions

Answer: D

81. During a soccer game a coach wants to call a "time out," so he holds up his hands to form the letter T. What type of gesture is the coach demonstrating?
    A. illustrator
    B. regulator
    C. adaptor
    D. kinesics
    E. emblem

H: Gestures, p. 227; C: conceptual; D: medium; L.O.: nonverbal codes

Answer: E

82. Your instructor explains the emergency escape route by saying, "Go out the door and take a right," and then pointing to the right. What function of nonverbal communication is he using?
    A. reiterating
    B. contradicting
    C. spotlighting
    D. replacing
    E. enhancing

    H: Conveying Meanings, p. 240; C: application; D: difficult; L.O.: nonverbal functions

    Answer: A

83. The two primary messages that posture can communicate are
    A. intimacy and dominance
    B. dominance and submissiveness
    C. submissiveness and intimacy
    D. immediacy and power
    E. weakness and power

    H: Posture, p. 227; C: conceptual; D: medium; L.O.: nonverbal codes

    Answer: D

84. You console your partner, whose grandmother just passed away, by holding his hand and giving him a hug. What communication space are you using?
    A. intimate
    B. personal
    C. social
    D. public
    E. none of the above

    H: Communicating through Personal Space, p. 232; C: application; D: difficult; L.O.: nonverbal codes

    Answer: A

85. According to the "Noh mask effect," facial expressions can
    A. substitute for verbal communication
    B. be ambiguous
    C. vary across cultures
    D. be viewed differently in Japanese culture
    E. change based upon one's point of view

    H: Facial Expression, p. 225; C: conceptual; D: medium; L.O.: nonverbal codes

    Answer: E

86. Which of the following behaviors would demonstrate the most power in the United States?
    A. feet planted firmly on the ground
    B. erect posture
    C. relaxed posture
    D. avoiding eye contact
    E. none of the above

H: Posture, p. 227; C: conceptual; D: medium; L.O.: nonverbal codes

Answer: C

87. If your friend Michael becomes impatient as you tell your story about a recent breakup, looks away, then points to his watch, what type of nonverbal communication is he using?
    A. illustrator
    B. regulator
    C. adaptor
    D. kinesics
    E. emblem

    H: Gestures, p. 227; C: application; D: difficult; L.O.: nonverbal codes

    Answer: B

88. Members of Japanese culture would rate which of the following behaviors as demonstrating the most power?
    A. feet up on the table
    B. erect posture
    C. relaxed posture
    D. avoiding eye contact
    E. none of the above

    H: Posture, p. 227; C: conceptual; D: medium; L.O.: nonverbal codes

    Answer: B

89. According to research by Mehrabian and others, what percentage of meaning is communicated nonverbally?
    A. 5%
    B. 19%
    C. 30%
    D. 93%
    E. 99%

    H: Nonverbal Communication Has More Meaning, p. 219; C: factual/definitional; D: medium; L.O.: nonverbal basics

    Answer: D

90. The primary determinant of the degree of intelligibility of one's speaking is
    A. speech rate
    B. tone
    C. vocabulary
    D. pronunciation and articulation
    E. pitch

    H: Speech Rate, p. 230; C: conceptual; D: medium; L.O.: nonverbal codes

    Answer: D

Short Answer

Briefly respond to the following questions in full sentences.

91. Define and give an example of an emblem.

    H: Gestures, p. 227; C: conceptual; D: medium; L.O.: nonverbal codes

    Possible Answer: A gesture with a specific verbal meaning. Example: flipping the bird.

92. Define and give an example of an illustrator.

    H: Gestures, p. 227; C: conceptual; D: medium; L.O.: nonverbal codes

    Possible Answer: A gesture that accents the verbal message. Example: your instructor pointing to the door while saying, "Please exit now."

93. Define and give an example of a regulator.

    H: Gestures, p. 227; C: conceptual; D: medium; L.O.: nonverbal codes

    Possible Answer: Nonverbal behavior that controls conversation. Example: pointing toward your watch.

94. Define and give an example of an adaptor.

    H: Gestures, p. 227; C: conceptual; D: medium; L.O.: nonverbal codes

    Possible Answer: A gesture that satisfies psychological or physical needs. Example: scratching your nose.

95. Define and give an example of vocalics.

    H: Communicating through Voice, p. 228; C: conceptual; D: medium; L.O.: nonverbal codes

    Possible Answer: Vocal characteristics used to communicate nonverbal messages. Example: loudness.

96. What is the Noh mask effect?

    H: Facial Expression, p. 225; C: conceptual; D: medium; L.O.: nonverbal codes

    Possible Answer: Our visual perspective affects how we view facial expression.

97. Explain how someone with M-time orientation can communicate effectively with someone with P-time orientation.

    H: Communicating through Time, p. 233; C: application; D: difficult; L.O.: nonverbal codes

    Possible Answer: Respect the other's time orientation and be willing to adapt your own use of time to match theirs.

98. Define and give an example of haptics.

    H: Communicating through Touch, p. 230; C: conceptual; D: medium; L.O.: nonverbal codes

    Possible Answer: The nonverbal behavior of touch. Example: a handshake.

99. How does culture affect one's nonverbal communication?

    H: Nonverbal Communication Is Influenced by Culture, p. 219; C: conceptual; D: medium; L.O.: nonverbal basics

Possible Answer: Cultural beliefs impact the way members use nonverbal communication such as eye contact, touch, or personal distance, which suggests that we need to learn about another culture before we can understand their nonverbal communication.

100. What does M-time mean? Provide an example of a culture that uses M-time.

H: Communicating through Time, p. 233; C: application; D: difficult; L.O.: nonverbal codes

Possible Answer: Adhering to strict schedules and time usage; used in the United States.

101. What does P-time mean? Identify a culture that uses P-time.

H: Communicating through Time, p. 233; C: application; D: difficult; L.O.: nonverbal codes

Possible Answer: A relaxed orientation to the use of time; used in African, Caribbean, and Latin American countries.

102. Explain what happens with mixed messages.

H: Nonverbal Communication Has More Meaning, p. 219; C: conceptual; D: medium; L.O.: nonverbal basics

Possible Answer: When someone's verbal and nonverbal behaviors contradict each other, we rely even more upon nonverbal behaviors.

103. What is an artifact? Give an example.

H: Communicating through Objects, p. 238; C: factual/definitional; D: easy; L.O.: nonverbal codes

Possible Answer: Objects that we possess that communicate our identity to others. Example: one's expensive watch or hybrid car.

104. Identify five ways nonverbal communication can be used to accent verbal communication.

H: Conveying Meanings, p. 240; C: conceptual; D: medium; L.O.: functions of nonverbal communication

Possible Answer: Reiterating, contradicting, enhancing, replacing, spotlighting.

105. What is an affect display? Give an example.

H: Expressing Emotion, p. 240; C: factual/definitional; D: easy; L.O.: nonverbal functions

Possible Answer: Intentional or unintentional nonverbal behaviors that display emotion; smiles, frowns.

Essay

Please respond to the following questions in paragraph form.

106. Define and explain proxemics and the four communication distances identified by Edward Hall.

H: Communicating through Personal Space, p. 232; C: conceptual; D: medium; L.O.: nonverbal codes

Possible Answer: Intimate space, distance of 0 to 18 inches; personal space, 18 inches to 4 feet; social distance, 4 to 12 feet; public space, 12 feet or more.

107. Compare and contrast the principles that define verbal and nonverbal communication.

H: Principles of Nonverbal Communication, p. 218; C: conceptual; D: medium; L.O.: nonverbal basics

Possible Answer: Nonverbal is more credible than verbal. Nonverbal is multichanneled; verbal is single-channeled. Nonverbal is more ambiguous than verbal, has fewer rules, and has perhaps more meaning than verbal.

108. What can you do to more effectively and responsibly manage your nonverbal communication?

H: Responsibly Managing Your Nonverbal Communication, p. 246; C: application; D: difficult; L.O.: manage your nonverbal communication

Possible Answer: The text offers four guidelines: when speaking with others, remember that your nonverbal behavior speaks louder than your verbal communication; remember that nonverbal communication is rooted in one's cultural orientation; remember to be sensitive to the demands of the interpersonal situation; and, finally, remember that communication is a package of both verbal and nonverbal messages.

109. How does gender affect nonverbal communication?

H: Nonverbal Communication Is Influenced by Gender, p. 220; C: conceptual; D: medium; L.O.: nonverbal basics

Possible Answer: Women are better than men at both sending and receiving nonverbal communication. Women are more facially expressive then men. Women gaze more than men, and, finally, men are more territorial than women.

Chapter 8: Developing Interpersonal Competence

Matching

Match the concept, term, or theory with its correct response or definition.

A. appropriateness
B. attributional complexity
C. communication apprehension
D. communication plans
E. control messages
F. conventional messages
G. defensive communication
H. dogmatic messages
I. effectiveness
J. ethics
K. ethnocentrism
L. expressive messages
M. flaming

N. high self-monitors
O. indifference messages
P. intercultural competence
Q. interpersonal communication competence
R. loneliness
S. low self-monitors
T. online disinhibition
U. rhetorical messages
V. shyness
W. superiority messages
X. verbal aggression
Y. world-mindedness

1. Communication that attacks others' self-concepts, not their positions or topics of conversation.
   H: Verbal Aggression, p. 275; C: factual/definitional; D: easy; L.O.: competence challenges
   Answer: X. verbal aggression

2. Messages in which a person dismisses constructive criticism or suggestions for improvement.
   H: Defensiveness, p. 272; C: factual/definitional; D: easy; L.O.: competence challenges
   Answer: H. dogmatic messages

3. The degree to which communication is in accordance with societal norms.
   H: Appropriateness, p. 255; C: factual/definitional; D: easy; L.O.: interpersonal communication competence
   Answer: A. appropriateness

4. A belief that one's cultural values, practices, beliefs, and attitudes are superior to others.

   H: Are You World-Minded? p. 268; C: factual/definitional; D: easy; L.O.: intercultural competence

   Answer: K. ethnocentrism

5. People who are not sensitive to norms and appropriateness of communication.

   H: Appropriateness, p. 255; C: factual/definitional; D: easy; L.O.: components of competence

   Answer: S. low self-monitors

6. The moral code that drives our communicative decisions.

   H: Ethics, p. 257; C: factual/definitional; D: easy; L.O.: components of competence

   Answer: J. ethics

7. Messages that aim to achieve our instrumental goals.

   H: Three Kinds of Messages, p. 259; C: factual/definitional; D: easy; L.O.: competent messages

   Answer: F. conventional messages

8. Messages that achieve the three criteria of communication competency: appropriateness, effectiveness, and ethics.

   H: Three Kinds of Messages, p. 259; C: factual/definitional; D: easy; L.O.: improving interpersonal communication competence

   Answer: U. rhetorical messages

9. Communicating in ways that are appropriate, effective, and ethical.

   H: What Is Interpersonal Communication Competence? p. 254; C: factual/definitional; D: easy; L.O.: components of competence

   Answer: Q. interpersonal communication competence

10. An anxiety or fear associated with anticipated or real communication with others.

    H: Communication Apprehension, p. 271; C: factual/definitional; D: easy; L.O.: competence challenges

    Answer: C. communication apprehension

11. Mental maps that lay out communication before it even occurs.

    H: Overcoming Communication Apprehension, p. 271; C: factual/definitional; D: easy; L.O.: competence challenges

    Answer: D. communication plans

12. The tendency for people to share personal information more openly and directly during online interactions.

    H: Adapting to Online Norms, p. 264; C: factual/definitional; D: easy; L.O.: online competence

    Answer: T. online disinhibition

13. Inappropriately aggressive online messages.

    H: Adapting to Online Norms, p. 264; C: factual/definitional; D: easy; L.O.: improving online competence

    Answer: M. flaming

14. A tendency to be reserved and talk less in the presence of others.

    H: Shyness and Loneliness, p. 272; C: factual/definitional; D: easy; L.O.: competence challenges

    Answer: V. shyness

15. Feelings of social isolation and lack of companionship.

    H: Shyness and Loneliness, p. 272; C: factual/definitional; D: easy; L.O.: competence challenges

    Answer: R. loneliness

16. The ability to use communication to achieve interpersonal goals.

    H: Effectiveness, p. 257; C: factual/definitional; D: easy; L.O.: components of competence

    Answer: I. effectiveness

17. Incompetent messages delivered in response to messages of suggestion or criticism.

    H: Defensiveness, p. 274; C: factual/definitional; D: easy; L.O.: competence challenges

    Answer: G. defensive communication

18. Messages implying that criticism is irrelevant or unimportant.

    H: Defensiveness, p. 274; C: factual/definitional; D: easy; L.O.: competence challenges

    Answer: O. indifference messages

19. Messages that convey our thoughts and feelings.

    H: Three Kinds of Messages, p. 259; C: factual/definitional; D: easy; L.O.: competent messages

    Answer: L. expressive messages

20. Ability to communicate appropriately, effectively, and ethically with people of diverse backgrounds.

    H: Improving Your Intercultural Communication, p. 267; C: factual/definitional; D: easy; L.O.: intercultural competence

    Answer: P. intercultural competence

21. Acceptance of and respect for other cultures.

    H: Are You World-Minded? p. 268; C: factual/definitional; D: easy; L.O.: intercultural competence

    Answer: Y. world-mindedness

22. A form of defensive communication conveyed when a person suggests he or she possesses special knowledge, ability, or status.

    H: Defensiveness, p. 274; C: factual/definitional; D: easy; L.O.: improving online competence

    Answer: W. superiority messages

23. Persons who are very sensitive to norms and appropriateness.

    H: Appropriateness, p. 255; C: factual/definitional; D: easy; L.O.: components of competence

    Answer: N. high self-monitors

24. The fact that the behaviors of others have multiple, complex causes.

    H: Remember: Check Your Perceptions and Practice Empathy, p. 269; C: factual/definitional; D: easy; L.O.: intercultural competence

    Answer: B. attributional complexity

25. Messages through which one seeks to squelch criticism by exerting power over the receiver.

    H: Defensiveness, p. 274; C: factual/definitional; D: easy; L.O.: competence challenges

    Answer: E. control messages

True/False

Please select whether the following statements are true or false.

26. One cannot improve or increase one's interpersonal communication competence.

    H: What Is Interpersonal Communication Competence? p. 254; C: conceptual; D: medium; L.O.: components of competence

    Answer: F

27. Interpersonal communication competence is simply a matter of acquiring knowledge about communication.

    H: What Is Interpersonal Communication Competence? p. 254; C: factual/definitional; D: easy; L.O.: components of competence

    Answer: F

28. Appropriateness takes into account the "shoulds," "shouldn'ts," and norms of communication.

    H: Appropriateness, p. 255; C: conceptual; D: medium; L.O.: components of competence

    Answer: T

29. A high self-monitor is likely not to change her communication behavior based upon the context or situation of communication.

    H: Appropriateness, p. 255; C: conceptual; D: medium; L.O.: components of competence

    Answer: F

30. Online disinhibition often leads to flaming, sending aggressive messages that wouldn't be conveyed face-to-face.

H: Adapting to Online Norms, p. 264; C: conceptual; D: medium; L.O.: improving online competence

Answer: T

31. Simply by focusing on appropriate communication, one would be considered a competent communicator.

H: What Is Interpersonal Communication Competence? p. 254; C: conceptual; D: medium; L.O.: components of competence

Answer: F

32. One of the benefits of online communication is that listservs, discussion groups, and blogs can bolster a real sense of community.

H: Adapting to Online Norms, p. 264; C: factual/definitional; D: easy; L.O.: components of competence

Answer: T

33. In practicing ethical communication, one needs simply to avoid doing harm.

H: Ethics, p. 257; C: conceptual; D: medium; L.O.: components of competence

Answer: F

34. The use of "elderspeak" is an example of respectful communication to use with the elderly.

H: Focus on Culture: Competence and Age, p. 261; C: factual/definitional; D: easy; L.O.: components of competence

Answer: F

35. "Elderspeak" is seldom used when seniors communicate with one another.

H: Focus on Culture: Competence and Age, p. 261; C: conceptual; D: medium; L.O.: components of competence

Answer: T

36. Conventional messages, because they focus on the achievement of instrumental goals, are considered to be the most competent form of communication.

H: Three Kinds of Messages, p. 259; C: conceptual; D: medium; L.O.: competent messages

Answer: F

37. Rhetorical messages, because they successfully blend all three elements of appropriateness, effectiveness, and ethics, are considered to be a form of competent communication.

H: Three Kinds of Messages, p. 259; C: conceptual; D: medium; L.O.: competent messages

Answer: T

38. The most effective method for managing communication apprehension is to develop competent communication plans.

H: Overcoming Communication Apprehension, p. 271; C: conceptual; D: easy; L.O.: competence challenges

Answer: T

39. A necessary step in communicating competently is to develop plan contingencies in which you plan out alternatives to your communication partner's potential reactions to help manage communication apprehension.

    H: Overcoming Communication Apprehension, p. 271; C: conceptual; D: medium; L.O.: competence challenges

    Answer: T

40. According to the textbook, shyness is the most common psychological disorder reported in the United States.

    H: Shyness and Loneliness, p. 272; C: factual/definitional; D: easy; L.O.: competence challenges

    Answer: F

41. Shyness and loneliness are linked to people's inability to create competent communication plans.

    H: Shyness and Loneliness, p. 272; C: conceptual; D: medium; L.O.: competence challenges

    Answer: T

42. Dogmatic messages are a type of defensive communication in which a person dismisses constructive feedback or criticism, believing that his or her behavior is acceptable.

    H: Defensiveness, p. 274; C: conceptual; D: medium; L.O.: competence challenges

    Answer: T

43. Defensiveness is usually fueled by anger.

    H: Defensiveness, p. 274; C: factual/definitional; D: easy; L.O.: competence challenges

    Answer: T

44. Verbal aggression is considered an example of communication competence because it is the tendency to attack issues and positions, not people or their self-concepts.

    H: Verbal Aggression, p. 275; C: factual/definitional; D: easy; L.O.: competence challenges

    Answer: F

45. We can increase our intercultural communication competence by practicing world-mindedness and acknowledging attributional complexity.

    H: Improving Your Intercultural Competence, p. 267; C: factual/definitional; D: easy; L.O.: intercultural competence

    Answer: T

Multiple Choice

Please choose the correct response to the following statements.

46. World-mindedness is
    A. demonstrating respect for other cultures
    B. acceptance of other people's expressions of their cultures
    C. avoiding the tendency to evaluate others' cultures

D. treating members of other cultures with respect

E. all of the above

H: Are You World-Minded? p. 268; C: conceptual; D: medium; L.O.: intercultural competence

Answer: E

47. The belief that one's own culture, including its values, beliefs, and practices, is superior to others' is

A. world-mindedness

B. ethnocentrism

C. superiority messages

D. dogmatic messages

E. intercultural competence

H: Are You World-Minded? p. 268; C: factual/definitional; D: easy; L.O.: intercultural competence

Answer: B

48. Interpersonal communication competence requires

A. awareness of accepted norms

B. a desire to achieve your goals

C. treating people with respect and honesty

D. all of the above

E. none of the above

H: What Is Interpersonal Communication Competence? p. 267; C: conceptual; D: medium; L.O.: components of competence

Answer: D

49. While visiting Thailand, Malo rethinks generalizations he has heard about Thai culture and finds himself observing a multitude of reasons for different behaviors exhibited by the locals. What quality is Malo acknowledging?

A. world-mindedness

B. ethnocentrism

C. attributional complexity

D. rhetorical messages

E. ethics

H: Remember: Check Your Perceptions and Practice Empathy, p. 269; C: application; D: difficult; L.O.: intercultural competence

Answer: C

50. What are some strategies that can be used to increase intercultural communication competence?

A. check your perceptions

B. check your ethnocentrism

C. demonstrate empathy

D. be flexible and open to new ideas

E. all of the above

H: Remember: Check Your Perceptions and Practice Empathy, p. 269; C: conceptual; D: medium; L.O.: intercultural competence

Answer: E

51. Which of the following is NOT an advantage of communicating online?
    A. relationships are based on what people say, not how they appear physically
    B. we can meet others not in our physical proximity
    C. others can judge us solely on the quality of what we say
    D. we don't have access to subtle nonverbal cues
    E. it can bolster a sense of community

    H: Improving Your Competence Online, p. 263; C: conceptual; D: medium; L.O.: online competence

    Answer: D

52. The norm of online disinhibition suggests
    A. we are more likely to disclose personal information online
    B. we are less likely to disclose personal information online
    C. we are more likely to disclose personal information face-to-face
    D. we are less likely to disclose personal information face-to-face
    E. none of the above

    H: Adapting to Online Norms, p. 264; C: conceptual; D: medium; L.O.: online competence

    Answer: A

53. Online disinhibition occurs because online communication
    A. is more anonymous
    B. lacks immediate feedback
    C. occurs in a different space
    D. all of the above
    E. none of the above

    H: Adapting to Online Norms, p. 264; C: conceptual; D: medium; L.O.: online competence

    Answer: D

54. Sending inappropriately aggressive online messages that are not typically communicated face-to-face is called
    A. defensive communication
    B. flaming
    C. dogmatic messages
    D. verbal aggression
    E. trolling

    H: Adapting to Online Norms, p. 264; C: factual/definitional; D: easy; L.O.: online competence

    Answer: B

55. Online communication, as compared to face-to-face interaction, is more likely to result in
    A. asking less personal questions
    B. higher amounts of disclosure on first encounters
    C. being less asynchronous
    D. sharing less intimate personal information
    E. none of the above

    H: Adapting to Online Norms, p. 264; C: conceptual; D: medium; L.O.: improving online competence

    Answer: B

56. Which of the following should be done when communicating online?
    A. create "draft" e-mails before sending
    B. remember your audience may be larger then intended
    C. talk to strangers
    D. know the code
    E. all of the above

    H: How to Communicate Competently Online, p. 264; C: conceptual; D: medium;
    L.O.: improving online competence

    Answer: E

57. Josh is very assertive and goal-oriented; however, he often forgets to consider the people he
    interacts with, who sometimes feel hurt or offended by his communication. What component
    of interpersonal communication competence is he lacking?
    A. appropriateness
    B. effectiveness
    C. ethics
    D. behavioral flexibility
    E. common sense

    H: Appropriateness, p. 255; C: application; D: difficult; L.O.: components of competence

    Answer: A

58. Melinda is so concerned about the thoughts and feelings of others that her own needs are
    rarely met and she is often seen as a doormat. What component of communication
    competence is she lacking?
    A. appropriateness
    B. effectiveness
    C. ethics
    D. behavioral flexibility
    E. common sense

    H: Effectiveness, p. 257; C: application; D: difficult; L.O.: components of competence

    Answer: B

59. If Aaron is very sensitive to and aware of the communication context and the
    appropriateness of his communication, he is
    A. demonstrating ethnocentrism
    B. demonstrating world-mindedness
    C. a flamer
    D. a low self-monitor
    E. a high self-monitor

    H: Appropriateness, p. 255; C: application; D: difficult; L.O.: components of competence

    Answer: E

60. Which of the following are NOT kinds of goals of the effectiveness component of competent
    communication?
    A. self-presentational goals
    B. social goals
    C. instrumental goals

D. relational goals

E. none of the above

H: Effectiveness, p. 257; C: conceptual; D: medium; L.O.: components of competence

Answer: B

61. Suppose you had been looking forward all month to seeing a show with your girlfriend; however, she is having a very bad week and needs your emotional support, so she chooses to stay home. You go see the show without her. What goals of effectiveness are you accomplishing?

A. instrumental goals

B. social goals

C. self-presentational goals

D. relational goals

E. emotional goals

H: Effectiveness, p. 257; C: application; D: difficult; L.O.: components of competence

Answer: A

62. If your partner, who would prefer to go out to a club, agrees to stay home and help you work on a presentation, what goals of effectiveness are your partner accomplishing?

A. instrumental goals

B. social goals

C. relational goals

D. self-presentational goals

E. emotional goals

H: Effectiveness, p. 257; C: application; D: difficult; L.O.: components of competence

Answer: C

63. As an employee for a cell phone company, Zach sells many phones by misleading customers about how much their monthly fees will be. What component of competent communication is Zach missing?

A. effectiveness

B. appropriateness

C. flexibility

D. instrumental goals

E. ethics

H: Ethics, p. 257; C: application; D: difficult; L.O.: components of competence

Answer: E

64. Ethics is

A. based upon moral codes

B. about avoiding intentionally hurting others

C. about treating others with respect

D. about treating others as valuable, worthy individuals

E. all of the above

H: Ethics, p. 257; C: conceptual; D: medium; L.O.: components of competence

Answer: E

65. Elderspeak is
    A. communication using a slower rate, increased pitch and volume, and simple words
    B. completely unlike baby talk
    C. an example of communication competence with the elderly
    D. specialized language used between elders
    E. specialized language used by elders to speak to young or middle-aged people

    H: Focus on Culture: Competence and Age, p. 261; C: conceptual; D: medium;
    L.O.: components of competence

    Answer: A

66. If a mother says to her young child, "Let's get ready to go for a little walky-walky," she is using
    A. elderspeak
    B. Esperanto
    C. communication competence
    D. expressive messages
    E. none of the above

    H: Focus on Culture: Competence and Age, p. 261; C: application; D: difficult;
    L.O.: competent messages

    Answer: E

67. Which of the following is NOT a reason defensiveness is considered incompetent communication?
    A. it violates norms for appropriate behavior
    B. it rarely achieves interpersonal goals
    C. it treats people disrespectfully
    D. it causes lower satisfaction in people's personal lives
    E. none of the above

    H: Defensiveness, p. 274; C: conceptual; D: medium; L.O.: competence challenges
    Answer: E

68. Your mother expresses her concern that your current romantic interest doesn't treat you respectfully and you respond, "I am so tired of hearing your opinion of my love life! Why can't you mind your own business?" What kind of message are you conveying?
    A. appropriate message
    B. conventional message
    C. rhetorical message
    D. expressive message
    E. none of the above

    H: Three Kinds of Messages, p. 259; C: application; D: difficult; L.O.: competent messages
    Answer: D

69. Verbal aggression can
    A. be appropriate toward other aggressive communicators
    B. stem from low self-esteem
    C. achieve short-term goals
    D. only manifest itself in verbal communication
    E. none of the above

H: Verbal Aggression, p. 275; C: application; D: difficult; L.O.: competent messages
Answer: C

70. Rhetorical messages are considered to be competent because they are
    A. appropriate
    B. effective
    C. ethical
    D. a successful blend of ingredients of competence
    E. all of the above
    H: Three Kinds of Messages, p. 259; C: conceptual; D: medium; L.O.: competent messages
    Answer: E

71. Which of the following is NOT considered a characteristic of a rhetorical message?
    A. uses neutral, nonjudgmental communication
    B. controls when you experience an emotion
    C. expresses empathy and perspective-taking
    D. offers specific solutions
    E. negotiates mutual consensus
    H: Three Kinds of Messages, p. 259; C: conceptual; D: medium; L.O.: competent messages
    Answer: B

72. Communication apprehension refers to
    A. fear before a speaking event
    B. fear after a speaking event and judgment made by an audience
    C. a phobia that cannot be managed
    D. anxiety associated with real or anticipated communication with others
    E. none of the above
    H: Communication Apprehension, p. 271; C: conceptual; D: medium; L.O.: competence challenges
    Answer: D

73. What do you need to map out when crafting a communication plan to combat communication apprehension?
    A. topics to discuss
    B. messages to use in relation to the topics
    C. the physical behaviors you will demonstrate
    D. all of the above
    E. none of the above
    H: Overcoming Communication Apprehension, p. 271; C: conceptual; D: medium; L.O.: improving communication competence
    Answer: D

74. What must you consider when thinking of contingencies to your communication plan?
    A. topics your partner will bring up
    B. other people who may join your conversation
    C. your partner's reaction to your communication
    D. both a and c
    E. none of the above

H: Overcoming Communication Apprehension, p. 271; C: conceptual; D: medium; L.O.: improving communication competence

Answer: D

75. Communication apprehension can result in
    A. increased blood pressure
    B. increased heart rate
    C. shakiness
    D. dry mouth
    E. all of the above

    H: Communication Apprehension, p. 271; C: conceptual; D: medium; L.O.: competence challenges

    Answer: E

76. If Sarah, who plans to break up with her boyfriend, devises messages based upon how she believes he will respond to her news, she is creating
    A. plan contingencies
    B. communication plans
    C. plan actions
    D. plan moves
    E. receiver communication

    H: Overcoming Communication Apprehension, p. 271; C: application; D: difficult; L.O.: competence challenges

    Answer: A

77. Shyness is
    A. associated with communication apprehension
    B. associated with loneliness
    C. a tendency to be reserved
    D. a tendency to talk less with others
    E. all of the above

    H: Shyness and Loneliness, p. 272; C: conceptual; D: easy; L.O.: competence challenges

    Answer: E

78. If Beth, who is feeling frustrated by her mother's criticism regarding her choice in friends, responds to her mother with: "I'm sorry . . . did I ASK you?" what type of defensive message is she sending?
    A. superiority message
    B. control message
    C. indifference message
    D. expressive message
    E. conventional message

    H: Defensiveness, p. 274; C: application; D: difficult; L.O.: competence challenges

    Answer: C

79. Which of the following is a type of defensive communication?
    A. dogmatic message
    B. superiority message

C. indifference message

D. control message

E. all of the above

H: Defensiveness, p. 274; C: factual/definitional; D: easy; L.O.: competence challenges

Answer: E

80. When Bobby tells his friend Marty that he's driving too fast through a neighborhood full of kids, Marty responds, "You better remember that you don't own a car and you depend on me for rides." Marty is demonstrating what type of communication?

A. dogmatic message

B. superiority message

C. indifference message

D. control message

E. all of the above

H: Defensiveness, p. 274; C: application; D: difficult; L.O.: competence challenges

Answer: D

81. During their first meeting, online conversation partners tend to

A. ask more personal questions of each other than face-to-face partners

B. ask fewer personal questions of each other than face-to-face partners

C. share less information with each other than face-to-face partners

D. lie more about personal information than face-to-face partners

E. none of the above

H: Adapting to Online Norms, p. 264; C: comprehension; D: easy; L.O.: online competence

Answer: A

82. When communicating online, you should

A. limit your use of capitalization and excessive punctuation

B. point out mistakes in grammar and spelling

C. not worry about the size of your audience

D. never speak to strangers

E. all of the above

H: How to Communicate Competently Online, p. 264; C: comprehension; D: medium; L.O.: online competence

Answer: A

Short Answer

Briefly respond to the following questions in full sentences.

83. Identify the four types of defensive communication.

H: Defensiveness, p. 274; C: factual/definitional; D: easy; L.O.: competence challenges

Possible Answer: Dogmatic message, superiority message, indifference message, and control message.

84. Give an example of two of the four types of defensive communication.

    H: Defensiveness, p. 274; C: conceptual; D: medium; L.O.: competence challenges

    Possible Answer: Dogmatic: "I don't need to change, you need to change, because I've always done it this way." Superiority: "I know more than you because I have been working with this client for years." Also possible: Indifference, control messages.

85. What are three ways one can deal with a verbally aggressive communicator?

    H: Verbal Aggression, p. 275; C: conceptual; D: medium; L.O.: competence challenges

    Possible Answer: Avoid communication such as teasing that may trigger verbal aggression, avoid contact, and remain polite.

86. How can you demonstrate world-mindedness?

    H: Are You World-Minded? p. 268; C: conceptual; D: medium; L.O.: intercultural competence

    Possible Answer: Accept others' communication as a reflection of their culture, avoid judging other viewpoints, and treat others with respect.

87. How is world-mindedness related to ethnocentrism?

    H: Are You World-Minded? p. 268; C: conceptual; D: medium; L.O.: intercultural competence

    Possible Answer: World-mindedness is the opposite of ethnocentrism.

88. Explain how recognizing attributional complexity can improve intercultural competence.

    H: Remember: Check Your Perceptions and Practice Empathy, p. 269; C: conceptual; D: medium; L.O.: intercultural competence

    Possible Answer: Recognizing that other people's behaviors can have a multitude of causes may reduce the likelihood of misunderstanding their behavior and cause us to carefully consider the reasons for their behavior.

89. How does online disinhibition impact our online communication?

    H: Adapting to Online Norms, p. 264; C: conceptual; D: medium; L.O.: online competence

    Possible Answer: We have the tendency to communicate and self-disclose more readily and openly in online than in face-to-face interaction.

90. Why is flaming considered a form of incompetent communication?

    H: Adapting to Online Norms, p. 264; C: conceptual; D: medium; L.O.: online competence

    Possible Answer: The lack of nonverbal cues increases the negative impact of such messages, and they are more readily perceived as personal attacks.

91. Identify the three criteria of interpersonal communication competence.

    H: What Is Interpersonal Communication Competence? p. 254; C: factual/definitional; D: easy; L.O.: components of competence

    Possible Answer: Appropriate (follows norms), effective (achieves goals), and ethical (treats people fairly).

92. Explain the difference between a low and high self-monitor.

    H: Appropriateness, p. 255; C: conceptual; D: medium; L.O.: components of competence

    Possible Answer: High self-monitors are sensitive and adapt to the appropriateness of context; low self-monitors are not sensitive to the appropriateness of particular situations.

93. Identify three types of interpersonal goals that effectiveness in competent communication helps achieve.

    H: Effectiveness, p. 257; C: conceptual; D: medium; L.O.: components of competence

    Possible Answer: Self-presentational goals, instrumental goals, and relational goals.

94. What are two ways to practice ethical communication?

    H: Ethics, p. 257; C: conceptual; D: medium; L.O.: components of competence

    Possible Answer: Do no harm and treat others with respect. See the NCA "Credo for Ethical Communication."

95. Why isn't "elderspeak" a form of communication competence with the elderly?

    H: Focus on Culture: Competence and Age, p. 261; C: conceptual; D: medium; L.O.: components of competence

    Possible Answer: It is not used among the elderly, only as a demeaning form of communication when younger people speak to elders; mimics the way adults talk to young children.

96. Describe the three ways that most people respond to difficult communication situations.

    H: Three Kinds of Messages, p. 259; C: factual/definitional; D: easy; L.O.: competent messages

    Possible Answer: Using expressive, conventional, or rhetorical messages.

97. Describe the two facets of a competent communication plan.

    H: Overcoming Communication Apprehension, p. 271; C: conceptual; D: medium; L.O.: competence challenges

    Possible Answer: First you must consider your plan actions, the "moves" you think you will use with your conversation partner. Then you must create plan contingencies, the messages you will use to respond to what your partner says.

Essay

Please respond to the following questions in paragraph form.

98. How can you demonstrate or improve your intercultural competence?

    H: Are You World-Minded? p. 268, and Remember: Check Your Perceptions and Practice Empathy, p. 269; C: conceptual; D: medium; L.O.: intercultural competence

    Possible Answer: By being world-minded, or demonstrating an openness to and respect for other cultures' norms, values, and customs, and through acknowledging attributional complexity, or understanding that a person's behavior may have myriad explanations or causes that you are not aware of.

99. Define and give examples of O'Keefe's three types of messages.

H: Three Kinds of Messages, p. 259; C: conceptual; D: medium; L.O.: competent messages

Possible Answer: Expressive messages convey thoughts and feelings ("I should never have trusted a loser like you."). Conventional messages focus on achievement of instrumental goals ("You are on our team and have a responsibility to the group to finish your portion of the project."). Rhetorical messages blend the three elements of competent communication: appropriateness, effectiveness, and ethics ("I know you are having trouble at home. Is there anything I can do to help out?").

100. Identify seven suggestions for increasing online communication competence.

H: How to Communicate Competently Online, p. 264; C: conceptual; D: medium; L.O.: improving online competence

Possible Answer: Match the gravity of the message to the communication medium, don't assume online communication is always more efficient, know the code, assume your audience is larger than intended, write drafts of e-mails, beware of the emotionally seductive quality of online communication, and talk to strangers.

101. What might a member of an individualistic culture do to be more effective in dealing with a member of a collectivistic culture and vice-versa?

H: Improving Your Intercultural Competence, p. 267; C: conceptual; D: medium; L.O.: intercultural competence

Possible Answer: The individualistic person may need to learn to be supportive of the group's decision and withhold personal opinion; a collectivistic person may need to be more expressive about his or her personal opinion or viewpoint.

102. Discuss some advantages and disadvantages of online communication.

H: Improving Your Competence Online, p. 263; C: conceptual; D: medium; L.O.: online competence

Possible Answer: Advantages—helps initiate and maintain relationships while transcending physical distance, bolsters sense of community, and allows us to be judged by what we say, not how we look. Disadvantages—lacks nonverbal communication, increases chance for misunderstanding, and allows messages to appear more important or intense than intended, creating unwanted results.

Chapter 9: Managing Conflict and Power

Matching

Match the concept, term, or theory with its correct response or definition.

A. accommodation
B. avoidance
C. collaboration
D. competition
E. complementary relationship
F. compromise
G. conflict
H. demand-withdraw pattern
I. dirty secrets
J. expertise currency
K. integrative agreements
L. intimacy currency
M. kitchen-sinking

N. personal currency
O. power
P. power-distance
Q. pseudo-conflict
R. resource currency
S. separation
T. skirting
U. sniping
V. social network currency
W. structural improvements
X. sudden-death statements
Y. symmetrical relationship

1. An approach to conflict in which one pursues his or her own goals to the exclusion of the goals of others.

   H: Competitively Managing Conflict, p. 297; C: factual/definitional; D: easy; L.O.: interpersonal conflict

   Answer: D. competition

2. Power that comes from belonging to a network of people who have substantial influence.

   H: Power Currencies, p. 291; C: factual/definitional; D: easy; L.O.: power in conflict

   Answer: V. social network currency

3. An approach to conflict in which one abandons one's own goals and acquiesces to the desires of another person.

   H: Accommodating Conflict, p. 297; C: factual/definitional; D: easy; L.O.: interpersonal conflict

   Answer: A. accommodation

4. Power that comes from having specialized skills or knowledge.
   H: Power Currencies, p. 291; C: factual/definitional; D: easy; L.O.: power in conflict
   Answer: J. expertise currency

5. A way of achieving conflict resolution that occurs when both parties change their goals to make them compatible.
   H: Short-Term Conflict Resolutions, p. 304; C: factual/definitional; D: easy; L.O.: conflict resolution and outcomes
   Answer: F. compromise

6. Accusations directed at one's partner that have little to do with a disagreement.
   H: Conflict in Relationships, p. 287; C: factual/definitional; D: easy; L.O.: nature of conflict
   Answer: M. kitchen-sinking

7. A relationship in which power is imbalanced.
   H: Power Is Always Present, p. 290; C: factual/definitional; D: easy; L.O.: power in conflict
   Answer: E. complementary relationship

8. A way of achieving conflict resolution in which both sides maintain their own goals and develop a creative solution to their problem.
   H: Short-Term Conflict Resolutions, p. 304; C: factual/definitional; D: easy; L.O.: conflict resolution and outcomes
   Answer: K. integrative agreements

9. A result of achieving resolution, if both parties change the basic rules governing their relationship to prevent future conflict.
   H: Short-Term Conflict Resolutions, p. 304; C: factual/definitional; D: easy; L.O.: conflict resolution and outcomes
   Answer: W. structural improvements

10. The degree to which a culture perceives the unequal distribution of power as acceptable.
    H: Power and Culture, p. 292; C: factual/definitional; D: easy; L.O.: power in conflict
    Answer: P. power-distance

11. An approach to conflict in which one ignores or communicates indirectly about a situation.
    H: Avoiding Conflict, p. 295; C: factual/definitional; D: easy; L.O.: interpersonal conflict
    Answer: B. avoidance

12. Power that comes from having money or property.
    H: Power Currencies, p. 291; C: factual/definitional; D: easy; L.O.: power in conflict
    Answer: R. resource currency

13. A type of avoidance in which one jokes about a serious source of conflict or changes the topic.
    H: Avoiding Conflict, p. 295; C: factual/definitional; D: easy; L.O.: interpersonal conflict
    Answer: T. skirting

14. Power that comes from having a close, personal bond with someone.

    H: Power Currencies, p. 291; C: factual/definitional; D: easy; L.O.: power in conflict

    Answer: L. intimacy currency

15. The perception that a conflict exists, when in fact it doesn't.

    H: Avoiding Conflict, p. 295; C: factual/definitional; D: easy; L.O.: interpersonal conflict

    Answer: Q. pseudo-conflict

16. Transactional process between people who perceive incompatible goals, scarce resources, or interference in achieving their objectives.

    H: What Is Conflict? p. 286; C: factual/definitional; D: easy; L.O.: nature of conflict

    Answer: G. conflict

17. Treating conflict as a mutual problem-solving challenge.

    H: Collaboratively Managing Conflict, p. 300; C: factual/definitional; D: easy; L.O.: interpersonal conflict

    Answer: C. collaboration

18. Pattern of conflict in which women pursue their goals by making demands and men withdraw from the encounter.

    H: Conflict and Gender, p. 309; C: factual/definitional; D: easy; L.O.: gender, culture, and technology

    Answer: H. demand-withdraw pattern

19. Declarations of the end of a relationship.

    H: Competitively Managing Conflict, p. 297; C: factual/definitional; D: easy; L.O.: interpersonal conflict

    Answer: X. sudden-death statements

20. A relationship in which power is balanced.

    H: Power Is Always Present, p. 290; C: factual/definitional; D: easy; L.O.: power in conflict

    Answer: Y. symmetrical relationship

21. Messages that are honest but have been kept hidden to protect a partner's feelings.

    H: Competitively Managing Conflict, p. 297; C: factual/definitional; D: easy; L.O.: interpersonal conflict

    Answer: I. dirty secrets

22. The sudden withdrawal of one person from a conflict.

    H: Short-Term Conflict Resolutions, p. 304; C: factual/definitional; D: easy; L.O.: conflict outcomes

    Answer: S. separation

23. Power that comes from possessing personal characteristics that are considered desirable within a culture.
    H: Power Currencies, p. 291; C: factual/definitional; D: easy; L.O.: power in conflict
    Answer: N. personal currency

24. A type of avoidance in which one communicates in a negative manner and then abandons the encounter.
    H: Avoiding Conflict, p. 295; C: factual/definitional; D: easy; L.O.: interpersonal conflict
    Answer: U. sniping

25. The ability to influence or control other people or events.
    H: Power and Conflict, p. 288; C: factual/definitional; D: easy; L.O.: power in conflict
    Answer: O. power

True/False

Please select whether the following statements are true or false.

26. High power-distance cultures can also be characterized as being highly authoritarian, believing authority figures should be obeyed.
    H: Power and Culture, p. 292; C: conceptual; D: medium; L.O.: power and conflict
    Answer: T

27. A key risk of engaging in competition as a strategy for managing conflict is escalation.
    H: Competitively Managing Conflict, p. 297; C: conceptual; D: medium; L.O.: interpersonal conflict
    Answer: T

28. Happy couples are more likely to avoid personal attacks during conflicts.
    H: Conflict in Relationships, p. 287; C: conceptual; D: medium; L.O.: nature of conflict
    Answer: T

29. Cumulative annoyance can result when relationship partners engage in avoidance as a conflict strategy.
    H: Avoiding Conflict, p. 295; C: conceptual; D: medium; L.O.: interpersonal conflict
    Answer: T

30. People from collectivistic cultures view direct messages about conflict as personal attacks.
    H: Conflict and Culture, p. 310; C: conceptual; D: medium; L.O.: gender, culture, and conflict
    Answer: T

31. Men tend to rely more on violence as a strategy to manage conflict than do women.
    H: Conflict and Violence, p. 303; C: conceptual; D: medium; L.O.: interpersonal conflict
    Answer: F

32. In Mexican culture, the value of *respeto* emphasizes symmetrical power relationships between elders and children.

    H: Power Is Always Present, p. 290; C: conceptual; D: medium; L.O.: power in conflict

    Answer: F

33. Power, in and of itself, is neither good nor bad.

    H: Power Can Be Used Ethically or Unethically, p. 290; C: factual/definitional; D: easy; L.O.: power in conflict

    Answer: T

34. Money, property, and food are examples of resource currency.

    H: Power Currencies, p. 291; C: conceptual; D: medium; L.O.: power in conflict

    Answer: T

35. An individual who is linked with a network of friends is considered to have intimacy currency.

    H: Power Currencies, p. 291; C: conceptual; D: medium; L.O.: power in conflict

    Answer: F

36. In Asian and Latino cultures, social network currency is more highly valued than resource currency.

    H: Power and Culture, p. 292; C: conceptual; D: medium; L.O.: power in conflict

    Answer: F

37. China has high power-distance, whereas the United States has moderate power-distance.

    H: Power and Culture, p. 292; C: conceptual; D: medium; L.O.: power in conflict

    Answer: T

38. One positive outcome of conflict managed by compromise is that both parties leave feeling fully satisfied.

    H: Short-Term Conflict Resolutions, p. 304; C: conceptual; D: medium; L.O.: conflict resolutions and outcomes

    Answer: F

39. Power is granted by those who relinquish control and allow others to exert influence over them.

    H: Power Is Granted, p. 291; C: conceptual; D: medium; L.O.: power in conflict

    Answer: T

40. Avoidance is the most frequently used approach to managing conflict.

    H: Avoiding Conflict, p. 295; C: factual/definitional; D: easy; L.O.: interpersonal conflict

    Answer: T

41. Pseudo-conflict is a risk that results from engaging in avoidance as a conflict strategy.

    H: Avoiding Conflict, p. 295; C: conceptual; D: medium; L.O.: interpersonal conflict

    Answer: T

42. In low power-distance cultures, differences in power are minimized, whereas in high power-distance cultures differences in power are accentuated.

    H: Power and Culture, p. 292; C: conceptual; D: medium; L.O.: power in conflict

    Answer: T

43. Accommodation is an approach to managing conflict that occurs when one refuses to give in to the needs or desires of one's relational partner.

    H: Accommodating Conflict, p. 297; C: conceptual; D: medium; L.O.: interpersonal conflict

    Answer: F

44. Conflict is often a result of long-term differences, but we usually don't attribute it to them.

    H: Barriers to Constructive Conflict, p. 303; C: conceptual; D: medium; L.O.: interpersonal conflict

    Answer: F

45. If your partner reports, "I have never really loved you," this is an example of a dirty secret that can result from conflict escalation.

    H: Competitively Managing Conflict, p. 297; C: conceptual; D: medium; L.O.: interpersonal conflict

    Answer: T

46. Collaboration is considered to be the most constructive approach to managing conflict.

    H: Collaboratively Managing Conflict, p. 300; C: factual/definitional; D: easy; L.O.: interpersonal conflict

    Answer: T

47. In a high power-distance culture such as China, professors are perceived as authority figures who should be believed and respected.

    H: Power and Culture, p. 292; C: application; D: difficult; L.O.: power in conflict

    Answer: T

48. In a demand-withdraw pattern, men often pursue conflict in attempting to meet their needs, whereas women respond by withdrawing from the episode.

    H: Conflict and Gender, p. 309; C: conceptual; D: medium; L.O.: gender, culture, and conflict

    Answer: F

49. Separation is an unproductive long-term strategy for dealing with conflict.

    H: Short-Term Conflict Resolutions, p. 304; C: conceptual; D: medium; L.O.: interpersonal conflict

    Answer: T

Multiple Choice

Please choose the correct response to the following statements.

50. If Mary and Marie believe their goals are incompatible, when in fact their goals are compatible, they are engaged in
    A. conflict
    B. escalation
    C. demand-withdraw pattern
    D. domination
    E. pseudo-conflict

    H: Avoiding Conflict, p. 295; C: application; D: difficult; L.O.: interpersonal conflict

    Answer: E

51. If Darcy has a long-term, committed relationship with her partner, what type of power currency is she likely to have?
    A. resource currency
    B. expertise currency
    C. social network currency
    D. personal currency
    E. intimacy currency

    H: Power Currencies, p. 291; C: application; D: difficult; L.O.: power in conflict

    Answer: E

52. Which of the following statements is NOT true about how gender influences conflict management?
    A. men are encouraged to avoid conflict
    B. women are encouraged to avoid conflict
    C. women are likely to accommodate
    D. men are likely to compete
    E. men are encouraged to use a violent approach in handling disputes

    H: Conflict and Gender, p. 309; C: conceptual; D: medium; LO.: gender, culture, and conflict

    Answer: A

53. Kitchen-sinking is
    A. holding a grudge against your relational partner
    B. dredging up unrelated problems in response to conflict
    C. an effective conflict management strategy
    D. an authoritative use of power
    E. an uneven distribution of household chores

    H: Conflict in Relationships, p. 287; C: conceptual; D: medium; L.O.: nature of conflict

    Answer: B

54. Jessica's boyfriend spends the day shopping for clothes when he's supposed to be looking for a job. When he comes home, she responds, "So you're buying a new wardrobe to stand in the unemployment line?" This is an example of what kind of conflict?
    A. déjà vu
    B. mock

C. sarcastic sniping

D. silent treatment

E. none of the above

H: Table 9.1: Types of Conflicts, p. 286; C: application; D: difficult; L.O.: nature of conflict

Answer: C

55. You're engaged in an online conflict with your friend when she writes a nasty comment about you and then signs off before you can reply. What conflict approach is your friend using?

A. sniping

B. skirting

C. cumulative annoyance

D. avoidance

E. withdrawal

H: Avoiding Conflict, p. 295; C: application; D: difficult; L.O.: interpersonal conflict

Answer: A

56. Conflict can be described as having all the following characteristics EXCEPT

A. transactional

B. occurs over time

C. proceeds through stages

D. grounded in objective reality

E. none of the above

H: What Is Conflict? p. 286; C: conceptual; D: medium; L.O.: nature of conflict

Answer: D

57. Which of the following is NOT true of conflict?

A. occurs most often outside the home

B. occurs between those who know each other well

C. occurs between those who have established relationships

D. occurs most often between family members and romantic partners

E. occurs between those who have disagreements over scarce resources

H: Conflict in Relationships, p. 287; C: conceptual; D: medium; L.O.: nature of conflict

Answer: A

58. If Don calls the shots and is the primary decision maker and his wife Kathy acquiesces to his decisions, what is being exemplified?

A. social network currency

B. symmetrical relationship

C. complementary relationship

D. resource currency

E. expertise currency

H: Power Is Always Present, p. 290; C: application; D: difficult; L.O.: power in conflict

Answer: C

59. If an auto repair shop charges high labor rates, yet you are willing to pay them because of their excellent reputation and skilled mechanics, what type of power currency is represented?
    A. resource currency
    B. expertise currency
    C. social network currency
    D. personal currency
    E. intimacy currency

    H: Power Currencies, p. 291; C: application; D: difficult; L.O.: power in conflict

    Answer: B

60. Which of the following statements regarding the relationship between culture and conflict is true?
    A. collectivists view direct messages as personal attacks
    B. individualists prefer to use avoidance
    C. collectivists prefer to use collaboration
    D. individualists prefer to use a third-party mediator
    E. collectivists are less concerned with nonverbal communication

    H: Conflict and Culture, p. 310; C: conceptual; D: medium; L.O.: gender, culture, and conflict

    Answer: A

61. A charismatic, extroverted personality would possess which type of power currency?
    A. resource currency
    B. expertise currency
    C. social network currency
    D. personal currency
    E. intimacy currency

    H: Power Currencies, p. 291; C: application; D: difficult; L.O.: power in conflict

    Answer: D

62. Andy makes demands of a friend, who in turn makes his own demands. Both parties eventually agree to make concessions by which neither friend gets exactly what he wanted. What type of resolution is being used?
    A. separation
    B. domination
    C. compromise
    D. competition
    E. accommodation

    H: Short-Term Conflict Resolutions, p. 304; C: application; D: difficult; L.O.: conflict outcomes

    Answer: C

63. The relationship between power and gender suggests that
    A. American women lead the world in political power
    B. women have lower resource, expertise, and social network power
    C. men and women have equal access to power currency

D. men tend to listen more closely to women than to other men

E. all of the above

H: Power and Gender, p. 294; C: conceptual; D: medium; L.O.: power in conflict

Answer: B

64. Structural improvements occur

A. when two people develop a creative solution to solve their problem

B. when one person gets his or her way

C. when one party withdraws from the conflict encounter

D. when people change the basic understanding of their relationship to avoid conflict

E. when one person uses accommodation and the other gets his or her way

H: Short-Term Conflict Resolutions, p. 304; C: conceptual; D: medium; L.O.: conflict outcomes

Answer: D

65. You take your new boyfriend to see a movie and are annoyed by kids behind you who talk incessantly and kick the back of your seat. You respond by turning around occasionally and fidgeting in your seat. What type of conflict management approach are you exhibiting?

A. collaboration

B. competition

C. accommodation

D. avoidance

E. withdrawal

H: Avoiding Conflict, p. 295; C: application; D: difficult; L.O.: interpersonal conflict

Answer: D

66. The new person you are dating keeps asking you about the status of your relationship and you respond by joking that committed relationships always end. What conflict approach are you using?

A. collaboration

B. skirting

C. accommodation

D. avoidance

E. withdrawal

H: Avoiding Conflict, p. 295; C: application; D: difficult; L.O.: interpersonal conflict

Answer: B

67. Which of the following is true of people who use collaborative approaches to manage conflict?

A. they are likely to see the same conflict resurface

B. they experience shorter and fewer disputes

C. they experience more mutual resentment

D. they are more likely to use separation in a positive way

E. all of the above

H: Long-Term Conflict Outcomes, p. 306; C: conceptual; D: medium; LO: conflict outcomes

Answer: B

68. Cumulative annoyance
    A. is a form of avoidance
    B. occurs when one communicates negatively
    C. occurs when repressed grievances accumulate
    D. occurs when one continually uses a competitive approach
    E. occurs when one jokes about or changes topic during a conflict episode

    H: Avoiding Conflict, p. 295; C: conceptual; D: medium; L.O.: interpersonal conflict

    Answer: C

69. If your supervisor asks you to work late and you agree, even though you have other plans, what conflict management style are you using?
    A. sniping
    B. competition
    C. accommodation
    D. avoidance
    E. withdrawal

    H: Accommodating Conflict, p. 297; C: application; D: difficult; L.O.: interpersonal conflict

    Answer: C

70. Which of the following strategies should a collectivist use to resolve a conflict with an individualist?
    A. recognize that conflicts can be separate from people
    B. use direct and assertive language
    C. focus on conflict, not personalities
    D. provide verbal feedback
    E. all of the above

    H: Conflict and Culture, p. 310; C: conceptual; D: medium; L.O.: gender, culture, and conflict

    Answer: E

71. When Jane sat down with Pat to discuss a disagreement over finances, Pat responded by bringing up old issues and problems that had long since been addressed. Pat is engaging in
    A. power distance
    B. sniping
    C. escalation
    D. dirty secrets
    E. kitchen-sinking

    H: Conflict in Relationships, p. 287; C: application; D: difficult; L.O.: nature of conflict

    Answer: E

72. On MTV's *The Real World*, what style of conflict management were Kevin and Julie using when they aggressively challenged one another?
    A. sniping
    B. competition
    C. accommodation
    D. avoidance
    E. withdrawal

H: Competitively Managing Conflict, p. 297; C: application; D: difficult; L.O.: interpersonal conflict

Answer: B

73. Escalation is
    A. a decrease in the intensity of a conflict
    B. a risk of engaging in competition
    C. a result of terminating a relationship
    D. people disclosing hurtful feelings about their partners
    E. none of the above

    H: Competitively Managing Conflict, p. 297; C: conceptual; D: medium; L.O.: interpersonal conflict

    Answer: B

74. If your faculty advisor, who is helping prepare your résumé, has many contacts in the business world, what type of power currency is he or she wielding?
    A. resource currency
    B. expertise currency
    C. social network currency
    D. personal currency
    E. intimacy currency

    H: Power Currencies, p. 291; C: application; D: difficult; L.O.: power in conflict

    Answer: C

75. When filing for divorce, your spouse says, "Let's try to figure out a way we can both end up happy and have joint custody of the kids." What conflict management style is he or she using?
    A. collaboration
    B. competition
    C. accommodation
    D. avoidance
    E. withdrawal

    H: Collaboratively Managing Conflict, p. 300; C: application; D: difficult; L.O.: interpersonal conflict

    Answer: A

76. While fighting with your new spouse, you yell, "I don't know why we even got married. We are so different." This is an example of
    A. dirty secret
    B. skirting
    C. sniping
    D. sudden-death statement
    E. pseudo-conflict

    H: Competitively Managing Conflict, p. 297; C: application; D: difficult; L.O.: interpersonal conflict

    Answer: D

77. According to research, what percentage of men reported that they had been physically assaulted during a conflict?
    A. 15%
    B. 52%
    C. 66%
    D. 85%
    E. 95%

    H: Conflict and Violence, p. 303; C: factual/definitional; D: medium; L.O.: interpersonal conflict

    Answer: C

78. Pseudo-conflict is
    A. an effective conflict management strategy
    B. a conflict that is resolved without incident
    C. the absence of conflict
    D. the perception that a conflict exists when it doesn't
    E. the perception that a conflict does not exist when it does

    H: Avoiding Conflict, p. 295; C: conceptual; D: medium; L.O.: interpersonal conflict

    Answer: D

79. Which of the following statements about conflict and violence is true?
    A. more than half of men and women have used violence to deal with conflict
    B. men are more likely to be injured or killed than women
    C. more gay men than lesbians experience violence in relationships
    D. women perpetrate about as much violence as do men
    E. gay men experience more violence than heterosexual men

    H: Conflict and Violence, p. 303; C: conceptual; D: medium; L.O.: interpersonal conflict

    Answer: D

80. Which of the following is true of members of a high power-distance culture?
    A. power is distributed equally among them
    B. they consider it unfair to emphasize power differences
    C. they value authoritativeness
    D. people of low and high status can relate equally
    E. they actively challenge authority

    H: Power and Culture, p. 292; C: conceptual; D: medium; L.O.: power in conflict

    Answer: C

81. Separation
    A. is a way for one party to get its way
    B. is both parties changing their conflict goals
    C. is the result of a failure to compromise
    D. is an effective method for dealing with conflict
    E. is a short-term resolution

    H: Short-Term Conflict Resolutions, p. 304; C: conceptual; D: medium; L.O.: conflict outcomes

    Answer: E

82. Integrative agreements occur
    A. when two people develop a creative solution to their problem
    B. when one person gets his or her way
    C. when one party withdraws from the conflict encounter
    D. when people change the basic understanding of their relationship
    E. when one person uses accommodation and the other gets his or her way

    H: Short-Term Conflict Resolutions, p. 304; C: conceptual; D: medium; L.O.: conflict outcomes

    Answer: A

83. Cheryl finds that she always has to remind her ex to pay child support, pick up their son, and be a good father. He ignores her repeated attempts to resolve their child care conflicts and says he is too busy to talk to or deal with his son. What is this couple experiencing?
    A. integrative agreement
    B. structural improvement
    C. separation
    D. demand-withdraw pattern
    E. escalation

    H: Conflict and Gender, p. 309; C: application; D: difficult; L.O.: gender, culture, and conflict

    Answer: D

84. Which of the following suggestions would you NOT recommend to an individualist manage a conflict with a collectivist?
    A. use a third-party mediator
    B. help the collectivist save face
    C. use indirect communication
    D. be careful using and observing nonverbal communication
    E. use an assertive style

    H: Conflict and Culture, p. 310; C: conceptual; D: medium; L.O.: gender, c conflict

    Answer: E

85. Collaborative conflict management means
    A. attacking the problem, not the person
    B. focusing on common interests
    C. developing creative options before making decisions
    D. evaluating your solutions
    E. all of the above

    H: Collaboratively Managing Conflict, p. 300; C: conceptual; D
    L.O.: interpersonal conflict

    Answer: E

86. If your parents provide you with food, clothing, shelter, and power currency do they have over you?
    A. resource currency
    B. expertise currency
    C. social network currency

Shor

Briefly

90. De

H:

Poss

scar

D. personal currency
E. intimacy currency

H: Power Currencies, p. 291; C: application; D: difficult; L.O.: power in conflict

Answer: A

87. Naja influences her partner's decisions and seems always to get her needs and wishes fulfilled. However, it seems her partner's goals are abandoned in order to do so. What is Naja demonstrating?
A. separation
B. domination
C. compromise
D. competition
E. accommodation

H: Short-Term Conflict Resolutions, p. 304; C: application; D: difficult; L.O.: conflict outcomes

Answer: B

88. Research on culture and conflict has found all of the following EXCEPT
A. individualists seem to prefer collaboration more than collectivists
B. collaboration is the preferred conflict management style for all cultures
C. collectivists seem primarily to use avoidance
D. collectivists view direct conflict styles as a personal attack
E. individualists prefer an assertive communication style, using "I" statements

H: Conflict and Culture, p. 310; C: conceptual; D: medium; L.O.: gender, culture, and conflict

Answer: B

89. Research suggests conflict over power
A. need not be destructive
B. can provide healthy change
C. can help resolve problems
D. can create new opportunities
E. all of the above

H: The Challenge of Managing Conflict and Power, p. 315; C: conceptual; D: medium; L.O.: conflict and interpersonal communication

Answer: E

t Answer

respond to the following questions.

fine conflict.

What Is Conflict? p. 286; C: conceptual; D: medium; L.O.: nature of conflict

ible Answer: A transactional process between people who perceive incompatible goals, e resources, or interference in achieving their goals.

91. Define radical pacifism and explain its relationship to accommodation.

H: Focus on Culture: Accommodation and Racial Pacifism, p. 298; C: conceptual; D: medium; L.O.: interpersonal conflict

Possible Answer: Radical pacifism is the belief that we have a moral obligation to behave selflessly and practice self-sacrifice in order to avoid conflict. Radical pacifism is an extreme form of accommodation.

92. What are five things one can do to more effectively manage online conflicts?

H: Conflict and Technology, p. 314; C: conceptual; D: medium; L.O.: managing conflict and power

Possible Answer: Wait and reread; assume the best and watch out for the worst; discuss the situation offline with someone you trust; craft a competent and supportive response; weigh your options carefully.

93. What is the difference between a high power-distance culture and a low power-distance culture?

H: Power and Culture, p. 292; C: conceptual; D: medium; L.O.: power in conflict

Possible Answer: High power-distance cultures accentuate differences in power based on social class or standing, whereas low power-distance cultures minimize such differences.

94. Define pseudo-conflict.

H: Avoiding Conflict, p. 295; C: conceptual; D: medium; L.O.: interpersonal conflict

Possible Answer: Perception that there is a conflict when there really is none. A risk of using an avoidance approach.

95. Why should we avoid kitchen-sinking with our relationship partner?

H: Conflict in Relationships, p. 287; C: conceptual; D: medium; L.O.: nature of conflict

Possible Answer: By virtue of being in a close, personal relationship with our partner, we possess personal information about him or her and may resort to using this information against him or her by making accusations unrelated to a present issue.

96. What is the difference between a symmetrical relationship and a complementary relationship?

H: Power Is Always Present, p. 290; C: conceptual; D: medium; L.O.: power in conflict

Possible Answer: In a symmetrical relationship, power is balanced; in a complementary relationship, power is unbalanced.

97. Identify and explain the most constructive approach to managing conflict.

H: Collaboratively Managing Conflict, p. 300; C: conceptual; D: medium; L.O.: interpersonal conflict

Possible Answer: Collaboration: when partners perceive conflict as a mutual problem-solving challenge. This approach increases relationship satisfaction, trust, and commitment.

98. What effect does gender have on violence in relationships?

H: Conflict and Violence, p. 303; C: conceptual; D: medium; L.O.: interpersonal conflict

Possible Answer: Both women and men use and receive violence in managing their conflicts.

99. How can structural improvements be used to manage conflict in our personal relationships?

    H: Short-Term Conflict Resolutions, p. 304; C: application; D: difficult; L.O.: conflict outcomes

    Possible Answer: When partners face intense conflict, they can manage their negative emotions and change basic rules of the relationship to help prevent further conflict.

100. How does the demand-withdraw pattern emerge?

    H: Conflict and Gender, p. 309; C: conceptual; D: medium; L.O.: gender, culture, and conflict

    Possible Answer: Because of power inequities between men and women that drive women to demand change while men are satisfied with the status quo. Also because women tend to deal with relationship issues, while men avoid them.

101. What are some ways to reduce the likelihood of violence in your relationship?

    H: Conflict and Violence, p. 303; C: conceptual; D: medium; L.O.: interpersonal conflict

    Possible Answer: Use anger management techniques, seek professional counseling or other help, and avoid or end the relationship.

102. What is a primary concern with relying upon compromise to manage conflict?

    H: Short-Term Conflict Resolutions, p. 304; C: conceptual; D: medium; L.O.: interpersonal conflict

    Possible Answer: When partners give up and cannot have their needs or goals met, they may resent their relational partners and hold it against them. This could breed potential future conflict and kitchen-sinking.

103. What are some advantages of managing conflict?

    H: The Challenge of Managing Conflict and Power, p. 315; C: conceptual; D: medium; L.O.: nature of conflict

    Possible Answer: Conflict can be constructive because it allows us to change and improve our relationships while also helping us better understand our own as well as our partners' needs and desires.

104. Identify three of the seven types of conflict defined by the text.

    H: Table 9.1: Types of Conflict, p. 286; C: factual/definitional; D: easy; L.O.: nature of conflict

    Possible Answer: Blow-up, civil, déjà vu, indirect, mock, sarcastic sniping, silent treatment.

Essay

Please respond to the following questions in paragraph form.

105. Identify and explain power and its defining characteristics.

    H: Power and Conflict, p. 288; C: conceptual; D: medium; L.O.: power in conflict

    Possible Answer: The ability to influence or control others. Power is always present; may be balanced or unbalanced in relationships; can be used either ethically or unethically; is granted, meaning it does not reside within individuals but is given by others; and it influences conflicts.

106. Define and give an example of the five power currencies used in our personal relationships.

H: Power Currencies, p. 291; C: conceptual; D: medium; L.O.: power in conflict

Possible Answer: Resource currency: material such as money or food; expertise currency: special skills or knowledge, such as certification by Microsoft; social network currency: a network of friends or contacts with significant influence, such as being friends with the president; personal currency: personal characteristics of an individual such as personality or communication style; intimacy currency: the connection and influence resulting from a close connection with another person, such as the power you wield over your partner.

107. Identify and explain the five primary conflict styles or approaches.

H: Handling Conflict, p. 295; C: conceptual; D: medium; L.O.: interpersonal conflict

Possible Answer: Avoidance: ignoring or communicating ambiguously about a conflict; accommodation: giving up goals in order to satisfy those of a partner; competition: confronting others in order to attain one's own goals to the exclusion of others'; compromise: changing goals to make them compatible with another's; collaboration: preferred approach to conflict management where partners treat a problem as a mutual problem-solving challenge.

108. Why is collaboration considered to be the most constructive strategy for managing conflict? Describe four strategies that can be used for collaboratively managing conflict.

H: Collaboratively Managing Conflict, p. 300; C: application; D: difficult; L.O.: handling conflict

Possible Answer: Collaboration tends to increase relationship satisfaction and enhance trust. First, attack problems, not people. Second, focus on common interests and long-term goals. Third, find creative options before arriving at decisions. Finally, critically evaluate the solution you have reached.

109. How do gender and culture impact conflict?

H: Conflict and Gender and Conflict and Culture, pp. 309–310; C: application; D: difficult; L.O.: gender, culture, and conflict

Possible Answer: In general, women are taught to avoid or suppress conflict, and to sacrifice their own goals. In close relationships with men, women tend to pursue conflict to demand that their goals be met. Men, on the other hand, tend generally to compete and to use aggression, but to avoid conflict in close relationships with women. Individualistic and collectivistic cultures manage conflict differently. Individualistic cultures prefer a more direct conflict approach, such as competition, whereas collectivistic cultures prefer a more indirect approach, such as avoidance.

Chapter 10: Relationships with Romantic Partners

Matching

Match the concept, term, or theory with its correct response or definition.

A. avoiding
B. beautiful-is-good effect
C. birds-of-a-feather effect
D. bonding
E. circumscribing
F. companionate love
G. differentiating
H. equity
I. experimenting
J. initiating
K. integrating
L. intensifying
M. liking

N. loyalty strategy
O. loving
P. matching
Q. mere exposure effect
R. passionate love
S. relational devaluation
T. relational maintenance
U. small talk
V. social exchange theory
W. stagnating
X. terminating
Y. voice strategy

1. Feeling of affection and respect we have for our friends.
    H: Liking and Loving, p. 322; C: factual/definitional; D: easy; L.O.: defining love
    Answer: M. liking

2. Intense emotional commitment that consists of intimacy, caring, and attachment.
    H: Liking and Loving, p. 322; C: factual/definitional; D: easy; L.O.: defining love
    Answer: O. loving

3. Relationship stage in which two people exchange demographic information with one another.
    H: Experimenting, p. 336; C: factual/definitional; D: easy; L.O.: development and deterioration
    Answer: I. experimenting

4. A passive approach to managing relationship crises in which a partner avoids direct confrontation.

    H: Loyalty Strategy, p. 347; C: factual/definitional; D: easy; L.O.: maintaining relationships

    Answer: N. loyalty strategy

5. The relationship stage in which the depth of personal disclosure increases.

    H: Intensifying, p. 336; C: factual/definitional; D: easy; L.O.: development and deterioration

    Answer: L. intensifying

6. An intense form of liking defined by emotional investment and intertwined lives.

    H: Different Types of Romantic Love, p. 322; C: factual/definitional; D: easy; L.O.: defining love

    Answer: F. companionate love

7. The relationship stage in which partners physically distance themselves from each other.

    H: Avoiding, p. 339; C: factual/definitional; D: easy; L.O.: development and deterioration

    Answer: A. avoiding

8. The realization that partners do not love and respect us as much as we thought they did.

    H: Betrayal, p. 351; C: factual/definitional; D: easy; L.O.: defining love

    Answer: S. relational devaluation

9. Forming long-term romantic relationships with people we perceive to be similar to us in physical attractiveness.

    H: Physical Attractiveness, p. 330; C: factual/definitional; D: easy; L.O.: romantic attraction

    Answer: P. matching

10. The initial stage of coming apart in which the differences between partners dominate their thoughts and communication.

    H: Differentiating, p. 338; C: factual/definitional; D: easy; L.O.: development and deterioration

    Answer: G. differentiating

11. The perceived balance of benefits and costs in a relationship.

    H: Resources, p. 331; C: factual/definitional; D: easy; L.O.: attraction

    Answer: H. equity

12. A phenomenon that suggests we are attracted to those we perceive as physically attractive because we think they are also intelligent and well-adjusted.

    H: Physical Attractiveness, p. 330; C: factual/definitional; D: easy; L.O.: attraction

    Answer: B. beautiful-is-good effect

13. We tend to be attracted to those we perceive as similar to ourselves.

    H: Similarity, p. 331; C: factual/definitional; D: easy; L.O.: attraction

    Answer: C. birds-of-a-feather effect

14. The relationship stage in which partners begin to mesh their identities.

    H: Integrating, p. 336; C: factual/definitional; D: easy; L.O.: development and deterioration

    Answer: K. integrating

15. Relationship stage in which we first meet and assess similarity between ourselves and others.

    H: Initiating, p. 334; C: factual/definitional; D: easy; L.O.: development and deterioration

    Answer: J. initiating

16. Communication of relatively safe information that lays the groundwork for a more intimate exchange.

    H: Experimenting, p. 336; C: factual/definitional; D: easy; L.O.: development and deterioration

    Answer: U. small talk

17. We are more attracted to those we see frequently than those we see less often.

    H: Proximity, p. 330; C: factual/definitional; D: easy; L.O.: attraction

    Answer: Q. mere exposure effect

18. Relationship stage in which partners formalize or make public their commitment to one another.

    H: Bonding, p. 337; C: factual/definitional; D: easy; L.O.: development and deterioration

    Answer: D. bonding

19. The relationship stage in which communication seems pointless.

    H: Stagnating, p. 339; C: factual/definitional; D: easy; L.O.: development and deterioration

    Answer: W. stagnating

20. A theory used to assess relational attraction by weighing costs and benefits.

    H: Resources, p. 331; C: factual/definitional; D: easy; L.O.: attraction

    Answer: V. social exchange theory

21. A state of intense emotional and physical longing for union with another.

    H: Different Types of Romantic Love, p. 322; C: factual/definitional; D: easy; L.O.: defining love

    Answer: R. passionate love

22. The final relationship stage, in which partners bring closure to the relationship.

    H: Terminating, p. 339; C: factual/definitional; D: easy; L.O.: development and deterioration

    Answer: X. terminating

23. Efforts designed to keep one's relationship in a desired state or condition.

    H: Maintenance Strategies, p. 342; C: factual/definitional; D: easy; L.O.: maintaining relationships

    Answer: T. relational maintenance

24. An approach to managing relationship crises in which partners talk directly about a problem.
    H: Voice Strategy, p. 346; C: factual/definitional; D: easy; L.O.: maintaining relationships
    Answer: Y. voice strategy

25. The relationship stage in which partners ignore relationship problems and spend less time together.
    H: Circumscribing, p. 339; C: factual/definitional; D: easy; L.O.: development and deterioration
    Answer: E. circumscribing

True/False

Please select whether the following statements are true or false.

26. Both the exit and loyalty strategies are passive approaches to relationship crises.
    H: Confronting Relationship Crises, p. 346; C: conceptual; D: medium; L.O.: maintaining relationships
    Answer: F

27. Men seem to possess more "starry-eyed" perceptions of love than women and are more likely to believe their partners are perfect and that "love at first sight is possible."
    H: Different Types of Romantic Love, p. 322; C: conceptual; D: medium; L.O.: defining love
    Answer: T

28. Loving is merely an intense form of liking.
    H: Liking and Loving, p. 322; C: conceptual; D: medium; L.O.: defining love
    Answer: F

29. Passionate love is a type of love that is specific to Western culture.
    H: Different Types of Romantic Love, p. 322; C: conceptual; D: medium; L.O.: defining love
    Answer: F

30. If Aaron longs to be with his partner, who is away on a summer internship, he is experiencing a loss of the caring component of love.
    H: Liking and Loving, p. 322; C: application; D: medium; L.O.: defining love
    Answer: F

31. Small talk is the trivial exchange of unimportant information that wastes a potential partner's time.
    H: Experimenting, p. 336; C: conceptual; D: medium; L.O.: development and deterioration
    Answer: F

32. If you perceive that costs and rewards are balanced between you and your partner, you are more likely to be happy in your relationship.
    H: Resources, p. 331; C: conceptual; D: medium; L.O.: attraction
    Answer: T

33. Liking is composed of feelings of affection and respect.
    H: Liking and Loving, p. 322; C: factual/definitional; D: easy; L.O.: defining love
    Answer: T

34. According to your text, passionate love is negatively related to relationship duration.
    H: Different Types of Romantic Love, p. 322; C: factual/definitional; D: easy; L.O.: defining love
    Answer: T

35. The loyalty strategy is the most active way to maintain a healthy relationship.
    H: Loyalty Strategy, p. 347; C: conceptual; D: medium; L.O.: defining love
    Answer: F

36. Women, more so than men, seem to experience pragma love.
    H: Different Types of Romantic Love, p. 322; C: conceptual; D: medium; L.O.: defining love
    Answer: T

37. Gay and lesbian couples experience falling in love, passion, and commitment differently than do straight couples.
    H: Diversity, p. 326; C: conceptual; D: medium; L.O.: defining love
    Answer: F

38. John and Abigail initially dislike one another. According to the mere exposure effect, they likely will find each other more attractive as they spend more time together.
    H: Proximity, p. 330; C: application; D: medium; L.O.: attraction
    Answer: T

39. If two people who have been dating begin to refer to one another as "sweet pea" and to identify as "we," not "you and I," they are probably in the intensifying stage of relationship development.
    H: Intensifying, p. 336; C: factual/definitional; D: easy; L.O.: development and deterioration
    Answer: T

40. If two partners disagree about the nature of their relationship, they do not have a romantic relationship.
    H: Key Elements of Romantic Relationships, p. 325; C: conceptual; D: medium; L.O.: defining love
    Answer: T

41. The effect of physical proximity reduces the likelihood of mixed-race romantic relationships in the United States because we tend to cluster in ethnically homogenous groups.
    H: Proximity, p. 330; C: conceptual; D: medium; L.O.: attraction
    Answer: T

42. Assuming the beautiful-is-good effect is operating, we are likely to see those who are physically attractive as more competent communicators.

    H: Physical Attractiveness, p. 330; C: conceptual; D: medium; L.O.: attraction

    Answer: T

43. The competing impulses, or tensions, between our selves and our feelings toward others are known as relational dialects.

    H: Tensions, p. 327; C: factual/definitional; D: easy; L.O.: defining romantic relationships

    Answer: T

44. The novelty versus predictability tension deals with how much of our selves we choose to share with our partners.

    H: Tensions, p. 327; C: factual/definitional; D: easy; L.O.: defining romantic relationships

    Answer: F

45. Judah tends to date only women he perceives to be much better looking than he is. He is demonstrating the matching concept of attraction.

    H: Physical Attractiveness, p. 330; C: application; D: difficult; L.O.: attraction

    Answer: F

46. Loving is based upon intimacy, caring, and attachment.

    H: Liking and Loving, p. 322; C: factual/definitional; D: easy; L.O.: defining love

    Answer: T

47. According to social exchange theory, we are more attracted to people we perceive as offering us benefits with few costs.

    H: Resources, p. 331; C: conceptual; D: medium; L.O.: attraction

    Answer: T

48. According to your text, the birds-of-a-feather effect suggests that a primary source of attraction is perceived similarity to others.

    H: Similarity, p. 331 C: conceptual; D: medium; L.O.: attraction

    Answer: T

49. Online communication helps with every component of the attraction process except proximity.

    H: Technology and Romantic Attraction, p. 332; C: conceptual; D: medium; L.O.: romantic attraction

    Answer: F

50. If Arya and Tatum travel to Massachusetts to obtain a license that allows same-sex couples to wed, they are in the bonding stage of relationship development.

    H: Bonding, p. 337; C: conceptual; D: medium; L.O.: development and deterioration

    Answer: T

Multiple Choice

Please choose the correct response to the following statements.

51. Loving
    A. is more intense than liking
    B. requires intimacy
    C. consists of caring
    D. includes attachment
    E. all of the above

    H: Liking and Loving, p. 322; C: factual/definitional; D: easy; L.O.: defining love

    Answer: E

52. Which of the following are tensions commonly found in romantic relationships?
    A. novelty versus predictability
    B. openness versus protection
    C. autonomy versus connection
    D. detachment versus empathy
    E. only A, B, and C

    H: Tensions, p. 327; C: conceptual; D: easy; L.O.: defining romantic relationships

    Answer: E

53. Gabriel and Harriett have been dating for almost two years. They have an intimate physical relationship and visit each other's parents on holidays. Recently, they bought a car and signed a lease on a new apartment together. What stage is this couple at?
    A. circumscribing
    B. experimenting
    C. integrating
    D. bonding
    E. intensifying

    H: Integrating, p. 336; C: application; D: difficult; L.O.: development and deterioration

    Answer: C

54. Which of the following is NOT considered a characteristic of passionate love?
    A. driven by idealization of the partner
    B. neither gender nor age change its experience
    C. positively related to relationship duration
    D. experienced by all cultures
    E. linked with sexuality and sexual desire

    H: Different Types of Romantic Love, p. 322; C: application; D: medium; L.O.: defining love

    Answer: C

55. According to social exchange theory, relational attraction can be described by all the following factors EXCEPT
    A. benefits
    B. costs

C. comparison level

D. uncertainty

E. rewards

H: Resources, p. 331; C: conceptual; D: medium; L.O.: attraction

Answer: D

56. Carolyn and Eric have gone out a couple of times. Their conversation is composed primarily of small talk, through which they learn about each other's similarities. Which stage best characterizes their relationship?

A. circumscribing

B. integrating

C. experimenting

D. bonding

E. intensifying

H: Experimenting, p. 336; C: application; D: difficult; L.O.: development and deterioration

Answer: C

57. Which of the following is true of companionate love?

A. the longer you are with your partner the less you feel it

B. it dominates media depictions of romance

C. it's less desirable than passionate love

D. it's an intense form of liking with emotional investment

E. it's not characteristic of long-term relationships

H: Different Types of Romantic Love, p. 322; C: conceptual; D: medium; L.O.: defining love

Answer: D

58. Which of the following statements about attraction is NOT true?

A. perceived similarity of attractiveness is not the same as actual similarity

B. we tend to underestimate our own physical attractiveness

C. similarity is important for more than just physical attraction

D. we tend to avoid people we view as less attractive than ourselves

E. you have to like a quality you possess to find it attractive in others

H: Similarity, p. 331; C: conceptual; D: medium; L.O.: attraction

Answer: B

59. Gael and Michelle have been dating for six months. They have disclosed a great deal of personal information to one another and even use pet names to refer to one another. Which of the following stages are they at in their relationship?

A. circumscribing

B. experimenting

C. integrating

D. bonding

E. intensifying

H: Intensifying, p. 336; C: application; D: difficult; L.O.: development and deterioration

Answer: E

60. Cael has been spending long nights at the office working with a coworker while his spouse is away on business. He's finding himself increasingly attracted to his coworker. Which of the following could explain his attraction?
    A. equity
    B. social exchange theory
    C. matching
    D. birds-of-a-feather effect
    E. mere exposure effect

    H: Proximity, p. 330; C: application; D: difficult; L.O.: attraction

    Answer: E

61. When Hessa wants to talk with Pat about how to compromise in managing money, Pat gets upset at their differences and claims they'll never be able to share a household if they can't agree on everything. Pat's attitude is an example of
    A. exit strategy
    B. mere exposure effect
    C. stagnating
    D. dysfunctional relationship beliefs
    E. betrayal

    H: Dysfunctional Relationship Beliefs, p. 349; C: conceptual; D: difficult; L.O.: relationship challenges

    Answer: D

62. Which of the following behaviors would NOT be considered an example of positivity?
    A. making sure your partner's family likes you
    B. making interactions enjoyable
    C. paying compliments to your partner
    D. trying to be romantic
    E. trying to be fun and interesting

    H: Positivity, p. 343; C: conceptual; D: medium; L.O.: maintaining relationships

    Answer: A

63. What is the most frequently reported relational maintenance strategy?
    A. openness
    B. positivity
    C. assurances
    D. sharing activities
    E. sharing tasks

    H: Positivity, p. 343; C: factual; D: easy; L.O.: maintaining relationships

    Answer: B

64. Which of the following are defining elements of a romantic relationship?
    A. perception and choice
    B. equity and communication
    C. diversity and equity
    D. communication and matching
    E. perception and exposure

H: Key Elements of Romantic Relationships, p. 325; C: conceptual; D: medium;
L.O.: defining love

Answer: A

65. In comparing gay and lesbian couples with cross-gender relationships, research suggests
    A. gay and lesbian couples are as "traditional" as cross-gender couples
    B. gay and lesbian couples place as much importance on their relationships as do cross-gender couples
    C. people in gay and lesbian relationships devote as much time to their relationships as cross-gender relationships
    D. gay and lesbian couples are as open as cross-gender couples
    E. all of the above

    H: Diversity, p. 326; C: conceptual; D: medium; L.O.: defining love

    Answer: E

66. If two people who have been dating for four years decide to get married, what relational stage have they reached?
    A. circumscribing
    B. experimenting
    C. integrating
    D. bonding
    E. intensifying

    H: Bonding, p. 337; C: application; D: difficult; L.O.: development and deterioration

    Answer: D

67. Which of the following best describes the "pragma" style of love?
    A. friendly love that is stable and predictable
    B. practical love that is logical and rational
    C. obsessive love that is intense and tumultuous
    D. forgiving love that is patient and selfless
    E. romantic love that is sentimental and idealistic

    H: Different Types of Romantic Love, p. 322; C: definitional; D: easy; L.O.: defining romantic relationships

    Answer: B

68. If your 8-year-old brother tells you he is in love with his teacher, you should treat his disclosure with respect and empathy because
    A. love is driven by the idealization of partners
    B. neither gender nor age affects how we experience passionate love
    C. love is negatively related to relationship duration
    D. love is experienced by all cultures
    E. love is linked with sexuality and sexual desire

    H: Different Types of Romantic Love, p. 322; C: application; D: difficult; L.O.: defining love

    Answer: B

69. What facet of attraction suggests that people will be drawn to others and will establish relationships with others if they believe the benefits and costs balance each other?
   A. uncertainty reduction
   B. equity
   C. social exchange
   D. relational dialectics
   E. matching

   H: Resources, p. 331; C: conceptual; D: medium; L.O.: attraction

   Answer: B

70. Which of the following factors is more important for initial attraction than for relational maintenance?
   A. physical attractiveness
   B. similarity
   C. complementary values
   D. shared interests
   E. intelligence

   H: Maintenance Strategies, p. 342; C: conceptual; D: medium; L.O.: attraction

   Answer: A

71. If Bill is more physically attracted to his new coworker than to his wife, what element(s) of social exchange theory is (are) influencing his attraction?
   A. costs
   B. proximity
   C. rewards
   D. comparison level of alternatives
   E. both C and D

   H: Resources, p. 331; C: application; D: difficult; L.O.: attraction

   Answer: E

72. According to social exchange theory, inequity results when
   A. your partner is too similar to you
   B. your partner is too different from you
   C. there is a balance of rewards and costs
   D. your partner provides fewer benefits than you do
   E. none of the above

   H: Resources, p. 331; C: conceptual; D: medium; L.O.: attraction

   Answer: D

73. Which of the following is a cause of tension among people using online dating sites?
   A. posting misleading or false information about physical appearance
   B. posting misleading or false information about marital status
   C. posting misleading or false information about age
   D. all of the above
   E. none of the above

   H: Technology and Romantic Attraction, p. 332; C: conceptual; D: easy; L.O.: romantic attraction

   Answer: D

74. Which of the following is NOT true of gender differences in love?
    A. women and men experience passionate love similarly
    B. women score higher than men on pragma love
    C. there is no difference between women's and men's experience of pragma love
    D. men tend to idealize their partners more than women do
    E. men tend to believe "there is only one true love for each person"

    H: Different Types of Romantic Love, p. 322; C: conceptual; D: medium; L.O.: defining love

    Answer: C

75. Romantic partners are happiest when
    A. they get more than they give
    B. they give more than they get
    C. there is a balance of giving and getting
    D. inequity is present
    E. none of the above

    H: Resources, p. 331; C: conceptual; D: medium; L.O.: attraction

    Answer: C

76. According to the mere exposure effect,
    A. decreases in contact lead to increases in attraction
    B. greater exposure leads to greater attraction
    C. less exposure leads to greater attraction
    D. equity must be achieved to increase attraction
    E. none of the above

    H: Proximity, p. 330; C: conceptual; D: medium; L.O.: attraction

    Answer: B

77. When the beautiful-is-good effect occurs, we tend to perceive others as
    A. physically appealing
    B. competent
    C. intelligent
    D. well-adjusted
    E. all of the above

    H: Physical Attractiveness, p. 330; C: conceptual; D: medium; L.O.: attraction

    Answer: E

78. Roberta's partner, Faith, has just moved out of the country; however, Roberta wants to maintain their relationship. Roberta regularly e-mails and sends instant messages to Faith, indicating that she wants this relationship to continue despite the physical distance between them. What relational maintenance strategy is Roberta using?
    A. positivity
    B. openness
    C. assurances
    D. sharing activities
    E. sharing tasks

    H: Assurances, p. 344; C: application; D: difficult; L.O.: maintaining relationships

    Answer: C

79. Joe is experiencing relationship problems with Carl and asks him to sit down and discuss their relationship. Carl avoids Joe and won't talk about the issues. What strategies are they using to manage their relational crisis?
    A. Joe loyalty, Carl voice
    B. Joe neglect, Carl exit
    C. Joe voice, Carl exit
    D. Joe exit, Carl loyalty
    E. none of the above

    H: Voice Strategy, p. 346; C: application; D: difficult; L.O.: maintaining relationships

    Answer: C

80. When matching occurs, we tend to
    A. desire those who are more attractive than us
    B. desire those are who less attractive than us
    C. desire those we perceive as conceited and sexually promiscuous
    D. desire those who are similar to us in physical attractiveness
    E. desire those who complement us

    H: Physical Attractiveness, p. 330; C: conceptual; D: easy; L.O.: attraction

    Answer: D

81. The higher divorce rate for interracial couples is largely due to
    A. inequity
    B. cultural disapproval
    C. dissimilarity in cultural values
    D. lack of communication
    E. the birds-of-a-feather effect

    H: Social Networks, p. 345; C: conceptual; D: medium; L.O.: attraction

    Answer: B

82. When we maintain a relationship with someone we perceive as similar to ourselves we
    A. are more likely to suffer boredom
    B. view predictability as a cost
    C. are likely to stay together longer
    D. tend to overestimate that similarity
    E. all of the above

    H: Similarity, p. 331; C: conceptual; D: medium; L.O.: attraction

    Answer: C

83. Which of the following stages are included in Mark Knapp's stages of coming apart?
    A. circumscribing
    B. experimenting
    C. integrating
    D. bonding
    E. intensifying

    H: Circumscribing, p. 339; C: factual/definitional; D: easy; L.O.: development and deterioration

    Answer: A

84. If Pascal perceives he is receiving fewer rewards than he gives to his lover he is likely to experience
    A. guilt
    B. sadness or anger
    C. equity
    D. happiness
    E. relational satisfaction and stability

    H: Resources, p. 331; C: application; D: difficult; L.O.: attraction

    Answer: B

85. Which of the following is a strategy you can use to defuse jealousy in a romantic relationship?
    A. self-reliance
    B. self-bolstering
    C. selective ignoring
    D. all of the above
    E. only A and B

    H: Jealousy, p. 350; C: conceptual; D: medium; L.O.: dark side of romantic relationships

    Answer: D

86. What percentage of American couples who marry end up divorcing?
    A. 25%
    B. 33%
    C. 40%
    D. 60%
    E. 75%

    H: Coming Apart, p. 337; C: factual/definitional; D: easy; L.O.: development and deterioration

    Answer: C

87. Alexander noticed Lai in his introductory speech communication class. He found her physically attractive and intelligent based upon her contributions to class discussion. He has introduced himself to her and is considering his next move. What stage of relationship development are they in?
    A. circumscribing
    B. initiating
    C. integrating
    D. bonding
    E. intensifying

    H: Initiating, p. 334; C: application; D: difficult; L.O.: development and deterioration

    Answer: B

88. Which of the following is NOT true about betrayal?
    A. betrayal can include sexual infidelity
    B. betrayal can include emotional infidelity
    C. betrayal can include disloyalty
    D. betrayal causes relational devaluation
    E. betrayal can be unintentional

H: Betrayal, p. 351; C: conceptual; D: medium; L.O.: dark side of romantic relationships

Answer: E

89. Henry and Josette have been married 10 years. Their marriage has reached the point where they both feel like they are just going through the motions. They use communication only when needed to maintain their household. What stage of relational coming apart are they experiencing?
   A. differentiating
   B. circumscribing
   C. stagnating
   D. avoiding
   E. terminating

   H: Stagnating, p. 339; C: application; D: difficult; L.O.: development and deterioration

   Answer: C

90. Which of the following is NOT true of sexual infidelity?
   A. the majority of people would consider divorce if their partner had a sexual affair
   B. women find emotional infidelity more distressing than sexual infidelity
   C. both men and women view emotional infidelity in the same way as sexual infidelity
   D. most people find a romantic date more of a betrayal than kissing
   E. relational devaluation is a common result of infidelity

   H: Sexual Infidelity, p. 351; C: conceptual; D: difficult; L.O.: relationship challenges

   Answer: C

Short Answer

Briefly respond to the following questions in full sentences.

91. Define social exchange theory.

   H: Resources, p. 331; C: conceptual; D: medium; L.O.: attraction

   Possible Answer: We are attracted to those we perceive as able to offer us more benefits than costs.

92. Why is similarity considered a primary source of attraction?

   H: Similarity, p. 331; C: conceptual; D: medium; L.O.: attraction

   Possible Answer: We are primarily attracted to those we perceive as similar to ourselves because they pose less uncertainty and their behavior seems easier to predict.

93. How does the mere exposure effect explain the importance of proximity to attraction?

   H: Proximity, p. 330; C: conceptual; D: medium; L.O.: attraction

   Possible Answer: The more we see someone or are in his or her physical space, the more likely we are to perceive him or her as attractive.

94. Identify the three strategies for reducing jealousy.

H: Jealousy, p. 350; C: conceptual; D: medium; L.O.: relationship challenges

Possible Answer: Self-reliance, self-bolstering, and selective ignoring.

95. Define small talk and explain its role in developing relationships.

H: Experimenting, p. 336; C: conceptual; D: medium; L.O.: development and deterioration

Possible Answer: Small talk is the disclosure of low-level information that doesn't risk alienating a potential partner and lays the groundwork for further exploration, self-disclosure, and interpersonal communication.

96. What is the impact of social networks on relational maintenance?

H: Social Networks, p. 345; C: conceptual; D: medium; L.O.: maintaining relationships

Possible Answer: Romantic relationships are more likely to survive if the partners' significant others, including friends and family, approve of the relationship.

97. What are two primary factors that determine whether a couple will stay together?

H: Deciding Whether to Maintain, p. 348; C: conceptual; D: medium; L.O.: maintaining relationships

Possible Answer: The degree to which they are in love, share equity and similarity, and have social network support.

98. What are some strategies for fostering supportive social networks?

H: Social Networks, p. 345; C: conceptual; D: medium; L.O.: maintaining relationships

Possible Answer: Tell your partner how much his or her family means to you; invite your partner's friends and family to spend time with you and your partner; sacrifice your own needs for those of your partner's friends and family.

99. Identify three of the five characteristics of passionate love.

H: Different Types of Romantic Love, p. 322; C: conceptual; D: medium; L.O.: defining romantic relationships

Possible Answer: Driven by idealization of partners; all cultures experience it; and no gender or age differences exist in how it is experienced.

100. Identify two active strategies for managing relational crises.

H: Confronting Relationship Crises, p. 346; C: conceptual; D: medium; L.O.: maintaining relationships

Possible Answer: Voice, an active, constructive strategy in which a couple addresses a problem without engaging in negative communication. Exit, an active, destructive strategy in which a partner threatens to or actually leaves a relationship.

101. Identify two passive strategies for managing relational crises.

H: Confronting Relationship Crises, p. 346; C: conceptual; D: medium; L.O.: maintaining relationships

Possible Answer: Loyalty, a passive, constructive approach in which partners avoid directly dealing with problems, hoping things will just get better on their own. Neglect, a passive, destructive strategy in which partners withdraw from one another and the relationship.

102. Which strategy for managing relational crisis is the most effective and why?

H: Confronting Relationship Crises, p. 346; C: conceptual; D: medium; L.O.: maintaining relationships

Possible Answer: The voice strategy: an active constructive strategy in which a couple addresses a problem without engaging in negative communication. It is associated with relational maintenance and happiness.

103. What are four criteria the author suggests we can use to determine whether to maintain a troubled relationship?

H: Deciding Whether to Maintain, p. 348; C: conceptual; D: medium; L.O.: maintaining relationships

Possible Answer: Do partners consider themselves "in love"; is there relational equity; are partners similar; do the partners' social networks approve of the relationship?

104. Define jealousy and the emotions it is composed of.

H: Jealousy, p. 350; C: conceptual; D: medium; L.O.: relationship challenges

Possible Answer: Jealousy is a protective reaction to a perceived threat to a valued relationship, and is a combination of negative emotions, including hurt, anger, and fear.

105. What are the five key elements of a romantic relationship?

H: Key Elements of Romantic Relationships, p. 325; C: conceptual; D: medium; L.O.: defining romantic relationships

Answer: Perception; diversity; choice; tensions; and communication.

Essay

Please respond to the following questions in paragraph form.

106. Identify the five common warning signs of an abusive partner.

H: Table 10.3: Five Common Warning Signs of an Abusive Partner, p. 358; C: conceptual; D: medium; L.O.: dating violence

Possible Answer: Isolates you from others; uses power to control you; frequently threatens you in various ways; uses emotionally abusive language; shifts blame to you.

107. Identify and describe the six forms of romantic love.

H: Table 10.1: Romantic Love Types, p. 325; C: conceptual; D: medium; L.O.: defining romantic relationships

Possible Answer: *Storge:* love is friendly, stable, and predictable; *agape:* love is unconditional, patient, and selfless; *mania:* love is intense, extreme, and consuming; *pragma:* love is logical, rational, and based upon common sense; *ludus:* love is fun and played like a game; and *eros:* love is sentimental, romantic, and idealistic.

108. Identify and briefly describe the five stages of coming together.

H: Coming Together, p. 334; C: conceptual; D: medium; L.O.: development and deterioration

Possible Answer: Initiating: first stage, in which you primarily observe the target person to discern if there is interest in pursuing a relationship. Experimenting: exchange of basic demographic information or small talk. Intensifying: the depth and breadth of self-disclosure increases and you begin to use personal terms of endearment for each other. Integrating: you are sexually active and strongly identify as a couple. Bonding: formal commitments are made to each other, such as marriage or a commitment ceremony.

109. Identify and briefly describe the five stages of coming apart.

H: Coming Apart, p. 337; C: conceptual; D: medium; L.O.: development and deterioration

Possible Answer: Differentiating: partners begin to recognize and focus on differences in values, beliefs, and attitudes. Circumscribing: active restriction of both quality and quantity of communication used with one's partner. Stagnating: virtually no communication occurs and partners feel stuck. Avoiding: partners physically distance themselves from each other. Terminating: a final encounter that draws the relationship to closure.

110. Describe and provide examples of three maintenance strategies.

H: Maintenance Strategies, p. 342; C: conceptual; D: medium; L.O.: maintaining relationships

Possible Answer: Positivity: communication using an upbeat, optimistic tone, and doing things for or giving unsolicited gifts to your partner, such as bringing home flowers or chocolates. Openness: a climate of security and trust in which feelings can be disclosed without negative repercussions, such as feeling comfortable disclosing a personal problem or issue. Assurances: messages that reaffirm the two partners' commitments to each other, such as telling your partner how much he or she means to you or how much you value the relationship.

Chapter 11: Relationships with Family and Friends

Matching

Match the concept, term, or theory with its correct response or definition.

A. agentic friendships
B. blended families
C. cohabiting couple
D. communal friendships
E. conformity orientation
F. consensual families
G. conversation orientation
H. courtship stories
I. extended family
J. family
K. family communication patterns
L. family communication rules
M. family rituals

N. family stories
O. friendship
P. friendship rules
Q. FWB relationships
R. gay or lesbian family
S. laissez-faire families
T. nuclear family
U. pluralistic families
V. positivity
W. protective families
X. single-parent family
Y. survival stories

1. Families who are low in both conversation and conformity.
   H: Laissez-Faire Families, p. 372; C: factual/definitional; D: easy; L.O.: defining family
   Answer: S. laissez-faire families

2. A family consisting of a husband, wife, and their biological children.
   H: Types of Family, p. 368; C: factual/definitional; D: easy; L.O.: defining family
   Answer: T. nuclear family

3. Friendships that focus on sharing time and activities together.
   H: Communal Friendships, p. 383; C: factual/definitional; D: easy; L.O.: defining friendship
   Answer: D. communal friendships

4. Two unmarried, romantically involved adults living together in a household, with or without children.

   H: Types of Family, p. 368; C: factual/definitional; D: easy; L.O.: defining family

   Answer: C. cohabiting couple

5. Beliefs about how family members should communicate with one another, and the communication that results from those beliefs.

   H: Communication Patterns in Families, p. 369; C: factual/definitional; D: easy; L.O.: defining family

   Answer: K. family communication patterns

6. Accounts families share about coping strategies they used to manage major challenges.

   H: Sharing Family Stories, p. 380; C: factual/definitional; D: easy; L.O.: maintenance strategies for families

   Answer: Y. survival stories

7. The degree to which families believe communication should emphasize similarity or diversity in attitudes, values, and beliefs.

   H: Communication Patterns in Families, p. 369; C: factual/definitional; D: easy; L.O.: defining family

   Answer: E. conformity orientation

8. Friendships in which participants engage in sexual activity without romantic attachment.

   H: Friends with Benefits, p. 388; C: factual/definitional; D: easy; L.O.: defining friendships

   Answer: Q. FWB relationships

9. Families who are high in both conversation and conformity.

   H: Consensual Families, p. 371; C: factual/definitional; D: easy; L.O.: defining family

   Answer: F. consensual families

10. A family in which relatives live together in a common household.

    H: Types of Family, p. 368; C: factual/definitional; D: easy; L.O.: defining family

    Answer: I. extended family

11. Families who are high in conversation but low in conformity.

    H: Pluralistic Families, p. 371; C: factual/definitional; D: easy; L.O.: defining family

    Answer: U. pluralistic families

12. Boundary conditions governing what family members can talk about, how they can discuss topics, and who should have access to information.

    H: Balancing Openness and Protection, p. 377; C: factual/definitional; D: easy; L.O.: maintaining family

    Answer: L. family communication rules

13. Narrative accounts shared repeatedly that bond a family together.

H: Sharing Family Stories, p. 380; C: factual/definitional; D: easy; L.O.: maintaining family

Answer: N. family stories

14. The degree to which family members perceive communication to be the primary means for maintaining family bonds.

H: Communication Patterns in Families, p. 369; C: factual/definitional; D: easy; L.O.: defining family

Answer: G. conversation orientation

15. Family stories about how parents fell in love.

H: Sharing Family Stories, p. 380; C: factual/definitional; D: easy; L.O.: maintenance strategies for families

Answer: H. courtship stories

16. A group of people who create and maintain a mutual identity, emotional bonds, and communication boundaries.

H: Defining Family, p. 366; C: factual/definitional; D: easy; L.O.: defining family

Answer: J. family

17. A family consisting of two people of the same sex who are parents for the biological or adopted children of at least one of them.

H: Types of Family, p. 368; C: factual/definitional; D: easy; L.O.: defining family

Answer: T. gay or lesbian family

18. Doing favors for family members without being asked is an example of this kind of maintenance strategy.

H: Positivity, p. 374; C: factual/definitional; D: easy; L.O.: maintenance strategies for families

Answer: V. positivity

19. A family type in which a husband and wife parent at least one child who is not the biological child of both adults.

H: Types of Family, p. 368; C: factual/definitional; D: easy; L.O.: defining family

Answer: B. blended family

20. Families that are low on conversation and high on conformity.

H: Protective Families, p. 371; C: factual/definitional; D: easy; L.O.: defining family

Answer: W. protective families

21. A voluntary relationship in which the partners like and enjoy each other's company.

H: Defining Friendship, p. 381; C: factual/definitional; D: easy; L.O.: defining friendships

Answer: O. friendship

22. Friendships in which the parties focus on helping each other achieve practical goals.
    H: Agentic Friendships, p. 384; C: factual/definitional; D: easy; L.O.: defining friendship
    Answer: A. agentic friendships

23. Principles that prescribe appropriate communication and behavior within a friendship.
    H: Abiding by Friendship Rules, p. 391; C: factual/definitional; D: easy; L.O.: maintaining friends
    Answer: P. friendship rules

24. A household in which one adult is the sole caregiver for the children.
    H: Types of Family, p. 368; C: factual/definitional; D: easy; L.O.: defining family
    Answer: X. single-parent family

25. Recurring and structured events that help solidify a family's emotional bonds.
    H: Communication Patterns in Families, p. 369; C: factual/definitional; D: easy; L.O.: defining family
    Answer: M. family rituals

True/False

Please select whether the following statements are true or false.

26. The nuclear family represents the majority of families in the United States.
    H: Types of Family, p. 368; C: conceptual; D: medium; L.O.: defining family
    Answer: F

27. More people in Asian countries than in European countries specify respecting privacy as a rule of friendship.
    H: Abiding by Friendship Rules, p. 391; C: conceptual; D: difficult; L.O.: defining friendship
    Answer: F

28. If, in your family, family comes before all outside relationships, you could be described as having a high conformity orientation.
    H: Communication Patterns in Families, p. 369; C: conceptual; D: medium; L.O.: defining family
    Answer: T

29. Friendships tend to be more power-imbalanced; family relationships tend to be more power-balanced.
    H: Defining Friendship, p. 381; C: conceptual; D: medium; L.O.: defining friendship
    Answer: F

30. Helicopter parents rely upon technology to keep in touch with their children.

    H: Focus on Culture, Autonomy and Class: Helicopter Parents, p. 378; C: conceptual; D: medium; L.O.: maintaining family

    Answer: F

31. If your family hosts a party each year for the Fourth of July and then goes to see fireworks together, they are demonstrating a family ritual.

    H: Communication Patterns in Families, p. 369; C: conceptual; D: medium; L.O.: defining family

    Answer: T

32. Communal friendships tend to fulfill the interpersonal need of companionship.

    H: The Different Forms of Friendship, p. 383; C: conceptual; D: medium; L.O.: defining friendship

    Answer: T

33. Families who are low on conversation and high on conformity are considered to be protective families.

    H: Protective Families, p. 371; C: conceptual; D: medium; L.O.: defining family

    Answer: T

34. Lower-income parents tend to be more involved in their children's lives than middle-class families.

    H: Focus on Culture, Autonomy and Class, p. 378; C: conceptual; D: medium; L.O.: maintaining family

    Answer: F

35. Families that are low in both conversation and conformity are considered to be laissez-faire families.

    H: Laissez-Faire Families, p. 372; C: conceptual; D: medium; L.O.: defining family

    Answer: T

36. Family communication rules govern not only what topics are appropriate for disclosure but also how such topics are broached.

    H: Balancing Openness and Protection, p. 377; C: conceptual; D: easy; L.O.: maintaining family

    Answer: T

37. Family communication rules can govern when, how, and to whom family members talk.

    H: Balancing Openness and Protection, p. 377; C: conceptual; D: medium; L.O.: maintaining family

    Answer: T

38. Families with a high conversation orientation are more likely to disclose personal information to one another.

    H: Communication Patterns in Families, p. 369; C: conceptual; D: medium; L.O.: defining family

    Answer: T

39. Positivity, openness, and assurances can be used to maintain both romantic and familial relationships.

    H: Maintenance Strategies for Families, p. 374; C: factual/definitional; D: easy; L.O.: maintenance strategies for families

    Answer: T

40. The majority of cross-sex friendships are motivated by sexual attraction.

    H: Gender and Friendships, p. 385; C: conceptual; D: medium; L.O.: defining friendship

    Answer: F

41. Nuclear families remain the most common family type in the United States.

    H: Types of Family, p. 368; C: factual/definitional; D: easy; L.O.: defining family

    Answer: F

42. Friendships are similar to other personal relationships in that they're difficult to break off.

    H: Defining Friendship, p. 381; C: conceptual; D: medium; L.O.: defining friendship

    Answer: F

43. In the twenty-first century, more than half of the children in the United States will grow up in blended families.

    H: Types of Family, p. 368; C: factual/definitional; D: easy; L.O.: defining family

    Answer: T

44. By the time we reach high school, we are more dependent on our friends than on our families.

    H: Defining Friendship, p. 381; C: conceptual; D: medium; L.O.: defining friendship

    Answer: T

45. When asked to identify the closest relationship in their lives, Javanese will select a friendship, whereas Americans tend to choose their romantic partner.

    H: Gender and Friendships, p. 385; C: conceptual; D: medium; L.O.: defining friendship

    Answer: T

46. Our friendships help us fulfill two primary interpersonal needs: companionship and the achievement of practical goals.

    H: The Different Forms of Friendship, p. 383; C: conceptual; D: medium; L.O.: defining friendship

    Answer: T

47. A family that is high in both conversation and conformity is considered a pluralistic family.

    H: Pluralistic Families, p. 371; C: conceptual; D: medium; L.O.: defining family

    Answer: F

48. In the United States, women's friendships tend to be communal, whereas men's friendships are usually agentic.

    H: Gender and Friendships, p. 385; C: conceptual; D: medium; L.O.: defining friendship

    Answer: F

49. Balancing autonomy and connection in families is most difficult in young adulthood.

    H: Balancing Autonomy and Connection, p. 376; C: factual/definitional; D: easy; L.O.: maintaining family

    Answer: F

50. Geographic separation is the most cited reason for the deterioration of a friendship.

    H: Maintaining Long-Distance Friendships, p. 392; C: factual/definitional; D: easy; L.O.: maintaining friendship

    Answer: T

Multiple Choice

Please choose the correct response to the following statements.

51. The balance between being more open versus being more private is expressed through
    A. family communication patterns
    B. family communication rules
    C. protective families
    D. family stories
    E. conversation orientation

    H: Balancing Openness and Protection, p. 377; C: conceptual; D: difficult; L.O.: maintaining family

    Answer: B

52. Scott and Mark have the same dad; however, they have different moms. What type of family do they share?
    A. nuclear
    B. extended
    C. blended
    D. gay or lesbian
    E. single-parent

    H: Types of Family, p. 368; C: application; D: medium; L.O.: defining family

    Answer: C

53. An important form of communication that helps maintain family relationships through the sharing of narrative accounts is
    A. family communication rules
    B. family communication patterns
    C. conversation orientation
    D. conformity orientation
    E. family stories

Answer: E

54. If Susan and Chris are being raised by their mother and her girlfriend Debbie, what type of family do they have?
    A. nuclear
    B. extended
    C. blended
    D. gay or lesbian
    E. single-parent
    H: Types of Family, p. 368; C: application; D: medium; L.O.: defining family

Answer: D

55. If you learn through experience that you should not ask your father for money or to borrow the car before he has gotten home from work and gone for a jog, what have you learned about?
    A. family communication rules
    B. consensual families
    C. protective families
    D. avoidant families
    E. family communication patterns
    H: Communication Patterns in Families, p. 369; C: application; D: difficult; L.O.: defining family

Answer: E

56. Which of the following is a characteristic that defines a family?
    A. bonds are emotionally intense
    B. uses interpersonal communication to define boundaries
    C. shares a history
    D. shares genetic material
    E. all of the above
    H: Defining Family, p. 366; C: conceptual; D: medium; L.O.: defining family

Answer: E

57. The degree to which families believe communication should emphasize similarity or dissimilarity in attitudes, values, and beliefs is called
    A. pluralistic family
    B. conversation orientation
    C. conformity orientation
    D. family orientation
    E. consensual family
    H: Communication Patterns in Families, p. 369; C: conceptual; D: medium; L.O.: defining family

Answer: C

58. Because of the prevalence of homophobia, Euro-American men in same-sex friendships
    A. are likely to assume traditional masculine gender roles
    B. are reluctant to demonstrate public affection

C. avoid verbal intimacy

D. avoid nonverbal intimacy

E. all of the above

H: Gender and Friendships, p. 385; C: conceptual; D: medium; L.O.: defining friendship

Answer: E

59. Maria's father died in an automobile accident and she is now being raised solely by her mother. What family type does she have?

A. nuclear

B. extended

C. blended

D. gay or lesbian

E. single-parent

H: Types of Family, p. 368; C: application; D: easy; L.O.: defining family

Answer: E

60. Monique's family is upset because she wants to skip her niece's christening to attend her boyfriend's graduation. "Family comes first," they say, "and he's not family yet." Monique's family could be described as having

A. low conformity orientation

B. high conformity orientation

C. high conversation orientation

D. low conversation orientation

E. high fluidity

H: Communication Patterns in Families, p. 369; C: application; D: difficult; L.O.: defining family

Answer: B

61. Families that are high in both conversation and conformity orientation are called

A. conformity orientation

B. laissez-faire families

C. consensual families

D. pluralistic families

E. protective families

H: Consensual Families, p. 371; C: conceptual; D: medium; L.O.: defining family

Answer: C

62. Najya and Sheehab live together with their biological parents. What family type do they have?

A. nuclear

B. extended

C. blended

D. gay or lesbian

E. single-parent

H: Types of Family, p. 368; C: application; D: medium; L.O.: defining family

Answer: A

63. Families that are high in conversation and low in conformity are called
    A. conformity orientation
    B. laissez-faire families
    C. consensual families
    D. pluralistic families
    E. protective families

    H: Pluralistic Families, p. 371; C: conceptual; D: medium; L.O.: defining family

    Answer: D

64. According to William Rawlins, friends who don't spend a lot of time together can still have a satisfying friendship if
    A. they view shared values as more important than shared time
    B. they agree on communication rules
    C. their friendship is agentic
    D. they perceive each other as "being there" when needed
    E. they communicate regularly

    H: Sharing Activities, p. 389; C: conceptual; D: difficult; L.O.: defining friendship

    Answer: D

65. Families raised with the beliefs that "Children should be seen and not heard" and "Children should speak when spoken to" are best described as
    A. conformity orientation
    B. laissez-faire families
    C. consensual families
    D. pluralistic families
    E. protective families

    H: Protective Families, p. 371; C: application; D: difficult; L.O.: defining family

    Answer: E

66. The degree to which family members believe communication is essential for maintaining family bonds is called
    A. family rituals
    B. conversation orientation
    C. conformity orientation
    D. family orientation
    E. consensual families

    H: Communication Patterns in Families, p. 369; C: conceptual; D: medium; L.O.: defining family

    Answer: B

67. Which of the following is NOT an important strategy for maintaining healthy family relationships suggested by your text?
    A. positivity
    B. evaluation
    C. openness
    D. assurances
    E. all of the above

H: Maintenance Strategies for Families, p. 374; C: conceptual; D: medium;
L.O.: maintaining family

Answer: B

68. Which of the following relational dialectics occurs most often within families?
    A. novelty vs. predictability
    B. autonomy vs. connection
    C. openness vs. protection
    D. both A and C
    E. both B and C

    H: Dealing with Family Tensions, p. 376; C: conceptual; D: medium; L.O.: maintaining family

    Answer: E

69. Which of the following statements about friendship most likely would be made by a Javanese person?
    A. My closest relationship is with my spouse.
    B. My closest relationship is with a same-sex friend.
    C. My friendships are short-lived.
    D. My best friend is of the opposite sex.
    E. none of the above

    H: Gender and Friendships, p. 385; C: application; D: difficult; L.O.: defining friendship
    Answer: B

70. Your younger brother, who is in high school, struggles with his desire to spend time with his friends, yet feels pressured to spend time with your family. What dialectic tension is he experiencing?
    A. novelty vs. predictability
    B. autonomy vs. connection
    C. openness vs. protection
    D. family vs. friends
    E. none of the above

    H: Balancing Autonomy and Connection, p. 376; C: application; D: difficult;
    L.O.: maintaining family

    Answer: B

71. Which of the following is considered to be a friendship rule that is applicable across cultures and within cross-sex friendships?
    A. respect privacy
    B. make your friends happy
    C. keep confidences
    D. seek support
    E. all of the above

    H: Abiding by Friendship Rules, p. 391; C: conceptual; D: medium; L.O.: maintaining friendship relationships

    Answer: E

72. Don and Sarah have been living together without being married for 20 years and have recently taken in a foster child. What kind of family do they have?
    A. cohabiting couple
    B. extended
    C. blended
    D. gay or lesbian
    E. single-parent

    H: Types of Family, p. 368; C: application; D: medium; L.O.: defining family

    Answer: A

73. Helicopter parents
    A. usually are from a lower socioeconomic class
    B. give their children independence starting in late adolescence
    C. aid their children's self-reliance skills
    D. often use technology to communicate regularly with their children
    E. none of the above

    H: Focus on Culture, Autonomy and Class: Helicopter Parents, p. 378; C: conceptual; D: medium; L.O.: maintaining family

    Answer: D

74. Mark's sister Trisha recently disclosed to him that she is involved in a same-sex relationship with a woman she met while away at college. Mark feels pressured to maintain his sister's confidence, yet also feels the desire to disclose this information to his parents. What dialectic tension is he experiencing?
    A. novelty vs. predictability
    B. autonomy vs. connection
    C. openness vs. protection
    D. family vs. friends
    E. none of the above

    H: Balancing Openness and Protection, p. 377; C: application; D: difficult; L.O.: maintaining family

    Answer: C

75. Family communication rules govern all of the following EXCEPT
    A. what family members can talk about
    B. how topics can be discussed
    C. with whom family members can talk
    D. where family members can talk about topics
    E. who has access to family-relevant information

    H: Balancing Openness and Protection, p. 377; C: conceptual; D: medium; L.O.: maintaining family

    Answer: D

76. If your parents enjoy telling you and your sister about how they met and proposed to one another at college, they are telling what kind of family stories?
    A. kinship stories
    B. survival stories
    C. courtship stories

D. birth stories

E. none of the above

H: Sharing Family Stories, p. 380; C: application; D: medium; L.O.: maintaining family

Answer: C

77. Karla was adopted by her parents at a very young age. When she asked about her birth parents, her adoptive parents explained that she was a special child who had been chosen from a roomful of babies. What kind of story are Karla's adoptive parents telling?

    A. kinship stories

    B. survival stories

    C. courtship stories

    D. birth stories

    E. none of the above

    H: Sharing Family Stories, p. 380; C: application; D: difficult; L.O.: maintaining family

    Answer: D

78. Which of the following family types are most likely to settle a disagreement by avoiding the topic?

    A. consensual families

    B. laissez-faire families

    C. pluralistic families

    D. protective families

    E. nuclear families

    H: Protective Families, p. 371; C: conceptual; D: medium; L.O.: defining family

    Answer: D

79. Friendships are different from family relationships because

    A. they are harder to end

    B. they are harder to maintain

    C. they are more likely to manifest open, public displays of affection

    D. they tend to be power-balanced

    E. none of the above

    H: Defining Friendship, p. 381; C: conceptual; D: medium; L.O.: defining friendship

    Answer: D

80. A communal friendship is one in which

    A. emotional support is the central aspect

    B. you share practical goals

    C. there's no expectation of sharing your time

    D. you're emotionally independent

    E. communication takes place over e-mail and the Web

    H: Communal Friendships, p. 383; C: conceptual; D: medium; L.O.: defining friendship

    Answer: A

81. Mohammad, his parents, his grandfather, and his aunt all live together in one house. What family type are they demonstrating?

    A. nuclear

    B. extended

C. blended

D. gay or lesbian

E. single-parent

H: Types of Family, p. 368; C: application; D: medium; L.O.: defining family

Answer: B

82. Your friend Ivan works full-time in the IT industry. You don't see him often; however, when you do he is always willing to fix your laptop computer or help you download software updates. What type of friendship do you have with Ivan?

A. virtual relationship

B. agentic friendship

C. communal friendship

D. avoidant friendship

E. collaborative friendship

H: Agentic Friendships, p. 384; C: application; D: difficult; L.O.: defining friendship

Answer: B

83. Taj was raised in a family in which communication was devalued. Sensitive topics and issues were not talked about; instead only safe topics, such as the weather and current events, were discussed. Taj's family could be described as having

A. low conformity orientation

B. high conformity orientation

C. high conversation orientation

D. low conversation orientation

E. none of the above

H: Communication Patterns in Families, p. 369; C: application; D: difficult; L.O.: defining family

Answer: D

84. What percentage of men report motives other than sexual as the basis for their friendships with women?

A. 10%

B. 25%

C. 50%

D. 70%

E. 90%

H: Gender and Friendships, p. 385; C: factual/definitional; D: medium; L.O.: defining friendship

Answer: D

85. What is the most common reason for the failure of FWB relationships?

A. disapproval from family and friends

B. lack of emotional satisfaction

C. one partner develops romantic feelings for the other

D. both A and B

E. both B and C

H: Friends with Benefits, p. 388; C: conceptual; D: medium; L.O.: defining friendship

Answer: E

86. When Jeremy began dating a Catholic girl, his parents sat him down and told him they expected him to marry a woman from their Mennonite community. This belief exemplifies which characteristic of families?
    A. families create identity through interpersonal communication
    B. families maintain emotionally intense bonds
    C. families use interpersonal communication to create boundaries
    D. families share a history
    E. family members share genetic material

    H: Defining Family, p. 366; C: application; D: difficult; L.O.: defining family

    Answer: C

87. Sabine enjoys being with her family, helps her parents out with her younger siblings, and tells her parents she appreciates everything they've done for her, but purposely keeps her life at college a secret from them. What family maintenance strategy could Sabine improve upon?
    A. communication
    B. assurances
    C. positivity
    D. openness
    E. equity

    H: Openness, p. 374; C: application; D: difficult; L.O.: maintaining family

    Answer: D

88. On Christmas Eve, Madison and her family go to midnight mass, come home, eat a pork dinner, and then each person opens one present of his or her choosing. These Christmas traditions are an example of
    A. family rituals
    B. conversation orientation
    C. conformity orientation
    D. family orientation
    E. consensual families

    H: Communication Patterns in Families, p. 369; C: application; D: medium; L.O.: defining family

    Answer: A

89. Families who are low in both conversation and conformity are called
    A. laissez-faire families
    B. protective families
    C. pluralistic families
    D. consensual families
    E. avoidant families

    H: Laissez-Faire Families, p. 372; C: conceptual; D: medium; L.O.: communication patterns in families

    Answer: A

Short Answer

Briefly respond to the following questions in full sentences.

90. What is a FWB relationship?

    H: Friends with Benefits, p. 388; C: conceptual; D: medium; L.O.: defining friendship

    Possible Answer: A relationship in which participants engage in sexual activity without the desire to progress to a romantic attachment.

91. What's the difference between communal and agentic friendships?

    H: The Different Forms of Friendship, p. 383; C: conceptual; D: medium; L.O.: defining friendship

    Possible Answer: Communal friendships are based on the sharing of emotional support, time, and activities. Agentic friendships are based more on the practical achievement of goals, or helping behaviors.

92. What are some challenges to maintaining cross-gender friendships?

    H: Gender and Friendships, p. 385; C: conceptual; D: medium; L.O.: defining friendship

    Possible Answer: Despite the fact that most cross-gender friendships are not motivated by sexual attraction, the public perception is that women and men can't be just friends. We have learned through socialization to segregate women from men. We have learned that friends are most often of the same sex.

93. What's the difference between a consensual family and a pluralistic family?

    H: Communication Patterns in Families, p. 369; C: factual/definitional; D: easy; L.O.: defining family

    Possible Answer: A consensual family scores high on both conversation and conformity, meaning they talk about a wide breadth of topics and use communication to emphasize their similarity with one another. A pluralistic family scores high on conversation but low on conformity, meaning they communicate openly and consider the children's contributions valuable to decision making.

94. What's the difference between a protective family and a laissez-faire family?

    H: Communication Patterns in Families, p. 369; C: conceptual; D: medium; L.O.: defining family

    Possible Answer: A protective family scores low on conversation but high on conformity, meaning there is a power imbalance between parents and children, and children are taught to quietly obey their parents. A laissez-faire family scores low on both conversation and conformity, meaning there is a sense of detachment between parents and their children.

95. Explain what a family story is and describe three types.

    H: Sharing Family Stories, p. 380; C: conceptual; D: medium; L.O.: maintaining family

    Possible Answer: Narrative accounts that bond family members to one another, courtship stories, birth stories, and survival stories.

96. Identify the three central aspects of friendship.

    H: Defining Friendship, p. 381; C: factual/definitional; D: easy; L.O.: maintaining family

    Possible Answer: They are voluntary, rooted in liking, and enjoyable.

97. What is conversation orientation?

    H: Communication Patterns in Families, p. 369; C: conceptual; D: medium; L.O.: defining family

    Possible Answer: The degree of fluidity with which family members converse and the breadth of topics they discuss.

98. What is conformity orientation?

    H: Communication Patterns in Families, p. 369; C: conceptual; D: medium; L.O.: defining family

    Possible Answer: The degree to which families use communication to emphasize similarity of attitudes, values, and beliefs.

99. Identify the three communication strategies that can be used to maintain healthy family relationships.

    H: Maintenance Strategies for Families, p. 374; C: factual/definitional; D: easy; L.O.: maintaining family

    Possible Answer: Positivity, openness, and assurances.

100. Identify the two relational dialectics that are most applicable to family relationships.

    H: Dealing with Family Tensions, p. 376; C: factual/definitional; D: easy; L.O.: maintaining family

    Possible Answer: Autonomy versus connection and openness versus protection.

101. What is a helicopter parent?

    H: Focus on Culture, Autonomy and Class: Helicopter Parents, p. 378; C: conceptual; D: medium; L.O.: maintaining family

    Possible Answer: Parents who hover over all aspects of their children's lives into young adulthood.

102. Explain how homophobia and traditional gender roles affect how men act in same-gender friendships.

    H: Gender and Friendships, p. 385; C: conceptual; D: medium; L.O.: defining friendship

    Possible Answer: Both factors cause men to avoid openly showing emotion and verbal and nonverbal intimacy, such as hugging and disclosing personal feelings.

103. Explain why, for most people, cross-gender friendships are more of a challenge than same-gender friendships.

    H: Gender and Friendships, p. 385; C: conceptual; D: medium; L.O.: defining friendship

    Possible Answer: Children are socialized through childhood to see genders as separate; society promotes same-gender friendships and cross-gender coupling as the only two options for relationships; family and friends may question the relationships.

Essay

Please respond to the following questions in paragraph form.

104. Define family and identify the five characteristics of a family.

    H: Defining Family, p. 366; C: conceptual; D: medium; L.O.: defining family

    Possible Answer: A group of people who create mutual identity, emotional bonds, and communication boundaries in the ways they interact with one another. 1) Family identity is created through interpersonal communication. 2) Family relationships are emotionally intense because we have been with the members of our family from an early age. 3) Families use interpersonal communication to define boundaries. 4) Families share a history. 5) Families share genetic material.

105. Describe the six different types of family.

    H: Types of Family, p. 368; C: conceptual; D: medium; L.O.: defining family

    Possible Answer: Nuclear family: husband, wife, and biological children. Gay or lesbian family: two people of the same sex who maintain a household and parent the children of at least one of them. Extended family: relatives living together in a common household. Blended family: a husband and wife who parent at least one child who is not the biological offspring of both adults. Cohabiting couples: two unmarried, romantically involved adults living together in a household. Single-parent family: one adult is the caregiver for the children.

106. Identify and explain the four family communication patterns.

    H: Communication Patterns in Families, p. 369; C: conceptual; D: medium; L.O.: communication patterns in families

    Possible Answer: Consensual families are high in both conversation and conformity. Pluralistic families are high in conversation but low in conformity. Protective families are low on conversation and high on conformity. Laissez-Faire families are low in both conversation and conformity.

107. How are friendships different from other relationships?

    H: Defining Friendship, p. 381; C: conceptual; D: medium; L.O.: defining friendship

    Possible Answer: Friendships are voluntary; unlike family members, you can choose friends. Friendships are easier to end than other relationships, such as with romantic partners or spouses. They are not as emotionally demanding as romantic relationships. They usually manifest fewer public displays of affection than do romantic relationships. Finally, friendships tend to be power-balanced, whereas family relationships tend be power-imbalanced.

108. Identify and provide an example of four of the ten friendship rules defined in the text.

    H: Abiding by Friendship Rules, p. 391; C: conceptual; D: medium; L.O.: maintaining friendship

    Possible Answer: Show support, seek support, respect privacy, keep confidences, defend your friends, avoid public criticism, make your friends happy, manage jealousy, share humor, and maintain equity.

Chapter 12: Relationships in the Workplace

Matching

Match the concept, term, or theory with its correct response or definition.

A. advocacy
B. control versus collaboration
C. defensive climate
D. density
E. detachment versus empathy
F. dogmatism versus flexibility
G. downward communication
H. evaluation versus description
I. hostile climate harassment
J. mixed-status relationships
K. organizational climate
L. organizational culture
M. organizational networks

N. professional peers
O. quid pro quo harassment
P. sexual harassment
Q. strategy versus spontaneity
R. superiority versus equality
S. supportive climate
T. upward communication
U. virtual networks
V. virtual peers
W. workplace abuse
X. workplace cliques
Y. workplace norms

1. A workplace's distinctive set of beliefs and practices.

   H: The Culture of the Workplace, p. 405; C: factual/definitional; D: easy; L.O.: workplace relationships

   Answer: L. organizational culture

2. Systems of communication linkages within organizations.

   H: Networks in the Workplace, p. 406; C: factual/definitional; D: easy; L.O.: workplace relationships

   Answer: M. organizational networks

3. The degree to which power differences are emphasized through communication.

   H: Superiority versus Equality p. 412; C: factual/definitional; D: medium; L.O.: workplace climate

   Answer: R. superiority versus equality

4. Unwelcome sexual advances, requests for sexual favors, or other verbal or physical conduct of a sexual nature.

H: Sexual Harassment, p. 426; C: factual/definitional; D: easy; L.O.: workplace abuse

Answer: P. sexual harassment

5. Groups of coworkers linked solely through e-mail and other Internet connections.

H: Networks in the Workplace, p. 406; C: factual/definitional; D: easy; L.O.: workplace relationships

Answer: U. virtual networks

6. The degree to which a person rigidly adheres to one solution or perspective or is willing to question opinions and decisions.

H: Dogmatism versus Flexibility, p. 409; C: factual/definitional; D: easy; L.O.: workplace climate

Answer: F. dogmatism versus flexibility

7. A workplace environment that is unfriendly, rigid, and unsupportive of professional and personal needs.

H: Supportive and Defensive Organizational Climates, p. 409; C: factual/definitional; D: easy; L.O.: workplace climate

Answer: C. defensive climate

8. People who hold positions of organizational status and power similar to your own.

H: Peer Relationships, p. 413; C: factual/definitional; D: easy; L.O.: peer relationships

Answer: N. professional peers

9. Coworkers who communicate mainly through phone, e-mail, and other communication technologies.

H: Types of Peer Relationships, p. 414; C: factual/definitional; D: easy; L.O.: peer relationships

Answer: V. virtual peers

10. Relationships between coworkers of different organizational status.

H: Mixed-Status Relationships, p. 418; C: factual/definitional; D: easy; L.O.: workplace strategies

Answer: J. mixed-status relationships

11. Communication from subordinates to superiors.

H: Managing Up, p. 419; C: factual/definitional; D: easy; L.O.: workplace strategies

Answer: T. upward communication

12. An effective form of upward communication through which a subordinate designs messages that will be well-received by his or her supervisor.

H: Managing Up, p. 419; C: factual/definitional; D: easy; L.O.: workplace strategies

Answer: A. advocacy

13. Communication from supervisors to subordinates.

    H: Communicating with Subordinates, p. 420; C: factual/definitional; D: easy;
    L.O.: workplace strategies

    Answer: G. downward communication

14. Verbal or nonverbal behavior that is hostile toward a person in an organization.

    H: Workplace Abuse, p. 426; C: factual/definitional; D: easy; L.O.: workplace abuse

    Answer: W. workplace abuse

15. An organization's expectations of what is appropriate interpersonal communication.

    H: The Culture of the Workplace, p. 405; C: factual/definitional; D: easy; L.O.: defining
    workplace relationships

    Answer: Y. workplace norms

16. The degree to which communication seems contrived and strategic rather than heartfelt.

    H: Strategy versus Spontaneity, p. 409; C: factual/definitional; D: easy; L.O.: workplace
    climate

    Answer: Q. strategy versus spontaneity

17. Networks of coworkers who share the same workplace values and broader life attitudes.

    H: Networks in the Workplace, p. 406; C: factual/definitional; D: easy; L.O.: workplace
    relationships

    Answer: X. workplace cliques

18. The degree to which problems are framed in terms of character defects rather than by
    objective language.

    H: Evaluation versus Description, p. 411; C: factual/definitional; D: easy; L.O.: workplace
    climate

    Answer: H. evaluation versus description

19. The product of an organization's culture, networks, and interpersonal interaction.

    H: Supportive and Defensive Organizational Climates, p. 409; C: factual/definitional;
    D: easy; L.O.: workplace climate

    Answer: K. organizational climate

20. The degree to which workers embrace professional detachment as opposed to supportive
    empathy.

    H: Detachment versus Empathy, p. 412; C: factual/definitional; D: easy; L.O.: workplace
    climate

    Answer: E. detachment versus empathy

21. A workplace environment that is warm and open.

    H: Supportive and Defensive Organizational Climates, p. 409; C: factual/definitional;
    D: easy; L.O.: workplace climate

    Answer: S. supportive climate

22. When a supervisor offers advancement or protection from layoffs in return for sexual favors.
    H: Sexual Harassment, p. 426; C: factual/definitional; D: easy; L.O.: workplace abuse
    Answer: O. quid pro quo harassment

23. Sexual behavior intended to disrupt a person's work performance.
    H: Sexual Harassment, p. 426; C: factual/definitional; D: easy; L.O.: workplace abuse
    Answer: I. hostile climate harassment

24. How connected, on average, each member of a network is to the other members.
    H: Networks in the Workplace, p. 406; C: factual/definitional; D: easy; L.O.: workplace relationships
    Answer: D. density

25. The degree to which communication is intended to control or to collaborate.
    H: Control versus Collaboration, p. 411; C: factual/definitional; D: easy; L.O.: workplace climate
    Answer: B. control versus collaboration

True/False

Please select whether the following statements are true or false.

26. The model minority myth is the belief that certain minority groups are unable to become reliable and technically proficient in the workplace.
    H: Focus on Culture: The Model Minority Myth, p. 422; C: conceptual; D: medium; L.O.: workplace relationships
    Answer: F

27. As with friendships, workplace relationships are based on equality.
    H: Defining Workplace Relationships, p. 404; C: factual/definitional; D: easy; L.O.: workplace relationships
    Answer: F

28. Norms, artifacts, and values are examples of an organization's culture.
    H: The Culture of the Workplace, p. 405; C: factual/definitional; D: easy; L.O.: workplace relationships
    Answer: T

29. Network density refers to the frequency and number of connections between people in a network.
    H: Networks in the Workplace, p. 406; C: conceptual; D: medium; L.O.: workplace relationships
    Answer: T

30. Organizational networks are characterized by the nature of the information that flows through them, the channels through which information flows, and network density.

    H: Networks in the Workplace, p. 406; C: conceptual; D: medium; L.O.: workplace relationships

    Answer: T

31. The rumor mill is a component of an organizational network through which workers pass on personal information about each other's personal and professional lives.

    H: Networks in the Workplace, p. 406; C: conceptual; D: medium; L.O.: workplace relationships

    Answer: T

32. Virtual networks are a type of organizational network in which workers communicate solely through e-mail and the Internet.

    H: Networks in the Workplace, p. 406; C: conceptual; D: medium; L.O.: workplace relationships

    Answer: T

33. Workplace cliques are formally defined networks of coworkers who share similar life values and attitudes.

    H: Networks in the Workplace, p. 406; C: conceptual; D: medium; L.O.: workplace relationships

    Answer: F

34. An organization's climate is composed of its culture, networks, and interpersonal interactions.

    H: Supportive and Defensive Organizational Climates, p. 409; C: conceptual; D: easy; L.O.: workplace climate

    Answer: T

35. A defensive climate is characterized by an unfriendly, unstructured, and unsupportive workplace.

    H: Supportive and Defensive Organizational Climates, p. 409; C: conceptual; D: medium; L.O.: workplace climate

    Answer: F

36. A supportive climate is characterized by a warm, open, and supportive workplace.

    H: Supportive and Defensive Organizational Climates, p. 409; C: conceptual; D: medium; L.O.: workplace climate

    Answer: T

37. A controlling communicator is one who uses pleasant messages that seem phony.

    H: Control versus Collaboration, p. 411; C: conceptual; D: medium; L.O.: workplace climate

    Answer: F

38. A dogmatic communicator is one who is rigid in his or her opinions and tends to be closed-minded.

    H: Dogmatism versus Flexibility, p. 409; C: conceptual; D: medium; L.O.: workplace climate

    Answer: T

39. Evaluation—the framing complaints about organizational problems in terms of character defects—is characteristic of defensive climates.

    H: Evaluation versus Description, p. 411; C: conceptual; D: medium; L.O.: workplace climate

    Answer: T

40. Supervisors who use the evaluation type of communication offer specific, timely, positive, and negative feedback and evaluation.

    H: Evaluation versus Description, p. 411; C: conceptual; D: medium; L.O.: workplace climate

    Answer: F

41. In a workplace climate characterized by detachment, supervisors treat employees with respect and understanding.

    H: Detachment versus Empathy, p. 412; C: conceptual; D: medium; L.O.: workplace climate

    Answer: F

42. Superiority is a characteristic of a defensive workplace climate, in which supervisors accentuate power differences between themselves and subordinates.

    H: Superiority versus Equality, p. 412; C: conceptual; D: medium; L.O.: workplace climate

    Answer: T

43. Empathy is a characteristic of a supportive workplace climate in which workers demonstrate care and understanding when communicating with one another.

    H: Detachment versus Empathy, p. 412; C: conceptual; D: medium; L.O.: workplace climate

    Answer: T

44. Professional peers are coworkers who hold positions of higher power than we do.

    H: Peer Relationships, p. 413; C: conceptual; D: medium; L.O.: peer relationships

    Answer: F

45. Information peers are those who have a similar status but with whom you communicate only about work-related content.

    H: Types of Peer Relationships, p. 414; C: conceptual; D: medium; L.O.: peer relationships

    Answer: T

46. Collegial peers are coworkers whom we consider friends and with whom we can disclose both work and personal matters.

    H: Types of Peer Relationships, p. 414; C: conceptual; D: medium; L.O.: peer relationships

    Answer: T

47. Professional peers are described as "blended" because they incorporate elements of both professional and personal relationships.

    H: Types of Peer Relationships, p. 414; C: conceptual; D: medium; L.O.: peer relationships

    Answer: F

48. Virtual peers can easily develop into virtual friends as the result of working together on shared tasks.

    H: Types of Peer Relationships, p. 414; C: conceptual; D: medium; L.O.: peer relationships

    Answer: T

49. The three dimensions of workplace relationships are status, gossip, and location.

    H: Defining Workplace Relationships, p. 404; C: conceptual; D: easy; L.O.: defining workplace relationships

    Answer: F

50. Workplace abuse may include either verbal or nonverbal behavior that is hostile and is directed at a person within an organization.

    H: Workplace Abuse, p. 426; C: factual/definitional; D: easy; L.O.: workplace abuse

    Answer: T

Multiple Choice

Please choose the correct response to the following statements.

51. Which of the following is NOT a dimension of a workplace relationship?
    A. status
    B. intimacy
    C. choice
    D. disclosure
    E. none of the above

    H: Defining Workplace Relationships, p. 404; C: factual/definitional; D: easy; L.O.: workplace relationships

    Answer: D

52. Which of the following is NOT a strategy that can be used to foster a supportive workplace climate?
    A. encouraging open, honest, spontaneous communication
    B. maintaining professional detachment with other workers
    C. adopting a flexible mind-set
    D. collaborating and seeking input and ideas
    E. describing and talking about issues in neutral terms

    H: Creating a Supportive Climate, p. 412; C: conceptual; D: medium; L.O.: workplace climate

    Answer: B

53. Which of the following is true of workplace abuse?
    A. nonverbal does not count
    B. must involve actual physical contact
    C. can include harmful communication
    D. usually done by subordinates to their supervisors
    E. less damaging than sexual harassment

    H: Workplace Abuse, p. 426; C: application; D: difficult; L.O.: workplace abuse

    Answer: C

54. Sexual harassment can include
    A. sexual advances
    B. sexual favors
    C. verbal statements
    D. physical conduct
    E. all of the above

    H: Sexual Harassment, p. 426; C: conceptual; D: medium; L.O.: workplace abuse

    Answer: E

55. At Brea's new job, she dressed formally to match her coworkers. However, on Fridays her peers dressed casually. What component of organizational culture does this switch pertain to?
    A. norms governing interpersonal communication
    B. norms governing personal relationships
    C. workplace artifacts
    D. workplace values
    E. all of the above

    H: The Culture of the Workplace, p. 405; C: application; D: difficult; L.O.: workplace relationships

    Answer: C

56. Organizational networks are composed of the following characteristics EXCEPT
    A. the physical space of the office
    B. network density
    C. nature of information
    D. media or channels
    E. frequency of connections

    H: Networks in the Workplace, p. 406; C: conceptual; D: medium; L.O.: workplace relationships

    Answer: A

57. You work for an IT company that has as its primary client a very large and powerful national bank. You provide technical support and project management. However, most of your work is done over the Internet via e-mail and through telephone conferences. What type of peer relationship do you have with the members of the bank?
    A. collegial
    B. information
    C. special
    D. blended
    E. virtual

H: Types of Peer Relationships, p. 414; C: application; D: difficult; L.O.: peer relationships

Answer: E

58. Ron is the chair of the English department at your local college. He is well liked by administrators, faculty, and students alike. He really seems to listen and understand when approached about academic or personal concerns. He supports his faculty and cares about them. What characteristic of a supportive workplace climate is Ron exhibiting?
    A. spontaneity
    B. flexibility
    C. collaboration
    D. empathy
    E. description

    H: Detachment versus Empathy, p. 412; C: application; D: difficult; L.O.: workplace climate

    Answer: D

59. You have just been assigned to a new project manager named Meka. When you approach Meka with questions or concerns, he seems to just give pat responses. In fact, you overheard your colleague approach him with a concern and Meka responded with the same line he used with you. What characteristic of a defensive climate is Meka manifesting?
    A. dogmatism
    B. strategy
    C. detachment
    D. control
    E. evaluation

    H: Strategy versus Spontaneity, p. 409; C: application; D: difficult; L.O.: workplace climate

    Answer: B

60. Your supervisor is known for seeking input from her subordinates and putting such suggestions to use. She often asks you, "How do you think we should handle this problem?" What characteristic of a supportive climate is your supervisor demonstrating?
    A. spontaneity
    B. flexibility
    C. collaboration
    D. empathy
    E. description

    H: Control versus Collaboration, p. 411; C: application; D: difficult; L.O.: workplace climate

    Answer: C

61. In your annual evaluation, your supervisor expressed concern that you are closed-minded and tend to be rigid in your thinking. What characteristic of defensive climates are you exhibiting?
    A. strategy
    B. dogmatism
    C. detachment
    D. evaluation
    E. description

H: Dogmatism versus Flexibility, p. 409; C: conceptual; D: medium; L.O.: workplace climate

Answer: B

62. The president of your company likes to remind employees, "I am the boss of this show and the buck stops here." He makes it clear that workers have lesser status than he does. What type of defensive climate is your president creating?
   A. strategy
   B. dogmatism
   C. detachment
   D. evaluation
   E. superiority

   H: Superiority versus Equality, p. 412; C: application; D: difficult; L.O.: workplace climate

   Answer: E

63. Sean works in a company that has an active rumor mill consisting of negative, pejorative statements such as "Can you believe how lazy our boss is?" and "I can't believe he didn't make the deadline again this month." This company is demonstrating which characteristic of a defensive climate?
   A. strategy
   B. dogmatism
   C. detachment
   D. evaluation
   E. superiority

   H: Evaluation versus Description, p. 411; C: application; D: difficult; L.O.: workplace climate

   Answer: D

64. In your company, personal business is to be left at home. Professionalism is of the utmost importance. Colleagues are anything but collegial. In fact, they are seen as distant and arrogant. What characteristic of a defensive climate best describes this company?
   A. strategy
   B. dogmatism
   C. detachment
   D. evaluation
   E. superiority

   H: Detachment versus Empathy, p. 412; C: application; D: difficult; L.O.: workplace climate

   Answer: C

65. Some high-tech companies have adopted an informal climate in which power and status differences are minimized and all layers of the organization have equal access to one another. It seems all employees are valued equally by these companies. What characteristic are these organizations demonstrating?
   A. spontaneity
   B. flexibility
   C. collaboration
   D. empathy
   E. equality

Answer: E

66. Professional peers are those
    A. in the organization who have higher status
    B. in the organization who hold similar status
    C. in the organization who have lower status
    D. with whom you share the workplace
    E. none of the above

    H: Peer Relationships, p. 413; C: conceptual; D: medium; L.O.: peer relationships
    Answer: B

67. In your office, there are several copy editors who are not only your professional peers but also your friends. You share both professional and personal information with them and sometimes eat lunch with them. What type of peer relationship do you have with them?
    A. collegial
    B. information
    C. special
    D. blended
    E. virtual

    H: Types of Peer Relationships, p. 414; C: application; D: difficult; L.O.: peer relationships
    Answer: A

68. May is your supervisor. Although she is very demanding, you appreciate the fact that she is very open-minded and not offended by your suggestions or questions about work policies. In fact, she readily seeks input, applies it, and acknowledges the source of the idea. May is demonstrating what characteristic of a supportive climate?
    A. spontaneity
    B. flexibility
    C. description
    D. empathy
    E. none of the above

    H: Dogmatism versus Flexibility, p. 409; C: application; D: difficult; L.O.: workplace climate
    Answer: B

69. If you prefer to have relationships with your peers at work in which you are equally comfortable talking about both work and personal issues, what type of peer relationship is your preference?
    A. information
    B. virtual
    C. blended
    D. special
    E. none of the above

    H: Types of Peer Relationships, p. 414; C: application; D: difficult; L.O.: peer relationships
    Answer: C

70. Which of the following maintenance strategies does your textbook especially recommend to maintain your collegial and special peer relationships?
    A. positivity
    B. empathy
    C. assurances
    D. do not define the other as just a coworker
    E. both C and D

    H: Maintaining Peer Relationships, p. 415; C: conceptual; D: medium; L.O.: peer relationships

    Answer: E

71. Cross-sex peers face which of the following challenge(s)?
    A. others view their relationship as sexual, not platonic
    B. must defend such relationships to peers
    C. may need to limit their time together
    D. the relationship may be the focus of workplace gossip
    E. all of the above

    H: Cross-Sex Peers, p. 416; C: conceptual; D: medium; L.O.: peer relationships

    Answer: E

72. Which of the following is NOT recommended as an effective method for maintaining a workplace romance?
    A. limit personal communication to e-mail
    B. leave your love at home
    C. communicate in a professional fashion with your romantic partner
    D. use e-mail judiciously
    E. avoid overly intimate or controversial topics

    H: Workplace Romances, p. 416; C: conceptual; D: medium; L.O.: peer relationships

    Answer: A

73. Caton was recently hired by a start-up company that provides technological assistance to small to midsize companies. He came from a job with the federal government in which he was used to a formal organizational culture. He used written memos and e-mails for all his communication, but was met with resistance because others in his new company preferred face-to-face communication. What component of organizational culture was a challenge for Caton?
    A. norms governing interpersonal communication
    B. norms governing personal relationships
    C. workplace artifacts
    D. workplace values
    E. all of the above

    H: The Culture of the Workplace, p. 405; C: application; D: difficult; L.O.: workplace relationships

    Answer: A

74. Organizational culture is influenced by
    A. norms governing interpersonal communication
    B. norms governing personal relationships

C. workplace artifacts

D. workplace values

E. all of the above

H: The Culture of the Workplace, p. 405; C: conceptual; D: medium; L.O.: workplace relationships

Answer: E

75. Mixed-status relationships in the workplace
    A. consist of relationships between coworkers of similar status
    B. consist of relationships between women and men
    C. consist of relationships between coworkers of different status
    D. consist of relationships between coworkers of different races
    E. none of the above

H: Mixed-Status Relationships, p. 418; C: conceptual; D: medium; L.O.: workplace strategies

Answer: C

76. Karla works at a large law firm with offices scattered across the United States. Her husband David just received a job offer in another state. She has appealed to her boss for a job transfer to work at the law firm in that state. What form of communication is she using?
    A. organizational communication
    B. horizontal communication
    C. downward communication
    D. upward communication
    E. none of the above

H: Managing Up, p. 419; C: application; D: difficult; L.O.: workplace strategies

Answer: D

77. A supportive climate is composed of all of the following EXCEPT
    A. spontaneity
    B. hierarchy
    C. collaboration
    D. empathy
    E. flexibility

H: Supportive and Defensive Organizational Climates, p. 409; C: conceptual; D: medium; L.O.: workplace climate

Answer: B

78. Advocacy is based on
    A. planning your pitch
    B. tailoring your message
    C. knowing your supervisor's knowledge
    D. creating coalitions
    E. all of the above

H: Managing Up, p. 419; C: conceptual; D: medium; L.O.: workplace strategies

Answer: E

79. The model minority myth suggests
    A. minorities have great barriers to overcome
    B. certain minority groups have overcome barriers and are hardworking
    C. minorities are less proficient and hardworking than the majority of the population
    D. certain minority groups need to be deported to their country of origin
    E. none of the above

    H: Focus on Culture: The Model Minority Myth, p. 422; C: conceptual; D: medium;
    L.O.: workplace strategies

    Answer: B

80. You work in the internal public relations department at a large manufacturing facility.
    However, you have a working relationship with peers who handle external relations, with
    whom you only discuss business. What type of peer relationship do you have with them?
    A. collegial
    B. information
    C. special
    D. blended
    E. virtual

    H: Types of Peer Relationships, p. 414; C: application; D: difficult; L.O.: peer relationships

    Answer: B

81. Which of the following is true of workplace abuse?
    A. can be verbal
    B. can be nonverbal
    C. can be more damaging than sexual harassment
    D. most often done by supervisors to their subordinates
    E. all of the above

    H: Workplace Abuse, p. 426; C: conceptual; D: medium; LO: workplace abuse

    Answer: E

82. Your officemate has become your best friend. You feel that you can tell him anything,
    whether or not it is work-related, and he reciprocates. You see him both inside and outside
    the office. What type of peer relationship do you have with him?
    A. collegial
    B. information
    C. special
    D. blended
    E. virtual

    H: Types of Peer Relationships, p. 414; C: application; D: difficult; L.O.: peer relationships

    Answer: C

83. A defensive climate is composed of the following characteristics EXCEPT
    A. detachment
    B. superiority
    C. control
    D. description
    E. none of the above

H: Supportive and Defensive Organizational Climates, p. 409; C: conceptual; D: medium; L.O.: workplace climate

Answer: D

84. Which of the following forms of harassment occurs most frequently in the workplace?
    A. verbal harassment
    B. quid pro quo harassment
    C. hostile climate harassment
    D. nonverbal harassment
    E. none of the above

    H: Sexual Harassment, p. 426; C: conceptual; D: medium; LO.: workplace abuse

    Answer: C

Short Answer

Briefly respond to the following questions in full sentences.

85. Identify the three components of organizational culture.

    H: The Culture of the Workplace, p. 405; C: factual/definitional; D: easy; L.O.: workplace relationships

    Possible Answer: Norms, artifacts, and values.

86. What are the three defining characteristics of organizational networks?

    H: Networks in the Workplace, p. 406; C: factual/definitional; D: easy; L.O.: workplace relationships

    Possible Answer: The nature of the information, the media or channels, and network density, or the frequency and number of connections among people.

87. Identify the three dimensions of a workplace relationship.

    H: Defining Workplace Relationships, p. 404; C: factual/definitional; D: easy; L.O.: defining workplace relationships

    Possible Answer: Status, intimacy, and choice.

88. What is an organization's climate composed of?

    H: Supportive and Defensive Organizational Climates, p. 409; C: factual/definitional; D: easy; L.O.: workplace climate

    Possible Answer: An organization's climate consists of its culture, networks, and interpersonal interaction within the organization.

89. What are the key characteristics of a supportive organizational climate?

    H: Supportive and Defensive Organizational Climates, p. 409; C: conceptual; D: medium; L.O.: workplace climate

    Possible Answer: A warm, open, and supportive workplace.

90. What are the key characteristics of a defensive climate?

H: Supportive and Defensive Organizational Climates, p. 409; C: conceptual; D: medium; L.O.: workplace climate

Possible Answer: An unfriendly, rigid, and unsupportive workplace.

91. How does a superiority climate differ from an equality climate?

H: Superiority versus Equality, p. 412; C: conceptual; D: medium; L.O.: workplace climate

Possible Answer: In a superiority climate, differences between employees' status are emphasized; in an equality climate, employees are treated similarly, emphasizing shared commitment, and minimizing rank and status.

92. Who is a professional peer?

H: Peer Relationships, p. 413; C: conceptual; D: medium; L.O.: peer relationships

Possible Answer: Workers who hold positions of similar organizational status and power to our own.

93. Who are collegial peers?

H: Types of Peer Relationships, p. 414; C: conceptual; D: medium; L.O.: peer relationships

Possible Answer: Coworkers we consider to be friends with whom we can discuss both work and personal issues.

94. Who is an information peer?

H: Types of Peer Relationships, p. 414; C: conceptual; D: medium; L.O.: peer relationships

Possible Answer: An equivalent-status coworker with whom we communicate only about work.

95. Who are virtual peers?

H: Types of Peer Relationships, p. 414; C: conceptual; D: medium; L.O.: peer relationships

Possible Answer: Coworkers who communicate mainly through e-mail, phone, and other technologies.

96. Define the two types of sexual harassment found in the workplace.

H: Sexual Harassment, p. 426; C: factual/definitional; D: easy; L.O.: workplace abuse

Possible Answer: Quid pro quo harassment is when a supervisor demands sexual favors in exchange for promotions or protection from layoffs. Hostile climate harassment is sexual harassment intended to disrupt a person's work performance.

97. What is upward communication?

H: Managing Up, p. 419; C: factual/definitional; D: easy; L.O.: workplace strategies

Possible Answer: Communication from subordinates to superiors.

98. What is advocacy?

H: Managing Up, p. 419; C: conceptual; D: medium; L.O.: workplace strategies

Possible Answer: A form of upward communication tailored to the communication preferences of your supervisor.

99. Define workplace abuse.

> H: Workplace Abuse, p. 426; C: conceptual; D: medium; L.O.: workplace abuse

> Possible Answer: Verbal or nonverbal behavior that is hostile toward a person within an organization.

Essay

Please respond to the following questions in paragraph form.

100. What are the characteristics of a supportive organizational climate?

> H: Supportive and Defensive Organizational Climates, p. 409; C: conceptual; D: medium; L.O.: workplace climate

> Possible Answer: Encourage spontaneity and honesty of expression, demonstrate flexibility, collaborate and seek ideas from others, describe challenges and use neutral language, offer empathy and concern, and finally, emphasize equality.

101. What are the characteristics of a defensive climate within an organization?

> H: Supportive and Defensive Organizational Climates, p. 409; C: conceptual; D: medium; L.O.: workplace climate

> Possible Answer: Strategic, calculated communication; believing only one idea, belief, or solution; seeking to control others; looking to assign blame; demonstrating professional detachment; and emphasizing superiority and power distance between supervisors and subordinates.

102. Define and identify the characteristics of and two types of sexual harassment.

> H: Sexual Harassment, p. 426; C: conceptual; D: medium; L.O.: workplace abuse

> Possible Answer: Sexual harassment includes unwelcome sexual advances, requests for sexual favors, and other verbal or physical conduct of a sexual nature when one must submit to such conduct as a condition of one's employment and such conduct interferes with an individual's work performance. Quid pro quo harassment occurs when a supervisor demands sexual favors in return for professional advancement or protection. Hostile climate harassment includes behavior that disrupts an employee's work performance.

103. What strategies can we use to maintain our peer relationships?

> H: Maintaining Peer Relationships, p. 415; C: conceptual; D: medium; L.O.: workplace strategies

> Possible Answer: Strategies include using positivity or communicating in an upbeat, optimistic manner and doing unasked-for favors for peers. Demonstrating openness so that peers feel comfortable disclosing information based upon a climate of trust. Next, use assurances to demonstrate your care and commitment to peers. Finally, treat peers as whole human beings, not just workers.

104. What are the principles of advocacy?

> H: Managing Up, p. 419; C: conceptual; D: medium; L.O.: workplace strategies

> Possible Answer: Plan your pitch, know why your supervisor should agree with you, tailor your message, know your supervisor's knowledge, create coalitions, and competently articulate your message.